ORIGINS OF OWNERSHIP

BY D. R. DENMAN

Estate Capital

Tenant-Right Valuation
in History and Modern Practice

Tenant-Right Valuation
and Current Legislation

ORIGINS OF OWNERSHIP

A BRIEF HISTORY OF
LAND OWNERSHIP AND TENURE
IN ENGLAND
FROM EARLIEST TIMES TO
THE MODERN ERA

BY

D. R. DENMAN

University Lecturer in Estate Management
University of Cambridge

Ruskin House
GEORGE ALLEN & UNWIN LTD
MUSEUM STREET, LONDON

TO J. D. D.

*Printed in Great Britain
in 11 point Pilgrim type
by East Midland Printing Company
Bury St. Edmunds and elsewhere in
the United Kingdom*

PREFACE

Many people have written much on the origins of land owner-ship in England but the stories are incidental themes of general histories. This book attempts, by dealing with the historical development of fundamental principles of proprietorship, to review briefly the stories as I have extracted them from the writings of recent authorities and to draw them together in a single narrative. My purpose is to introduce the reader to the themes of current debate as acknowledged, modern authorities on economic, legal and social history see them.

My debt is great to the historians whose works I cite and whose thoughts I endeavour to follow. Care has been taken to avoid misquotation. If at any point I have not understood a writer's thought and my words misrepresent him, I crave indulgence as my intention is primarily to introduce his thoughts to those who will make their own judgements. Here and there I have given my own constructions of the historical evidence for what they are worth, and I would ask the reader to bear kindly with the *a posteriori* reasoning of the chapter on prehistory. As far as possible I have avoided over-emphasizing particular views, although I admit a certain readiness to incline to the Germanic theory of the origin of manors.

What I have to say about Norman feudalism and the develop-ment of the land law in the Middle Ages owes a great deal to the generous help and valuable suggestions I received from Professor T. F. T. Plucknett, F.B.A., who kindly criticised the text of these chapters and read over the typescript of the others. I am deeply grateful to him and to the many friends who read and criticised the proofs.

Cambridge, 1957   D. R. DENMAN

CONTENTS

CONTENTS

CHAPTER ONE

PREHISTORY

The Evidence. It may well be asked whether prehistory can provide a prologue to a story of landownership. What can be told rests solely upon archaeological evidence but the testimony of archaeology is more fluent than might be supposed. A wealth of evidence tells in a hesitant but nonetheless reliable way something of the life and social order of Britain during the two and a half millennia before the Belgic invasion. And among this evidence can be found traces of earliest land use and settlement.

Principles of landownership obviously cannot be known. But pointers are discernible, suggestive of sources of land law and custom. Patterns of land use contiguous to each other are signposts. Evidence of coeval nomadism and permanent settlements sharing a land area is ground for thinking of the settlers as the political superiors of the nomads and hence the makers of law which creates and controls the system of landownership. The nomads must recognise and honour the boundaries of the settled land. Alternative to this is an entente between tribesmen and settlers. Although work-a-day agreements are known to have existed among nomadic folk,[1] a universal entente is an unlikely contingency. And where the archaeological evidence reveals the existence of mighty monuments and towering buildings expressive of huge and highly organised labour forces there is additional reason to suppose a well developed society dominant over the nomadic tribesfolk. Moreover the extent of the building development and the size of the buildings are indicative of the proportions of the population and the land area over which the builders have jurisdiction. When the spade therefore exposes the foundations and lesser traces of a virile and massive architecture there is revealed by the same event a memorial to a populous, legislating people among whose edicts and over whose wide-ranging lands a land law would not have been wanting. Lesser buildings are signposts pointing to a correspondingly limited political and legislative autonomy.

Sites of isolated buildings contrast with those of group habitation. A single dwelling surrounded by a defence work can betoken possession by rule of might and not rule of law — "he who owns the stick owns the cow". But grouped habitations are evidence of a land law emanating from a higher authority than the pos-

---

[1] Toynbee: *A Study of History* (abr. Somervell) pp. 166-171.

sessor of each dwelling. Likewise extensive cattle enclosures and forts point either to voluntary cooperation or to ownership sprung of a dominating lawgiver.

Although undefended boundaries are strong evidence of law-protected possession, especially where other signs point to a dense population, they are not unequivocable evidence. Much depends upon the nature of the property. Land may be undefended because its secrets and wealth yield themselves only to the skill of craftsmen who can win them — flint, zinc and copper mines in the early cultural ages are examples. In these and other ways archaeological evidence is suggestive of the prehistoric origins of landownership.

EARLIEST SETTLEMENT PATTERNS

Nomadism, hoe-agriculture and hunting. Histories of civilisations have accepted agriculture as a logical step in progress from a state of nomadism. Professor Toynbee[2] questions the idea. Agriculture for him is a matrix in which nomadism is born. Anchored to the soil, emancipated in some measure from the total servitude which a hunting and food-gathering economy demands, man groped towards stock husbandry and pastoralism.

Simple nomadism is unknown to the archaeological record of Britain. Certain authorities[3] suggest that the course of events in the earlier ages bore out Toynbee's sequence. The Early Bronze Age appears more pastoral and nomadic than the immediately preceding Neolithic Age; lack of Early Bronze Age settlement sites and evidence of meat, not corn, as the staple diet are responsible for this opinion. Nothing is certain. Other archaeologists[4] hesitate to assign the evidence of primitive settlements exclusively to Neolithic times and accept it as valid for all the cultural ages from the Neolithic advent to the coming of the Deverel-Rimbury plough-teams in the Late Bronze Age. However the pendulum of fashion may have swung between hoe-agriculture and nomadic pastoralism during the fifteen hundred years which span those epochs, all authorities are agreed that the rural economy of prehistoric England was a tapestry of both types of enterprise, relieved by hunting, fishing and food-gathering.

[2] Toynbee: op. cit., p. 168.
[3] cf. Childe: *Prehistoric Communities of the British Isles*, p. 98.
[4] Curwen: *Air-Photography and the Evolution of the Corn-field*, p. 11.

Hoe-agriculture is evinced by traces of small, irregular corn-plots. In location, plots are confined to the moors of Cornwall, Devon and Yorkshire, but ubiquitous grinding querns and frequent imprints of grain in pottery clay are indirect testimony to a widerspread practice. At one place the plots are discrete, at another knit together, but everywhere their outline is an irregular curve, the work of antler pick and digging stick. As the digger loosened surface stones he tossed them into heaps along the plot perimeters. There they have remained, to give away to the inquisitor of today the secrets of two thousand years[5].

In size the plots vary; at Trowlesworthy Warren House the average size is about half an acre[6]. Associated with the plots are numerous hut-circles, the remains of shelters and dwellings. The hut-circles far exceed the plots in number. If the huts and the plots were contemporary the division of the land among the inhabitants would have been very intense. A hut would represent a minute area of cultivated land; at Trowlesworthy no more than one-tenth of an acre. Modern intensive agriculture would find so tiny an allotment inadequate for family needs. It would not have warranted the labour spent on it in a primitive economy whose catalogue of cultivated plants was limited to primitive wheat and barley[7]. The evidence clearly points to associated nomadism. The hut-sites were probably not of contemporary buildings. They represent successive periods of occupation of the area and at each period the plots were dug over after years of fallow. Some groups of hut-circles are not associated with agricultural life. Protecting walls surround the group and these clusters were either homes of early food-gatherers[8] or, more likely, hutments similar to Hebridean shielings, for the shelter of herdsmen tending their animals on the remote summertime pasture grounds.

Dwellings. Round or oval huts were characteristic of the dwellings of the cultural ages, and to some extent of early historic times. Domestic buildings seem to have degenerated rather than advanced after Neolithic times. One of the earliest dwellings, unanimously accepted as Neolithic[9], was a timber framed affair, the like of which is not subsequently known until Roman times. The normal curvilinear hut was built either of loose stones and turf or of wattle or other light material fastened to stakes.

Dwellings were not always clustered in groups. Isolated sites

[5] Clark : *Prehistoric England*, p. 20.   [8] Curwen : op. cit., p. 8.
[6] Curwen : op. cit., p. 9.   [9] Clark : op. cit., p. 30.
[7] Hawkes, J. and C. : *Prehistoric Britain*, p. 33.

have been discovered. At the other extreme is evidence for a conventional village. At Skara Brae[10], in Orkney, is something more than a collection of huts, huddled together within the circumvallation of a protecting wall. Seven or eight mono-cellular structures are linked in an alinement by paved and roofed alleys. Some cells are used for 'industrial' purposes[11] and others as dwellings. Storage and sanitation are not wanting and the entire assemblage is drained by sewers.

Causewayed camps. Dwellings are found associated with what the archaeologist calls the causewayed camp. These camps are a feature of the earliest recognisable traces of land settlement in Britain and probably preceded the megalithic tombs, although both are accepted features of the so-called Windmill Hill culture[12]. Each camp comprises a series of annular, concentric ditches quarried in downland chalk. Excavated material is banked against the inward lip of the ditch and forms a plinth supporting a stockade. Gaps are left at intervals in the irregular banks and provide causeways leading to the heart of the enclosure. Design and size are not uniform. At one site the innermost enclave is 2 acres and the entire camp covers nearly six times that area; at another place the central arena is 3 acres and the whole encampment 14 acres. Evidence of dwelling sites is never found within the arenas; the bric-a-brac of human occupation is plentiful enough, but it lies in the camp ditches.

Tombs and temples. Necropolis and temple shadow the camps and cornplots of the early cultural ages. A time may have been when this was not so. There are indications of the megalithic tomb-builders coming as invaders to dominate the people of the causewayed camp[13]. Temples are probably the work of Beaker Folk in the Early Bronze Age. Recently doubt has been expressed [14] of the validity of the evidence by investigators who think the megalithic tombs were built by people of the Early Bronze Age under the cairns and long barrows of Neolithic times. An exact chronology is not important. Although great variety inspired the builders, both types of tomb are alike in the enormous demand the con-

---

[10] The Skara Brae village appears to have been the work of refugees fleeing northwards through Britain from the Beaker migrations on the Continent, and it is reasonable to assume that their culture was expressed in less durable dwellings among the lowland marshes and forest clearings : Childe : *Prehistoric Communities of Britain*, p. 86.
[11] Childe suggests the workshop of a chert-knapper : op. cit., p. 85.
[12] Op. cit., pp. 34-53.
[13] Op. cit., p. 78.
[14] cf. op. cit., p. 50.

struction made upon labour; and this is the significant feature when tracing the story of landownership. Some long barrows extend to 400 feet in length, and one stretches for nearly three furlongs. Both long barrow and cairn give evidence of discriminate planning and careful construction. The ground on which they stand appears to be consecrated by oblation and sacrifice and the early sacring of the ground is an abiding influence. Not only are long barrows found in the company of each other, but instances occur[15] where the less impressive round barrows of a later age keep company with long barrows and within the purlieus of the sacred area are the temenos of temple sites.

The temples of prehistory have left an awe-inspiring epitaph in monolith, stone circle and henge. For the most part these antiquities lie among the western hills[16], not because the westerners of the Early Bronze Age were more pious than their eastern contemporaries but for them the giant stones were ready to hand. Analogous sites have recently been discovered, from the air, among the lowlands of the eastern counties. And fossed annular embankments in the loose, geological formations of the downlands may be the expressions of a similar religious architecture.

The boss of the chalk and oolite hills, where they fuse together at Salisbury Plain, is the focus of early cultural tradition. The landscape is peppered with round barrows and within hailing distance of each other are Avebury circle, and Stonehenge; two outstanding monuments to prehistoric religious zeal and authority.

Avebury is pre-eminent. It is not the conception of one generation; it is a contribution from many ages. In its final splendour the layout resembled a chimerical beast of giant head and long, sinuous, ring-tipped tail, sprawling a mile and more over the land. Today the head is sound, and is the largest megalithic circle in Europe; over 1,100 feet in diameter, enclosed by an abraded bank and silted fosse, originally 50 feet from crown to ditch-bottom, the whole encircling some 28½ acres; within the largest circle are two smaller ones and traces of a third cut its circumference. A winding alinement of megaliths, the backbone of the beast, once joined the head with the rest of the anatomy—two concentric stone circles known as the Sanctuary. Near to Avebury stands Silbury Hill, a perfectly moulded, grass-decked pyramid and one of Europe's profoundly mysterious antiquities; a giant mudcast from the pudding basin of the gods. Stonehenge also is an expression of successive generations of worshippers and architects.

[15] Hawkes, J. and C.: op. cit., p. 40.
[16] Clark: op. cit., p. 103.

When the first circular ditch was cut it encompassed an arena within which all future developments took place. Within the temenos later worshippers erected the massive, inter-locked stones and trilithons, the traditional image of Stonehenge. At some time, possibly later still, a circle and horseshoe of blue-stones were added. The blue-stones excite even greater wonder than the mammoth blocks. The blocks are local; they suggest a bowed humanity harnessed to their massive bulk, easing the stones inch by inch from a natural bed to the glory of the temple. But the blue-stones, though much smaller, are the rocks of South Wales, and demand an almost unbelievable feat of transportation, ingenuity and organization[17].

EARLIEST LANDOWNERSHIP

Dominance of hierarchical ownership. The archaeological record of the Early and Middle Bronze Ages shows a land divided between the sacred sites of burial grounds and temples, and the pastoral wanderings of nomads. In places the boundaries are contiguous; sacrosanct marches divide hoof-trodden from holy ground. The contrast hardens as the centuries pass. Nomadism becomes more vigorous, stimulated by a progressive stock husbandry, and the sacred areas establish and extend themselves as temple succeeds temple. Had the burial barrows not clustered together in the purlieus of the temples, and had agriculture instead of nomadism been the prevailing mode of rural economy, the picture would have been less definite and its evidence more difficult to deduce.

If the hypothesis of the opening paragraphs is sound, the facts point to legislative power in the hands of a hierarchy responsible for temple construction and the preservation of burial sites. Such land law as there is emanates from the priesthood. No evidence from the sacred sites suggests otherwise. Defence works would have required a different interpretation. Admittedly the temples have embankments, but if the bank at Avebury is a guide the temple embankment is an elevated auditorium rather than a defence glacis. Moreover, if the sacred sites were kept inviolate from the nomadic peoples by force of arms there would be evidence of an associated agriculture without which the religious communities could not have survived. The nomads in some manner provided food for the sedentary priesthood who must have had political power over them. The massive architecture of the temple sites and burial grounds supports the supposition.

[17] Childe : op. cit., p. 105.

Those cyclopean structures could not have been built without organised labour on a vast scale; nor could the blue-stones of Stonehenge have been transported from South Wales without an extensive, authoritative command of economic resources in the hands of the priesthood. Labour organisation would be necessary to reconcile the demands of a primitive agriculture and virile nomadism with the conflicting demand of the building activities[18]. Seasonal requirements of husbandry would aggravate the problem and lift it altogether beyond the possibility of nomadic tribes to solve.

The more the facts are pondered, the more cogent does argument for an hierarchical, political authority and legislature become. The argument goes further than the case for a ruling priesthood creating laws to secure the ownership of the sacred sites. The intricacies of labour organization and the extent of economic control which the structure and siting of the great temples indicate are strong grounds for postulating a central authority whose word of law fashions not only the principles of ownership for the sacred sites but governs remotely all dealings in land, even the temporary tenements of moving herdsmen. Something closely approaching this is known in tribal lands to-day. Landownership is linked to religious practice and ordinance; before a land grant can be sanctioned an officiating priest will propitiate the local deities, and thus the ultimate dominion over the land is vested in the priestly lord[19].

Ownership of causewayed camps. The argument for a central legislative priesthood stands upon the existence of the great temple buildings and extensive sacred sites. If such authority did in fact exist, its growth would be gradual, moving in step with the development of the architecture. Neolithic days would have known nothing of it. The Neolithic tombs seem to fit into a narrow, religious jurisdiction within tribal limits where the local chief is both priest and king[20]. This dual role throws light upon the ownership of the contemporary causewayed camps. Some archaeologists seek no other purpose for the camps than the herding of cattle. Others, notably Childe, see them as military establishments, fortified strong points. This view is logical. Nomadism is incessantly active. The camps cannot have been night

---

[18] There is reason to think that parts of the temples were more elaborate than their remains lead a casual observer to believe, and the timber erections would understandably require continual maintenance.
[19] cf. Liversage : *Land Tenure in the Colonies*, p. 6.
[20] Childe : op. cit., pp. 77, 78.

shelters or even occasional shelters for cattle[21]. As central rallying grounds, in use at branding seasons, they raise more difficulties than they solve; herding cattle together before branding them would confuse the identities of ownership and defeat the very purpose of the branding, unless the owner of the camp were also the owner of the cattle. The military theory assumes that the concentric ditches and mounds are ramparts manned by herdsmen and warriors defending the cattle herded in the innermost arena. Only in times of danger are the camps used; then animals and men are ensconced within the ramparts. If such were the case ownership rights would probably be fashioned by tribal custom. Something approximating to plenary power over the camps must vest in the tribal chief as supreme military commander, but he will have had to recognise the right of his fellow tribesmen to the protective shelter of the ramparts. On him will fall the responsibility for maintenance; and the traces of dwellings sited between the annular banks may be evidence of resident garrisons, responsible for repairing the ramparts. Local military authority over the fortresses would not have been tolerated by a central legislative authority, and this may account for the abandonment of the camps in the days of the Beaker folk and later hierarchies. The sites in those days were used to some purpose, possibly as occasional shelters, but they never regained a military use[22].

Ownership of isolated dwellings and group habitations. In the days of the causewayed camps it is probable that no word of law or custom subjected the tribesmen to a higher authority. But there must have been a seat of authority within the tribe or social group. Without it society would crumble into the granular independence of the Homeric Cyclops:

> Mootless are they and lawless — On the peaks
> Of mountains high they dwell, in hollow caves,
> Where each his own law deals to wife and child
> In sovereign disregard of all his peers.

How far tribal custom or law governed ownership it is impossible to say. The simplest hutment cannot be the property of its possessor without the sanction of landright. Some law or custom must have defined the principles of tenure by which the Neolithic tribesmen held their scattered and clustered dwellings.

In theory the tribesman can hold his home in an absolute ownership of natural law, in which possession and ownership are one, where rights of ownership are what it is physically and practically

---

[21] Hawkes, J. and C.: op. cit., p. 30.   [22] Childe: op. cit., p. 98.

possible to do unmodified by the abstract sanctions of positive law. Isolated dwellings may be taken as evidence of a natural order. But unless each property shows signs of defence works and self-supporting enterprise, it is absurd to interpret the evidence that way. Neolithic Britain was not Arcady. A rule of law or custom must have secured the ownership of the undefended homesteads.

Dwellings in groups suggest the existence of tribal law, for a different reason. What appears to be a casual scattering of huts and corn plots cannot in fact have originated fortuitously. Tribal groups move together. A loose assortment of men has no voice of authority of itself; its acts and speech are the policy and opinion either of a leader or of individual members to whom sovereign powers are given to legislate and act in concert. Individual or plural authority within the group will choose the settlement sites and in so doing will condition the rights of ownership that eventually fall to the several members of the group. Settlement sites that show signs of design and order, such as the arrangement at Skara Brae[23], were probably chosen and arranged by one and the same authority. Skara Brae and the less conventional clusters of hutments are human communities. Differences that divide neighbours will divide these. Law must run and adjudicate between parties; and that law as well as the original siting and layout of the settlement will influence the rights of ownership in the several dwellings and corn plots.

Ownership of isolated and grouped dwellings in post-Neolithic times would feel the authority of the dominant priesthood but control was probably very remote and would allow ample room for the development of tribal law and custom.

Ownership of mines. Dwellings and camps were not the only secular institutions occupying land. There were mines; not for metal but for flints. The miners have left traces of dwellings which suggest the existence of mining colonies. The workings are intricate. Only highly skilled craftsmen could have operated them. A specialised craft has also left its sign in the rational sorting of the flints in the proximity of the mines. Archaeologists believe the miners were a coterie. Their special skill probably made them a law unto themselves and was a natural safeguard of the mines and mineral wealth against petty pillage and pilfering. Flint mines, however, in Neolithic times, would be of strategic economic and military importance. The miners would seek the military protection of warrior chieftains, who, in turn, would be anxious to

[23] cf. p. 4 ante.

B

engender the goodwill of the craftsmen. It is reasonable to suppose that whatever law governed the ownership of dwellings and corn plots within a tribal area would also govern the ownership of the tribal mines. In the Bronze Ages flint mines continue to be worked but have lost their strategic character, and the natural protection of the trained craftsman is probably of greater consequence, although the influence of a powerful, dominant priesthood must not be overlooked.

FIRST PLOUGHLANDS

Deverel-Rimbury ploughteams. Antiquarians have woven a coat of many colours for the prehistoric cultural ages; the silver-flint Stone Ages, the bronze and iron-grey of more advanced cultures. But cultural change does not match the changing patterns of land use. Nomadism and hoe-agriculture characteristic of the Stone Ages continue well into the Late Bronze Age. And that epoch, in its middle age, suddenly opens a new chapter in the land story. Two and a half centuries before the first Iron Age[24], ploughmen escaped hither from the southern and eastern shores of the continent. Nomadic shepherds, accustomed to the age-old traditions of the Island, would find the ploughman, his queer implement and his docile beast, profoundly disturbing. But these first ploughmen, whom archaeologists call the Deverel-Rimbury folk, had come to stay and to prosper, and to sow in strange, straight furrows the seeds of a new civilization.

No plough-relic of that age has been discovered in Britain. Classical evidence for the momentous revolution in agrarian life is the traces of field systems that grid-mark the downlands. Continental discoveries, associated with similar topographical marks, have yielded evidence of the plough itself; an uninspiring construction, no more than an elaborate digging-stick harnessed between a pair of oxen, pointed in metal and shafted to give the entire device into the hand of the ploughman. Only light, bodiless soils were tractable, and the newcomers tended to cultivate the lands of the scratch-agriculturalists. Poor mountain soils could be worked but not where the soil was pitched at acute angles or lay deep in pockets among the rocks. The new implement may have suffered considerable modification among the hills of the west. In the isles and western Highlands, even in modern times, crofters have

[24] Childe : op. cit., p. 187.

used the caschrom, and Curwen[25] has likened this Celtic digging tool to the main plough part of the ancient two-oxen plough. He argues that the Deverel-Rimbury innovation, proving too cumbersome for the mountains, was divested of its oxen and cross-shafting and converted to a hand implement. Of course a reverse process may have accounted for the plough: the two-oxen plough might have evolved from the digging stick.

Early plough and caschrom. Childe[26] calls attention to the later hoe-plots of the Middle Bronze Age and points to them as the possible work of caschrom digging. But these plots are curvilinear in outline and the caschrom stitches straight. This important fact led Curwen to link the caschrom so completely with the plough and to date it in the plough-age. An implement capable of breaking the sod with geometrical precision must belong to the ages that run forward from the first plough-furrow. Plough and caschrom have the furrow in common. Yet they differ in the cultivation patterns they make. The plough makes a rectilinear patchwork on open ground. The work of the caschrom can be square, rectangular, polygonal or triangular, a variety of straight-sided patches. The earliest plough is a sorry tool by modern standards, but it surpasses the caschrom in speed and possibly in efficiency of working where the soil suits it. The prehistoric ploughmasters did not have mouldboard, plough-brest, coulter or broad ploughshare and, although their naked implement is the acknowledged, honourable ancestor of the fully caparisoned plough, it was incapable of turning a furrow.

Ploughing patterns. Original or maiden ploughing appears, from the markings of the earliest ploughfields, to have been cross-ploughed. The tilth must have been a sorry sight, even where the soil was exceptionally friable. Cross-ploughing probably accounts for a tendency in the plough-plots to be rectangular and not square. If the length of a furrow is the distance a ploughteam can traverse without pause, the maiden furrows will be shorter than the cross-furrows; the width of the plough-fields probably measures the run of the maiden furrows and the length of the field the run of cross-furrows. The rectangular plots butt end to end and form chains running parallel and perpendicular to the contours of the downland. As the soil was loosened it gravitated down the hillside and formed terraces or lynchets. These are the bold, hori-

[25] Curwen: op. cit., p. 24.
[26] Op. cit., p. 157.

zontal ribs of the tell-tale grid markings. The terminals of the furrows that ran parallel with the hill contours threw up loose banks of stones and flints, to provide a light cross-ribbing between the horizontal lynchets, so giving the grid effect.

Settled agriculture. What is now known of the new economy refutes the idea of Earnle and other historians who thought of the cultivators of the rectangular fields as practising "wild field grass" husbandry; a predatory system of breaking virgin land, cropping it to capacity, abandoning it to natural fallow and breaking it again after a period of recuperation. Wild field grass husbandry requires movement. It is in keeping with the hoe-agriculture of the earliest times and the semi-nomadism of the western mountains, but not with deepset lynchets. These are the hall-marks of a settled agriculture.

The sedentary nature of the new economy is suggested also by evidence of permanent homesteads, corn silos and cattle enclosures, associated with the square and rectangular fields[27]. The earliest evidence is a group of enclosures comprising what were probably banked and palisaded enclaves, each containing a dwelling hut and storage buildings. Later evidence shows elaboration[28]. One of the most closely investigated discoveries is the site of an Early Iron Age settlement at Britford near Salisbury[29]. This appears to have been a holding of 15 to 20 acres with a farmstead of a commodious, round-shaped dwelling and minor buildings surrounded by a paled fence. The corn silos are sunken pits in which grain is stored after winnowing and drying. Each pit works effectively for a few years and is then abandoned. On the small farm at Britford as many as 360 silos have been discovered; this is strong evidence for the continuous occupation of the site over three centuries.

The cattle kraals and boundaries of far-flung ranches lie on the shadow side of the hills, whose sunnier faces have been ploughed into patchwork. Both kraals and boundary marks are of plough origin. The kraals are rectangular in plan and vary in area to a maximum of two acres. Their sides are straight banks and ditches, probably set out in the first place by ploughing a furrow slice round the enclosure. Nothing suggests that the embankments are defence works or that the kraals are analogous to the ancient causewayed camps. Ranch boundaries are also marked by

[27] Childe : op. cit., p. 190.
[28] Hawkes, J. and C. : op. cit., p. 93.
[29] Clark : op. cit., p. 24.

wide, straight ditches, doubtless of plough origin. Most authorities
think these wide-bottomed cuts and the low banks on one or both
sides of them had other functions beside boundary demarkation.
They were perhaps trackways along which cattle herded in defile.

The sum of the evidence leaves little doubt that agriculture
became settled under the two-oxen plough. At first the homesteads were isolated or in twos and threes. Eventually, and certainly by the Early Iron Age, extensive groupings developed and
some venture to speak of these as nucleated villages[30].

OWNERSHIP AND SECULAR LAW

Settled peace. When the Deverel-Rimbury ploughteams came
to these shores the country had known a thousand years free of
invasion. The millennium favoured the growth of local custom and
law. The newcomers trespassing as they did upon the open hill
lands of the native Urn folk, must have presented a formidable
challenge to established proprietary rights. Despite what was probably a deep laceration of tribal country, the new settlers have
left no evidence of defence works, guarding their square fields, wide
pastures and settled homesteads against a hostile native population.
Ditches, embankments and fences abound, but they are not formidable enough to be military defences; they point to an active
livestock husbandry. It is significant that four hundred years later,
when the descendants of these Deverel-Rimbury folk, and the Hallstatt ploughmen who followed them, were in their turn threatened
by invaders from the Continent, defences were erected outside the
fenced boundaries of the homesteads[31]. The defenceless farms of the
first ploughmen may be a peace memorial, a token of accord
between invaders and invaded, or silent witnesses to a total
subjection of the native folk. It is hard to imagine the native Urn
folk giving open-armed welcome to the invaders, but the weight of
evidence[32] suggests that in the long run the two peoples settled
down together.

Evidence of a secular land law. The undefended boundaries do
not only speak of peace: they bear testimony to a rule of law.
Light palisades are the signs of a settled stock husbandry; the
terraced lynchets are the terminals of the new plough furrows; but
the long, low banks and ditches stretching for miles between

[30] Childe : op. cit., p. 195.   [32] Op. cit., p. 188.
[31] Op. cit., p. 195.

cattle ranches can only be explained as boundaries recognised and protected by property law. From whence comes the new law? From the ancient hand of priestly rulers; or from another source?

Ancient temples, massive and dominating, have suggested a political and social order in which the priests were sovereign. Law comes from those whose authority and interest marshalls labour masses to build giant tombs and mammoth temples. Ownership is the creation of the religious powers. Nomadism developed tribal customs and faltering notions, but it did not bind its peoples by a code of law universally honoured over wide areas. Only the hierophants of the temples had the wisdom and power for that.

Now in the latter days of pre-history are found permanent boundaries separating nomads from settlers of a different way of life. The ploughmen do not bury their dead in mighty mausoleums but in level urnfields. No priest-king dragoons them to erect great temples. The great monuments of the past are used by them, but not copied and repeated and there is nothing in these latter days to take their place as evidence of an hierarchical supremacy[33]. It is possible, therefore, that custom and land law came from a secular sovereignty. The decline in religious architecture points that way, and of far greater significance are the impressive hill forts erected late in the period as military measures against the last invaders of prehistoric Britain.

MILITARISATION AND THE GROWTH OF VILLAGES

Hill forts. Here and there the uplands of southern England are puckered by deep folds, as if some Titaness had smocked the smooth fabric of the open hills. Authorities agree that these earthworks are the relics of once extensive hill forts peculiar to the Iron Ages of prehistoric Britain. The earliest of them were the Island's answer to yet another threatened invasion.

Towards the middle of the third century B.C. the tranquillity of half a millennium, in which the traditions of the Deverel-Rimbury and Hallstatt ploughmen had matured, was rudely shattered by warriors from the Middle Rhine. Northwards, beyond the Lincoln Wolds, they were successful. In the south their way was contested and their progress halted by formidable hill-forts.

The structure and design of the forts were remarkably uniform. In extent they varied from 8 to 60 acres.[34] Even to-day what remains of the ramparts are high flung glissades. In their first

[33] Hawkes J. and C.: op. cit., p. 97.   [34] Childe: op. cit., pp. 196, 197.

glory capped with towering palisades they would present a spectacle of stupendous strength. In width they allow manoeuvre and fighting and about the entrance to the fort the great ramparts turn inwards to give an easily defended bottleneck. Highest points were not always chosen as the sites for for the hill forts. They occupy places of advantage commanding the widest panorama. They do not appear to be linked as units in a general strategic plan; each plays its own part. Size is, therefore, a criterion of responsibility and a pointer to the extent of the tribes and population groups within the defended aegis. The number and size of the forts suggest that the population of these later Iron Ages substantially exceeded earlier populations. A 60-acre fort at Cissbury, according to one estimate, meant the excavation and embanking of 35,000 cubic yards of virgin chalk and the erection of 10,000 heavy timber piles as a retaining wall. Forts were enlarged from time to time; one fort covered 230 acres in its final form. Later the ramparts of many were multiplied in number; and it is this elaboration which is responsible for the smocking effect. The early forts are impressive in their simple, majestic strength. The elaborate achievements of the last days would have beggared belief had not their gargantuan features cut deeply and permanently the smooth cheek of the hills.

Circular forts of Cornwall. In the tin areas of Cornwall comparatively small, circular forts or castles exceptionally wrought and presenting an architecture quite different from the hill-forts are noteworthy features of Iron Age land use. Only one, Chun Castle, a landmark at Land's End, has been fully studied[35]. In its prime the place was a bluff, impregnable fortress. Great granite blocks face two concentric ramparts of dry masonry of which the inner one is some 15 feet thick enclosing a circular court 170 feet in diameter. Ditches augment the defences between the ramparts and beyond the outer wall. No one can tell the original height of the inner walls; as late as a century ago the ruins stood twelve feet out of the ground. Chun Castle is by no means the largest of its type, others are twice or three times as large and boast ramparts of greater complexity.

Hill forts and urban centres. Hill forts and the granite-faced castles give evidence of human habitation within the inner keeps. Some attempt has been made[36] to ascribe to the hill fort the

[35] Childe, op. cit., p. 228.   [36] Op. cit., p. 199.

origin of urban life: the fort stands aloof from the square-field husbandry. Evidence does not readily support the theory. Hut sites are few within the forts and such as there are nestle against the ramparts. The forts do not appear to be cities of jostling populations. Whoever lived within the protected enceinte followed a life very similar to that of the husbandmen in the homesteads[37]. In some forts there is evidence of the corn silos of Early Iron Age culture. The silos may have been peculiar to wartime but whatever explanation may be given for them, they do not support the hypothesis of a densely populated urban centre. Unfinished workings, completed works never used, and signs of periodic neglect and restoration[38] support the notion that the hill-forts were centres of great military consequence and not permanent habitations. Anomalies in the evidence warn against too certain a confidence. It is not beyond the realms of probability or the nature of the evidence to suppose that the security of the forts attracted merchants and markets[39] much as the peace of the old English burghs did centuries later.

Villages of the Iron Age. Hill-forts, even if they were urban centres, did not accommodate the major part of the population. Ordinary folk inhabited clustered dwellings which Childe, as previously noted[40], does not hesitate to call nucleated villages. Clusters of primitive dwellings were no new thing. What is noteworthy of the closing centuries of pre-history is a definite tendency for the clusters to increase in size as though social structure had become more complex.

Three main types of village have been identified — the open, the walled and the lacustrine — and all three associate with the practice of square-field husbandry. One open village has been systematically and thoroughly excavated[41]. Eight asymmetric courtyard dwellings, each with an irregular garden plot, were discovered arranged in parallel formation about a common street. The settlement shows signs of repeated rebuilding and long occupation, probably from the second century B.C. to the third century of the Christian era. The walled villages were not defended strong points[42]. In plan they resemble a communal farmstead. Usually one hut sited in the centre of the compound dominates the others. Smaller huts, less prominent, within and without the stone walls cluster about the entrance of the village. Among the

[37] Op. cit., p. 200.
[38] Clark: op. cit., pp. 86, 87, 89.
[39] Childe: op. cit., p. 242.
[40] cf. p. 13 ante.
[41] Childe: op. cit., p. 230.
[42] Clark: op. cit., p. 34.

lacustrine settlements the most informative sites are those of the Iron Age lake villages of Glastonbury and Meare in Somerset. The Glastonbury site contained at one time no less than 60 households actively engaged in industrial crafts, trade and square-field husbandry[43]. A palisade of heavy timbers protected and supported the foundations of the crannog or artificial island and each dwelling house was built upon a timber platform supported and reinforced by stakes of its own. The buildings were doubtless light affairs and many of them appear to have been the subjects of endless rebuilding. The village is a masterly demonstration of early engineering; and life there must have called for a developed social consciousness and high code of responsibility.

SECULAR SOVEREIGNTY AND LAND LAW

The meaning of the hill-forts. The contribution of the hill-forts to the evidence for a secular land law in later prehistoric times at first sight is not convincing. Ramparts and defended palisades speak more of anarchy than the run of law, of a people possessing land by main force. Hitherto the argument of the chapter accepts defended boundaries as the sign-manual of the absence of law.

The hill-forts, however, present an altogether different set of circumstances. Had the builders who laboured to build the forts permanently occupied them, they could well betoken an age of anarchy. Admittedly, signs of habitation are found within them, but these signs lose all significance when it is remembered how great must have been the labour forces harnessed to the task of construction. The forts cannot have been permanently occupied by the communities responsible for building them. Permanent occupation within walls fortified against the immediate neighbourhood would have necessitated within the defended area an agriculture of great intensity. Intense agriculture would have been quite impossible if the forts were permanently occupied by the teeming population. The labour invested in the forts stands as a guide-post, pointing in the same direction as the giant temples of old to a social and political unity. Dominance of temple and tomb betoken an hierarchical sovereignty; but forts are not temples. Even if the kings who constructed them had been priestly persons, the purpose of their building was essentially and primarily secular. The forts imply a secular sovereignty and source of law. Care is

[43] Childe : op. cit., p. 235.

needed lest imagination overreaches what the facts allow. Secular sovereignty is a reasonable deduction, but to assume a national unity is going too far. The hill-forts stand alone, sentinels over autonomous domains. Military strategy does not join one to another in a vast defence system. Each defends its own lands. Some areas are larger than others; Cissbury casts its shoe over 35 square miles[44]. Doubtless some minor forts were subject to the hegemony of the greater, but as a general rule political and legal sovereignty is local, in the hands of the warriors who planned, built and administered the forts. From these authorities came the land law.

Deverel-Rimbury lawgivers. How far the threat of invasion and the defence programme that answered it were responsible for the origin of secular, political and legislative power cannot be known. If the argument from the boundary forms of Deverel-Rimbury and Hallstatt cattle ranches[45] is valid, the ploughmen must have been legislators centuries before they were fort-builders. If the lawgivers were secular lords, as the facts of the later centuries imply, they were probably an aristocracy ruling the ruck of ploughmen. Archaeology has valuable corroborative evidence to support this notion; traces of an aristocratic society who knew nothing of hill forts have been found.[46] The evidence is later than the true Deverel-Rimbury period, but before the time of multivalate forts. The aristocrats were invaders from the Marne. Invasion and conquest and the call for leadership tend to throw up an aristocracy of a military ruling class. So might it have been with the Deverel-Rimbury invaders, whose descendants became the fort-builders.

Landownership in the later villages.   The open, walled and lacustrine villages of the Late Bronze and Iron Ages in the companion-ship of the square-fields add something to the evidence for a land law. They cannot help to solve the problem of sovereignty and source of law. But their settlement patterns point to a more circumscribed ownership. The evidence is not different in principle from the testimony of the corn-plots and hut-circles of Neolithic times. It has a different vogue. The settlement patterns are larger and more closely knit. The greater the degree of compactness in land settlement the more confined are the rights of ownership. The owners of dwelling houses ranged wall against wall along

[44] Op. cit., p. 199.   [45] cf. pp. 13, 14 ante.
[46] Hawkes, J. and C., op. cit., p. 109.

the streets of the open villages and packed on the water-lapped platforms of the lacustrine villages must have suffered a restriction which cramped the freedom and plenary rights of natural ownership. Ownership would be confined and jealously guarded in these advanced villages and because of this would be more precisely defined. Whatever its form and content the land law was probably the creation of a secular aristocracy whose area of jurisdiction was determined by military circumstances.

CHAPTER I

SELECT BIBLIOGRAPHY

Bowen, E. G.: *Prehistoric South Britain* (Historical Geography of England, ed. H. C. Darby, 1948).

Childe, V. Gordon: *Prehistoric Communities of the British Isles* (3rd Ed., 1949).

Clark, Grahame: *Prehistoric England* (4th Ed., 1948).

Curwen, E. Cecil: *Air-Photography and the Evolution of the Cornfield* (2nd Ed., 1938).

Daniel, G. E.; Clark, J. G. D.; et al.: *The Heritage of Early Britain* (1952).

Hawkes, Jacquetta and Hawkes, Christopher: *Prehistoric Britain* (1947).

CHAPTER TWO

ROMAN BRITAIN

EVIDENCE MAINLY ARCHAEOLOGICAL

Marked advances have been made in the study of Roman Britain since the opening years of the present century. For the most part the new knowledge has been induced from the rewards of patient spade-work. Epigraphic evidence of value has been found but nothing documentary and the comment which Haverfield[1] made in 1905 lamenting the scanty evidence of land tenure in the province could for like cause be made to-day. An attempt to trace the lineaments of landownership in Roman Britain must, in consequence, depend a great deal upon inference and conjecture, the two guides who made progress possible through prehistory.

Compared with prehistory the extent of archaeological evidence is impressive. But the very fact that it lies on the near side of history's horizon brings dangers unknown to the undocumented ages. There is a temptation to suppose a similarity between the state of affairs in Britain and the economic and social conditions in other parts of the Roman world. In the archaeological record Romano-British villas may closely resemble their archetypes about the Imperial City, but that is no ground for assuming a similitude of tenure or ownership. The imperial ownership of military and certain other institutions might be sufficient to support analogies, but it would not be wise to postulate them where the only common feature is imperial law, as Roman law was not uniform throughout the Empire. Even literary references are uncertain guides. The Theodosian Code mentions *coloni* in Britain but it does not follow that the British colonate was identical in every respect with the colonate of Etruria[2] and elsewhere; local tribal custom may influence and conflict with Roman principles of land law.[2a]

Caution also is needed when reading classical agronomists: they know the husbandry of their own countries but not that of Britain. Attempts have been made[3] to make dry bones live by

---

[1] Haverfield (revised Macdonald): *The Romanisation of Roman Britain* (4th Ed.), p. 65.
[2] Haverfield (revised Macdonald): *The Roman Occupation of Britain*, p. 233.
[3a] cf. Stevens: *Journal of Roman Studies*, Vol. XXXVII, p. 132.
[3] cf. Seebohm: *The English Village Community*, and *The Tribal System in Wales.*

clothing the skeletal knowledge of land divisions in Roman Britain with the codified Celtic traditions of medieval times, but the effect is not convincing. What follows in this chapter is adduced primarily from local archaeological evidence.

LAND USE IN ROMAN TIMES

Salient Motifs. An eloquent testimony to archaeology is the fullness of detail which makes the Ordnance Survey Map of Roman Britain[4] so worthwhile a publication. Sufficient is shown for the main pattern of land use to be quickly seen. All cartographical representations of history suffer from either one or another of two inevitable defects: either the passage of time is telescoped until all historical perspective is lost, or one period is abstracted and past and future neglected. The Ordnance Survey of Roman Britain telescopes the centuries. Consequently the picture presents geographical, economic, political and social features as they would appear at the end of a development process growing steadily more complex. As it was, history did not proceed in this manner. Care, therefore, must be exercised when interpreting the map. Allowance must be made for the fact that probably at no time were all the villas and towns shown on it flourishing together; the time of villa prosperity coincided with the decay and even abandonment of many urban centres.[5] Nor can the map show the details that distinguish private villas from imperial concerns. But allowing for this and similar shortcomings, and for the long flowing and short ebbing of the Roman tide from the first century B.C. to the fifth century A.D., the map shows clearly the salient motifs of land use.

The most striking feature is the distribution of villas and villages on the one hand and fortifications and military works on the other. Assuming a divide from Tees Bay to Lyme Bay, slightly convex in its northern half, villas and villages with but few exceptions lie to the south-east, while the great fortified areas occupy the opposite side. Exceptions among villa and village sites are found more frequently along the margins of the Welsh mountains, among the fortifications in the vicinity of Eburacum[6] and along the Saxonicum Litus.[7] The military zone for the most part is co-extensive with the rugged terrain of the

---

[4] *Ordnance Survey Map of Roman Britain* (2nd Ed.)
[5] Frank (ed.): *An Economic Survey of Ancient Rome* (Vol. III), pp. 12, 13.
[6] York.   [7] The Saxon Shore.

ancient rocks; the Pennine backbone, the two clenched massifs of
Cumbria and Snowdonia and the knotty limbs of the Brecon
Hills and the South Western highlands. The civil zone is a rolling
country of soft lined hills, wide valleys and broad plains. Geological formations have played a significant part — a truth made
classical by Haverfield, Fox and other authorities.

Although Roman towns and villas are scarce in the highlands
proper, the map shows clearly how in the lowlands the slopes
of the chalk and limestone ridges and of the Downland plateaux
were favourite sites. Summits are avoided. In this the Romano-
Celts differ from the earlier Celts and follow the pioneering Belgae.
A side of a hill is the ideal. Settlements in valleys and plains
skirt the dense woodlands and deep marsh in favour of easier and
more friable driftlands. Celtic village sites also follow the alignment of the hills, but are not shy of hill-tops and river valleys;
a distribution to be expected from what is already known of
prehistoric fields and settlements.

Villas and villages are emblematic of the new and old
civilizations respectively. The villa is not invariably of
Roman occupation nor the village essentially Celtic. Rome, after
conquest, romanised those elements of a native population willing
to be taught her ways. Villa occupants are as a general rule
Romanised Celts. And so with the cities. Many have names
obviously romanised eponyms, inspired by the Celtic tribes
whose activities centred on them. Only a few attracted high
constitutional status. One, Verulamium, the tribal capital of the
strong Catuvellauni, alone acquired the rank of *municipium*[8]
a mark that the place was of native origin and of sufficient
importance for constitutional favours. Other towns of rank
are the *coloniae* — a term indicative of a more definite Roman
origin.[9] Attainment of rank, either as municipium or colonia,
is, as with the boroughs of a later day, not governed by size or
commercial significance, a fact so obvious in the failure of
Londinium, the greatest town in Britain, to obtain constitutional
standing.[10]

The limitation of villas and civilian life by the south-eastern
divide did not mean that the military zone knew nothing of
Roman civilization save the austerity of barrack-room and drill-

[8] Haverfield (revised Macdonald): op. cit., p. 190. There is some doubt
whether Verulamium was ever a true municipium (cf. Richmond: *Roman
Britain*, p. 77).
[9] Haverfield (revised Macdonald): op. cit.. p. 188.
[10] Gilbert: *The Human Geography of Roman Britain* (*Historical Geography
of England*, ed. Darby), p. 61.

square. Rigours of conquest gave way to easier days.[11] Trade and a semblance of Roman civilian life gathered about the larger auxiliary forts.[12] And in any event it was an inherent feature of the Roman military system to require auxiliary forts to be industrially and perhaps agriculturally self-supporting;[13] a policy which gave rise to special village settlements, or *vici*, in the neighbourhood of military establishments. Moreover, the mass of military reserve was quartered not on the restless frontiers but in the slack immediately to the rear. Here the great legionary fortresses become civilian and administrative landmarks.

Apart from this intermingling of civilian and military life, the civil and military zones have one common feature of major importance: the road system. Of proverbial directness the arterial roads run the length and breadth of the land linking forts, cities, villages and ports. The ancient, prehistoric track-ways are ignored. Often the roads appear, as in the Fen country and among the deep woodlands of the wet clays, to cleave for miles a most inhospitable country, but there is purpose in every mile. Another common feature are the mines which frequently account for exceptional settlement sites.

Such are the grand motifs of the land pattern, a loose tracery of new and old woven upon a vast fustian of forest and mountain and fen.

Agriculture. Of the more intimate features of the land pattern, the agricultural systems of Roman Britain are of undoubted importance. Urban and industrial life are relatively of less importance and in themselves agricultural and pastoral activity are outstanding achievements. Strabo, in the days before the Roman Conquest, refers to the export of corn from Britain. Diodorus refers to cutting it green to be stored in pits — the silos of prehistory.[14] Caesar writes of dense populations of men and cattle. And in the days of the Conquest and Occupation not only does the province feed the army and its dependants (estimated at 100,000)[15] but corn is exported for the relief of the Rhineland[16] and wool to eastern Europe.[17]

The bounty of Britain in her light, warm arable lands is

[11] Wheeler: *Prehistoric and Roman Wales*, p. 233.
[12] Richmond: *Ancient Rome and Northern England*, Ant. Vol. XIV, p. 297.
[13] Frank: op. cit., pp. 73, 91.
[14] Op. cit., p. 71.
[15] Collingwood: *Town and Country in Roman Britain*, Ant. Vol. III, p. 276.
[16] Randall: *Population and Agriculture in Roman Britain*, Ant. Vol. IV., p. 86.
[17] Haverfield (revised Macdonald): op. cit., p. 220.

notorious in these first days of her history. There was, however, more than one way to cultivate the soil. Three different systems of agriculture have been identified in Roman Britain. Little is known of two of them, the obscure techniques of the Belgae and the Roman villas. The third is the way of the ancients, the square-field husbandmen whose patchwork fields and lynchetted grids originate with the prehistoric ploughteams.

Until recent times historians supposed that the long, sinuous striplands characteristic of Anglo-Saxon agriculture were of Saxon origin. They were Saxon because the heavy, broad-shared, wheeled ploughs which formed them were Saxon. Recently doubt has been cast on this.[17a] Traces of heavy ploughs have been discovered associated with Belgic lands,[18] and strange elongated ploughings neither true Celtic nor true Saxon, disturb square-field lynchets on the Hampshire and Wiltshire Downs. The meaning is obscure. The inference authorities[19] are tempted to draw invests with the heavy plough the semi-Teutonic Belgae who immediately preceded the Romans in the invasion of southern Britain. The heavy plough, unlike the light two-oxen instrument, is formidable, strong enough to break a furrow through the dense soils of deep valleys and felled woodlands. The heavy instrument would enable the Belgae to open up the lower virgin lands and give cause for Caesar to remark that "they have begun to till the land." Evidence, how-ever, is very meagre. No trace of strip-systems comparable to the Saxon is known.

Another cause of obscurity is the relationship of the villa land economy and the square-field systems. On the map of Roman Britain are shown wide areas, notably Salisbury Plain, in which the only settlements are villages closely associated with the square-field system. There the traditional Celtic square-fields were not harnessed to the new villa economy, although there is evidence in other places of villas displacing primitive holdings and in others of villas associated with native hut sites in some way.[19a] Collingwood[20] argues that the villa owners operated an open-field system. He supports his case by a theory that open-fields are characteristic of the isolated holdings of prehistory and on some of them villas were set up in Roman times.

[17a] Hunter Blair : *An Introduction to Anglo-Saxon England*, p. 271.
[18] Curwen : *Air-Photography and The Evolution of the Cornfield* (2nd Ed.), p. 15.
[19] Barger : *The Present Position of Studies in English Field Systems*, E.H. Rev., Vol. LIII, 1938, p. 103.
[19a] Richmond : *Roman Britain*, pp. 124-128.
[20] Frank : op. cit., pp. 81, 82.

The Celtic square-fields. What the square-field system was is by no means clear. The almost regular grid lynchets by which the ancient workings are to-day identified cannot have been the coincidence of unregulated ploughing. Ploughmen know how little consistency there is between each day's ploughing. One day may favour the plough, another hinder it; beasts pull well in some hours and fail in others; seasons are bewitched by accident or blessed by ordered progress. A day's work is a margin of more or less about a common average. The sun never obediently sets as the last furrow of a constant, daily number runs out on the headland. If the lynchets are the termini of ploughing work, the grid layouts must have been predetermined for the ploughman. The lynchets are not the fortuitous expression of day work meeting day work. Someone must have set out the square-fields.

None can tell with any finality what notions of mensuration prompted the layouts. Western Europe recognised a day's work in diverse ways. The Romans called it *actus quadratus*; a rectangular plot representing twice the square of a two-oxen plough furrow (by modern standards approximately 120' x 240').[21] The square-fields of Britain do not exhibit a regularity suggestive of layouts carefully co-related to a common standard of this measure, although Curwen has indicated a tendency for the plots to vary in size about a norm which could be a crude multiple of *actus quadratus* or some similar measure.

The grid formation is the result of chains of plots running at right-angles to each other. The widths of the chains often bear definite proportions to each other; some chains are twice or three times the width of others. Frequently they narrow to one end, not acutely but with sufficient consistency to support the idea that each link in the chain has meaningful alignment with its neighbour. The chain alignments were probably set out before the traverse divisions which divide them into the familiar squares and rectangles. Some lynchet systems[22] show a marked tendency for squares of uniform size to be arranged in groups of two or three, and it is not too fanciful to see in this evidence for rotational cropping.[23] Certainly the divisions have an origin other than the

---

[21] Curwen : op. cit., p. 19.
[22] Notably that of Buckland Bank, Falmer (Cf. Holleyman : *The Celtic Field-System in South Britain*, Ant. Vol. IX, pp. 443-454).
[23] Curwen has shown that this is in fact the purpose of similar divisions in remote Celtic lands today.

common termini of furrow cuts and in some parts they have been made permanent by megalithic boundary stones.[24]

Villas. Whatever the agricultural secrets of the square-field husbandmen may have been there is little to show that they shared them with the owners of the Roman villas. The villa is not a town-house in the modern sense. A certain looseness in handling the word has prompted authorities to attempt definitions. Collingwood,[25] in one place, equates villa with "any house of the Roman period . . . provided that it was the dwelling of people, somewhat romanised in manners, who farmed a plot of land; as opposed to a town-house on the one hand and a cottage on the other." In another place [26] he makes it clear that the occupier of a villa need not be an agriculturalist, provided his occupation showed some affinity with agriculture. Haverfield[27] has a wider definition which embraces any agricultural building. The term seems to throw a promiscuous embrace over all residential, agrarian units isolated and distinct from the Celtic square-field holdings. Villas are Roman, not, as formerly supposed, the property of true Romans. Authorities are agreed that Roman occupation was the exception, and in the normal event, the occupier or proprietor was a romanised Briton.

Villas vary in size from humble husbandry units to enormous concerns housing vast labour forces. Magnificent villas are the achievement of a developed culture and rural economy[27a]. A considerable degree of self-sufficiency is characteristic especially of the great establishments, although the higher the culture and standard of living the more insistent become the demands for exotic luxuries. Some of the more extensive villas seem to have produced home-made cloth, tiles and metal-work.[28] Here and there proud dominating villas have enlarged their borders and gathered humbler establishments about themselves to form compound properties.[29] The policy is exceptional. Normally the villa economy focusses upon a farmstead independent of off-premises and lesser dwellings. But the influence of a substantial villa must have radiated far. The commerce, comfort and culture of the Empire is there in micro-

---

[24] Raistrick and Chapman : *The Lynchet Groups of Upper Wharfedale, Yorkshire*, Ant. Vol. III, pp. 165-181.
[25] Collingwood : *The Archaeology of Roman Britain*, p. 113.
[26] Frank : op. cit., p. 80.
[27] Haverfield (revised Macdonald) : op. cit., p. 224.
[27a] Richmond : *Roman Britain*, p. 109.
[28] Frank : op. cit., p. 79.
[29] Op. cit., p. 80.

cosm. Villas are the hall-marks of civilization and the symbols of prosperity in rural areas.

Unfortunately, little is known of the layouts of villas, apart from the fact that a farmstead is the central point about which the agricultural economy turns. Only the humblest villas have farmsteads of a single building.[30] Usually, barns, stores, boxes, stabling and even small dwellings are ranged about the principal dwelling house. In southern Britain grassland tended to replace an arable agriculture on the villa lands while in the north a reverse process took place.

Rural dwelling houses were of three main architectural types:[31] the courtyard house, the corridor house and the basilican house. Superior villas were built to a courtyard pattern. A villa at North Leigh,[32] Oxfordshire, is a good example. A square courtyard, approximately 190 feet by 160 feet, is enclosed by ranges of buildings about three of its sides, and gives a sense of compactness to the whole. In the house the main rooms face the open end of the courtyard. The wings comprise less elaborate living quarters and what appear to be farm buildings. From what is known of the place it seems reasonable to assume that it housed an entire land staff animals and equipment. Ward-Perkins[33] has identified and described a Roman villa at Lockleys in Hertfordshire as one which provides "a fair picture of the type of small farmhouse that was the backbone of the Roman villa-system in this country." Here the house is a modest corridor pattern, containing about a dozen rooms mainly at ground level. Not every room is used for a domestic purpose; some are rough-floored and give the impression of belonging to a farmstead under a roof common with the residence. No other buildings have been discovered, but there is reason to suppose from analogous sites that somewhere within the enceinte of the surrounding fence and ditch additional steading had been erected. Structure, like design, portrays wealth and taste, although local building materials often determine the construction of a place. The majority of villas were timber framed erections standing upon brick or masonry foundations; this certainly was so of Lockleys. A high degree of comfort, outmoding the typical accoutrements of modern farmhouses, was reached in all but the humblest villa; rooms were heated by hypocausts, and bath-suites provided even in the servants' quarters.

[30] Collingwood : op. cit., p. 134.
[31] Op. cit., p. 114.
[32] Op. cit., p. 126.
[33] Ward-Perkins : *Roman Villa, Lockleys, Welwyn*, Ant. Vol. XIV, pp. 317-320.

Urban centres. Rural villas were never jealous of the domestic architecture of the urban areas. Throughout the province the total urban area probably never exceeded 2,560 acres,[34] and much of this was *rus in urbe.* The urban areas were sufficiently distinct from rural life to develop an architecture and landownership peculiar to themselves. They are the logical outcome of Roman civilisation and were designed, constituted and planned to reflect in a thousand mirrors the strategy, commerce and culture of the great Civitas. The manner of their ordaining and the nature of their affinity with tribal centres were not the same in each province. In the province of Britain three main classes have been identified[35] : the municipium and colonia; Romanised tribal centres; and other centres of importance.

By the time of the Claudian invasion (A.D.43) the Belgae settled in the south-east had built up a cohesive state centred at Camulodunum.[36] Previously the centre of government had been the flourishing but less conspicuous Verulamium. Verulamium lost political prestige, but in Roman eyes the place was sufficiently notorious and worthy to attract the rank of municipium. Camulodunum was made a colonia and became Colonia Victricensis, the first colonia in Britain, and the first tribal centre to receive municipal rank. A colonia is an urban centre built and administered for the benefit of time-expired legionaries; an essential which distinguishes coloniae from municipia is the apparentation of the army.[37] Three other coloniae sprang up in the wake of the legions; Lindum,[38] Glevum,[39] and Eburacum.[40] Politically the difference between the conceptions of legal status is slight.[41] Both types of city are governed by municipal officers and an *ordo,* or senate, and the inhabitants have the status of Roman citizens. Within a relatively wide circumference, the municipal government extends to the countryside. Roman polity abhorred the indefinite administration of rural government. But the effective range of a moderate municipality is limited, [42] and in a land like Britain of well organised tribal government, concessions had to be made.

There arose a quasi-municipal administration based upon tribal

---

[34] Gilbert : op. cit., p. 65.
[35] Gilbert : op. cit., p. 43.
[36] Colchester.
[37] Haverfield (revised Macdonald) : op. cit., p. 188.
[38] Lincoln.   [40] York.
[39] Gloucester.   [41] cf. p. 22 ante.
[42] Haverfield (revised Macdonald) : *The Romanisation of Roman Britain* (4th Ed.), p.58.

areas.[43] It was in these areas that the Romanised tribal towns were established. History endorses the evidence of pre-history: the Romans found a country divided among tribes, each wielding political power over a large or small area defended by a ramparted hill-fort or open site. The wider the area of country through which a unified law ran the greater was the distance between the hill-forts and the more advanced the development of statecraft; the Brigantes of the north and the Belgae of the south were outstandingly advanced.[44] Rome failed to municipalise in an orthodox manner the political and social centres of the tribes. The conquerors drove the tribesmen from the hill-top defences to lower sites and wove the tribal territories into a pattern of administrative cantons each centred upon a tribal capital. There are twelve of these capitals. During the Occupation they affect a tribal nomenclature:[45] the Iceni look to Venta Icenorum;[46] the Silures to Venta Silurum;[47] the western Belgae to Venta Belgarum;[48] the Atrebates to Calleva Atrebatum;[49] and so on. The compulsory toga was but lightly worn and when Rome finally withdrew the garment was laid aside with almost indecent haste.[50]

The tribal centres were artefacts of Roman colonisers. Other lesser towns were not so. Their growth was more natural. They developed not according to factitious planning but out of "groups of houses clustered by the side of a road or at a place where two roads meet, or where a road crosses a river".[51] There were many of these towns. It was from such unpretentious beginnings that the two greatest cities of the Province eventually blossomed; in the west Corinium Dobunorum[52] and in the south-east Londinium.[53] Other towns were fostered for specific purposes exemplified by Ariconium[54] an iron smelting centre, and Aquae Sulis,[55] a health spa.

Siting, design and structure. Recent excavations at Belgic Camulodunum have revealed only one major occupation site. Whatever stood upon it was too thoroughly destroyed to leave

---

[43] Op. cit., p. 62.
[44] Childe: *Prehistoric Communities of the British Isles*, p. 254.
[45] Gilbert: op. cit. p. 43.   [48] Winchester.
[46] Caistor-by-Norwich.   [49] Silchester.
[47] Caerwent.
[50] Haverfield attributes the rapid abandonment of the tribal suffixes in the nomenclature to tribal indifference, but the change may have been a consequence of Saxon domination: [Haverfield (revised Macdonald): op. cit., p. 61.]
[51] Collingwood: op. cit., p. 92.
[52] Cirencester.   [54] Weston under Penyard.
[53] London.   [55] Bath.

any indication of structure. Elsewhere buildings were either simple huts or larger, asymmetrical timber constructions scattered indiscriminately. Strategical placements can be discerned, but no evidence of architectural site-planning. Scholars who undertook the excavations when reporting their discoveries make the categorical statement that " of a house of civilised build there is no sign";[56] and yet they sum up their evidence by concluding that Camulodunum was more deeply influenced by Rome than any other British centre of its time. What is true of Camulodunum is true also of Verulamium. Dr. Wheeler's[57] account of that Belgic city gives little evidence of domestication and architectural advance.

The vast earthworks of Verulamium and Camulodunum resemble in many respects the great ramparts of the ancient hill forts. The cities are characteristically sited away from hill summits in woodland clearings but apart from this feature, which made their locations attractive to the Romans, there is little that gave them *pas* in native eyes. The relatively lowland pitches of these Belgic *oppida* did not save them from the Roman policy of abandonment and re-siting.[58] Removal was less dramatic than the wholesale descent from the hill-tops but it was nevertheless complete. The Roman municipium of Verulamium lies clear of the Belgic embankment by 300 yards.[59] And Colonia Victricensis lies about 880 yards to the east from Sheepen, the original site of Camulodunum.[60] Apparently in the far west, beyond the civil zone, Rome counted her fortifications and military placements sufficient to wink at the contemporary erection of native fortified towns of traditional style among the hill-tops.[61] The slight but definite removes of the Roman developments at Belgic centres were the nearest the Empire ever came to honouring native sites in Britain. At all points cities and towns of Roman Britain are founded upon virgin soil.

In the past similar conclusions were deduced from the rigid, symmetrical grid-pattern of Roman town-planning.[62] To-day this evidence is suspect. So much more is known of the origin of Roman towns and the chess-board town-plan is not within the new knowledge. Londinium, in the view of Dr. Wheeler,[63] grew

[56] Hawkes and Hull : *Camulodunum*, p. 50.
[57] Wheeler, R.E.M., and T.V.: *Verulamium; A Belgic and Two Roman Cities.*
[58] Gilbert : op. cit., p. 42.
[59] Wheeler, R.E.M. and T.V.: op. cit., plt. CXVIII.
[60] Hawkes and Hull : op. cit., plt. I.
[61] Wheeler : *Prehistoric and Roman Wales*, p. 259.
[62] Haverfield : *Ancient Town Planning*, p. 129.
[63] Wheeler : *London in Roman Times*, p. 22.

an inchoate, struggling parasite about London Bridge. Not until the old city had been sacked and razed to the ground by Boudiccan patriots in A.D.61 did the comprehensively planned port, displaying the classical chess-board street system, arise. The first Roman Verulamium was probably a free developing growth of humble dwellings and other buildings about a favoured section of the Watling Street, displaying perhaps hydra-headed ribbon-development. Its story is not the beatific vision of town planning idealists.[64] Silchester also:[65] the extreme conformity of chess-board orthodoxy which the street-plan displays was apparently a feature of later days, when in some mysterious manner streets running perpendicular to each other were interlaced among the earlier structures. Something of a comparable tale is told of Camulodunum.[66] Whatever may have been the form and plan of the first colonia, the Roman edifices built upon the Belgic location were most haphazardly sited. While recent knowledge tends to contradict the opinion that the first serious establishment of towns in Roman Britain took place in the Flavian period, it sees in that period the beginnings of serious town-planning on the chess-board principle.[66a] The early opinion had been largely influenced by a reference in Tacitus to Agricola who boldly states that it was he who "encouraged them by personal advice and public assistance to build temples, fora and houses".[67]

One of the most incongruous features of many cities whose interior plans conform to the orthodox chess-board layout is the irregularity and lack of symmetry of the boundary walls. Meaningless outlines, polygonal and curvilinear, defeat the logical aspirations of the chess-board planners. Various interpretations have been offered to account for this roguish disregard of planning convention. An early theory places the orthodox Roman planning within the baroque, native embankments. The virgin sites of Roman colonisation explode this theory. And they do more: they confound the notion that the Roman architect is a greater visionary than a realist. Virgin sites are a heaven on earth for town-planners; who could fail to make dreams come true on open land unencumbered by the agglomerations of past generations? And yet Rome

[64] Wheeler, R.E.M. and T.V.: op. cit., pp. 25, 75.
[65] Fox, A.: The Early Plan and Town Houses of Silchester, Ant. Vol. XXII, pp. 172-8.
[66] Hawkes and Hull: op. cit., pp. 51-56.
[66a] Collingwood and Myres: Roman Britain and the English Settlements (2nd Ed.), p. 191.
[67] Frank: op. cit., p. 48.

failed. The first towns in Britain lacked logical precision and gave
way to wild abandonment about their perimeters.

The case is worsened when archaeologists discover considerable
time gaps between the inauguration of chess-board planning and
the erection of city walls. At Silchester[68] the walls have been
assigned to the later half of the 2nd century, but chess-board
planning was introduced in the first half of the century. The
massive walls of the later Roman city at Verulamium were erected
by the Emperor Hadrian to embrace a virile urban area of fifty
or more years growth.[69] The walls of Caerwent may well have
been contemporary with those of Verulamium but the Roman
planning was probably Flavian.[70] Londinium too had been given
walls, but subsequent to the city's spread.[71] The concensus of
evidence strongly supports a theory put forward by Haverfield[72]
with less data to instruct him, that in Britain the boundary lines
of cities were "drawn simply to enclose the necessarily shapeless
areas which had come to be occupied by houses." Land contours
and military considerations doubtless had some bearing upon
the ultimate alignment of city walls. But walls that were the mere
panache of an emperor, as the case was at Verulamium,[73] must
have followed the outline of a city inconsiderate enough to cock a
snook at the chess-board ideal.

Apart from what appears to be a lack of continuity in planning
policy, it does not require a minute examination of city layouts
where orthodox planning has been introduced to observe a
measurable disregard of street alignment and planning ideals. Where
Roman influence was more dominant, as at Caerwent,[74] the
anomalies are less noticeable; elsewhere, especially at Silchester,[75]
they are quite bold. There some aberrations are due to the
superimposition of an orthodox street plan upon an irregular
layout, but other deviations display what appears to be a wanton
disregard of street alignment. When the orthodox, chess-board
street plan was adopted the public baths were apparently mutilated
and forced into conformity with the new plan, but existing
domestic buildings were not the subject of such a Procrustean
method.

[68] Fox, A., op. cit., p. 172.
[69] Wheeler, R. E. M. and T. V.: op. cit., pp. 6, 27.
[70] Wheeler: *Prehistoric and Roman Wales*, p. 243.
[71] Wheeler: *London in Roman Times*, p. 24.
[72] Haverfield (revised Macdonald): *The Roman Occupation of Britain*, p. 203.
[73] Wheeler, R. E. M. and T. V.: op. cit., p. 76.
[74] Wheeler: *Prehistoric and Roman Wales*, p. 249.
[75] Fox, A.: op. cit., p. 173.

Town houses. Town houses in Roman Britain differ from rural villas although rural designs are found among them. The distinctive type of town house has its entrance through the gabled end of a rectangular building sited more or less perpendicularly to the street axis. Some have elaborations or wings. Exactly when programmes of ambitious house design and construction and splendid public buildings commenced it is not possible to say.[75a] In their hey-day the Romano-British cities boast a not unenviable magnificence, and yet "Ichabod" is soon written over many a proud city. Roman cities decayed quickly in Britain, victims of native apathy and over-expenditure of public and private wealth. Rural villas flourished in their stead.

Military works. Many urban areas were less than 50 acres in extent, smaller than the legionary fortresses of the military zone. Within that zone the greatest demand for habitable land came from the great fortresses. They differed from the cities of the civil zone, not only in essential purpose and function, but in appearance; they were more faithful to preconceived and formal planning. That this should be so is readily understood. Planning as an abstract idea has no virtue in itself; virtue withholds her accolade until the purpose of the plan is. known and deemed worthy. The military engineers who planned and built the great fortresses[76] of Isca Silurum,[77] Deva,[78] and Eburacum[79] understood the purpose of their labours and planned accordingly. Consequently, a marked feature of the Roman legionary fortresses of Britain is uniformity of site plan. In size they average about 50 acres within rectangular earthern ramparts. Later, stonework revetments were introduced and finally, about the opening of the third century, all walls and buildings were rebuilt in stone. Internally the fortresses tend to follow the plan of the small forts although the commandant's quarters probably permitted a higher standard of living.

The legionary forts were invariably manned by Roman citizens, but the smaller forts, as distinct from temporary campaigning camps, housed either infantry cohorts or cavalry levied from recently conquered tribes. Some forts carried a nominal strength of 500 men and others twice the number. The nominal housing capacity determines the size of the fort; the smaller types vary between 3-4 acres, while the larger range between 4-6 acres.

[75a] cf. C. A. F. Berry, *The Dating of Romano-British Houses,* Journal of Roman Studies, Vol. XLI, p. 25.
[76] Collingwood: op. cit., pp. 14-24.
[77] Caerleon-on-Usk.   [78] Chester.   [79] York.

There is no fixed standard. Forts of later years tended to be more extensive. As with the fortresses, the earthworks and timber rein-forcements gave place in time to stone revetments and to struc-tures entirely of masonry. A fort was generally rectangular although irregularity was a feature of the earliest types and certain forts of the late-Empire on the Saxon Shore.

Fortresses and forts demanded more land than the actual fortified area. Self-sufficiency was a maxim of Roman military policy.[80] Economically each establishment reaches out for itself. Agriculture and pastoral husbandry are practised and tileries are developed. At least one set of mineral workings has been iden-tified as the industrial activity of a fortress.[81] These adventitious enterprises of permanent garrisons were responsible for the growth of affiliated villages for relatives, dependants, agriculturalists and others attached to the garrison. In later times garrisons were wont to quit the ramparts for the villages or *vici* beyond.[82] Two vici subsequently flourished into important cities; one against the Ouse under the shadow of the north-eastern legionary fortress became the city of York; and the other, a trading vicus against Hadrian's Wall, is now the city of Carlisle.

Hadrian's Wall girdled the province in the north between Tyne and Solway. The Vallum or ditch ran parallel with it half-a-mile to the south. Wall and Vallum were military works of exception.[83] Eight score signal towers and half as many sub-forts or mile-castles were interspersed between seventeen auxiliary forts, and the whole was harnessed together from sea to sea by 73 miles of solid masonry. Along the outer front ran a defence ditch, and to the rear ran the Vallum, 30 feet wide and 7 feet deep, with its own complement of forts, milecastles and causeways. The entire complex made peculiar demands upon the frontier land. Not only are all the usual impacts traceable but in addition gaunt quarries and disused limekilns tell something of the price paid in terms of land wealth.

Roads. In its demand made for stone and minerals the great Wall resembles another important military feature, the network of major roadways.[84] Minor ways have been lost to history, but it is reasonable to suppose they covered an impressive mileage and con-tributed no small weight to the general pressure upon land re-

[80] Richmond : *Ancient Rome and Northern England*, Ant. Vol. XIV, p. 293.
[81] Frank : op. cit., p. 41.
[82] Collingwood : op. cit., pp. 19, 25.
[83] Frank : op. cit., p. 53.
[84] Collingwood : op. cit., pp. 1-4.

sources. As the frontiers were pushed westwards and northwards the military roads accommodated civilian traffic. Little reparation work was undertaken in the civil zone until the launching, in the third century, of a general road reparation and construction policy.[85] The demand for road metals in the military zone has, of course, always to be reckoned with.

Mines. Over the southern roads pigs of lead have been discovered, sufficient in number to indicate trade routes and the location of lead mines.[86] Lead and its associates, silver and zinc, were the most important minerals mined in Roman Britain, although iron ore and coal were widely exploited and copper was also worked.[87] The tin streams of Cornwall were neglected until the evening years of the Empire. Gold, one of the lures of the conquest, was probably mined at Dolaucothy in Wales.[88] Little is know of actual mining sites. Coal shafts have been found indicative of open-cast workings. Slag heaps and furnaces often associated with vast woodland clearances betoken smeltings;[89] and articles of Roman usage in ancient workings are tell-tales of mining ways. Where sites have been definitely identified only two — a Mendip lead mine and the gold settlement in Wales — display evidence of architectural and technical practice and social conventions comparable with Roman standards and genius. Here and there, especially in the north, the discovery of mineral workings associated with vici sites suggests local mines opened for the benefit of the garrisons.[90] Usually the mining settlements are native villages resembling those in the company of the square-field agriculture. In some parts native miners probably lived in the shafts of the mine.[91] Mining villages as a general rule seem to have had Roman oversight, but essentially they are Celtic interests and lead pigs and other prepared metals have been found bearing tribal names.[92]

LAND TENURE

The testimony of graphic evidence. Gaulish schoolmasters, it is said,[93] taught British lawyers. Whatever may be the truth in this statement, nothing of their pedagogy has been discovered. Nowhere is the land law of Roman Britain revealed. Literary and

[85] Frank : op. cit., p. 26.
[86] Gilbert : op. cit., p. 73.
[87] Frank : op. cit., p. 38.
[88] Wheeler : op. cit., p. 273.
[89] Gilbert : op. cit., p. 71.
[90] Frank : op. cit., p. 42.
[91] Frank : op. cit., p. 38.
[92] Op. cit., pp. 43, 45.
[93] Haverfield (revised Macdonald) : op. cit., p. 245.

epigraphic evidence has been preserved sufficient in range and depth of detail to identify three great categories of proprietorship: imperial, incorporate and private.

Imperial ownership. Imperial rights of ownership are traceable over agricultural lands, mines, other industrial establishments and roads. A historian writing of the Boudiccan revolt identifies the prime cause as the confiscation of property[94] which the Emperor Claudius had previously given the king of the Iceni.[95] Imperial ownership of land must, therefore, have been established prior to the gift.

An inscription found near Bath reads:"for the welfare of the Emperor Caesar Marcus Aurelius Antoninus, pious, fortunate, invincible, august; Naevius, freedman of the Emperor and assistant to the procurators, rebuilt from the ground the principia which had become dilapidated". This epigraph has been taken by Collingwood[96] as referring to the rebuilding of a bailiff's courtyard villa on imperial land. The evidence of imperial ownership of mines is limited to lead mines and consists of the Emperor's name stamped upon lead pigs.[97] Imperial proprietorship of other industrial concerns is deduced from a reference in the *Notitia Dignitatum* to the imperial manager of weaving-mills at Venta[97a] in Britain, and from the names of emperors stamped upon building tiles.[98] A proprietary responsibility for arterial roads has been assumed where imperial milestones record construction and repair at the hand of an emperor.[99] All these sources are too exiguous for any definition of the law of ownership, but they point to an imperial order of ownership.

Corporate ownership. One of the most telling inscriptions indicative of communal action and proprietary interest is the commemoration of the forum at Wroxeter:[100] "In honour of the Emperor Caesar Trajanus Hadrianus, son of the divine Trajanus Parthicus, grandson of the divine Nerva, pontifex maximus, in

---

[94] Carey's translation of Dio's history at this point refers to confiscations of money, which Claudius had given, but it is difficult to imagine how money *qua* money could be confiscated nearly twenty years after the gift.

[95] Frank : op. cit., p. 15.   [96] Frank : op. cit., p. 80.

[97] Haverfield, op. cit., p. 258.

[97a] This is almost certainly Venta Belgarum. (Cf. Richmond, *Roman Britain*, p. 132.)

[98] Frank : op. cit., pp. 102, 106.

[99] Collingwood : op. cit., p. 5.

[100] Frank : op. cit., p. 49.

the fourteenth year of his tribunician power, thrice consul, father of his country; erected by the civitas of the Cornovii". Here the Cornovii seem to be acting with a sense of bodiliness, although there is no evidence of the *persona ficta* of medieval times. Nevertheless the epigraph is a testimony to joint action by a Celtic tribe and, read in conjunction with the reference[101] of Tacitus to the granting of public assistance for the erection of temples and fora, points firmly to something in the nature of corporate ownership of public buildings. The public assistance of which Tacitus writes may have been given indirectly in the form of military labour,[102] but it probably consisted of grants from government funds; at all events there is room for both interpretations. Other evidence also points to corporate ownership. The community of the Silures erect a monument at Caerwent;[103] and the Respublica Glevensium apparently own a tilery.[104] Repair responsibility for sections of Hadrian's frontier wall is assigned to the civitates of certain cities in the south and north of the province. And tribal interest in mining wealth is probable.

Private ownership. Evidence of corporate action undertaken by a guild of artificers in the earliest days of the occupation has been found at Chichester.[105] The inscription is noteworthy as it also alludes to private ownership in the following words: "This temple was erected to Neptune and Minerva, for the welfare of the Imperial family, by authority of Tiberius Claudius Cogidubnus, King and Imperial legate in Britain, at the expense of the guild of artificers and its members, the site presented by Clemens, son of Pudentinus." Literary evidence for private ownership occurs in the text already quoted describing the gifts of land to the king of the Iceni. And the Theodosian Code refers to the private land both in hand and occupied by *coloni* of tax-paying decurions in Britain;[106] an insufficient reference upon which to build precise notions of tenure, but indicative of a colonate system of some kind.

It has been suggested[107] that Caesar's allusion to *creberrima aedificia* is sufficient to admit the presumption of self-contained land holdings in pre-Roman Britain, but the evidence is not very convincing. Of greater cogency are the names of private persons

---

[101] p. 31 ante. [102] Frank: op. cit., p. 52.
[103] Wheeler: op. cit., p. 244.
[104] Haverfield (revised Macdonald): *The Romanisation of Roman Britain*, p. 63.
[105] Frank: op. cit., p. 57. [106] Haverfield: op. cit. p. 65.
[107] Frank: op. cit., p. 81.

stamped upon lead pigs and copper ingots; these suggest limited private interests in the lead minings and even a greater degree of private ownership in copper workings.[108]

The testimony of analogy. The danger and usefulness of analogy as a means of throwing light upon landownership in Roman Britain have already been mentioned.[109] The danger cannot be over emphasised. But as graphic evidence points to three classifications of property it is surely safe to seek a similar classification in the better documented lands of the Empire.

Imperial property. Consider first of all imperial property. The first emperors had considerable wealth in land but nothing comparable with the vast imperial landed interests created by confiscation and other means from the days of Tiberius until Septimus Severus.[110] Severus attempts to distinguish what he is pleased to call *res privata* from other imperial wealth because, since the establishment of a fiscus by Claudius, imperial revenue from many sources gravitated into the personal hand of the emperor. Fortresses and forts with their annexed lands and interests and all roads constructed for military purposes were imperial property. A policy to place control of gold and silver mines in the hands of the Emperor also dates from Tiberius. Here is evidence enough to support in a general way a tentative case for imperial property in Britain. General documentary sources which permit this view also make it plain that at no time is there an attempt to standardise tenure.[111] Political, geographic, economic, climatic and other factors make it impossible to do so, even within the otherwise homogeneous category of imperial possessions.

Roads are no exception. Great roads were built by Hadrian across Spain, Africa and Asia probably by military labour at his own expense, but the same Emperor extracted a road charge of one-third of the cost of construction from the owners of land adjoining the Appian way.[112] It is reasonable to suggest that proprietary rights were more uniform where the property was essentially military. Rome never creates a sharp antithesis between her ways and the ways of the provinces.[113] Whatever may have constituted imperial military ownership in Mauretania was doubtless of different mould in Brigantia.

[108] Frank: op. cit., pp. 38, 44   [109] cf. p. 20 ante.
[110] Frank: op. cit. (Vol. V), pp. 16, 87.
[111] Op. cit. (Vol. II), p. 74 et seq.
[112] Op. cit. (Vol. V), p. 72.
[113] Haverfield (revised Macdonald): *The Roman Occupation of Britain,* p. 175.

Municipal property. At the heart of the Empire municipalities held land corporately by ancient tradition. From these lands public revenue is raised to meet expenditure upon a wide range of urban services — walls, streets, bridges, water supplies, theatres, baths, sewers, monuments and so on.[114] New municipalities appear to be similarly financed. Not only did ownership of public land bring financial benefit, it gave the municipal authorities considerable control over landed interests both within and without the urban area. Nothing is known of the manner or degree in which the system was adopted in Britain, but it would be over-timid to refuse, for want of direct evidence, any recognition of the policy. The existence of colonia and the public actions of the *civitates* living within them are attested beyond cavil. Details of law and the niceties of rights of ownership cannot be expected but it is reasonable to postulate the existence of the system in the coloniae and perhaps at Verulamium. Absence of legal status makes it wise to abstain from pressing the analogy in favour of other towns, and especially in the direction of the Celtic cantons.

Private property. If analogy is so barren towards municipal and imperial tenures, there is perhaps little point in raising the question of private property. But the Empire does most readily recognise private landed wealth, and supports vast private possessions. Wide ranging possessions called *latifundia* are countenanced in Italy and Sicily.[115] They are extensive areas in private ownership comprising smaller units or *fundi*. The possessions were built up of lesser properties and eventually led to an agricultural tenantry. There seems to have been something like a tenurial chain of lord, mesne tenant and tenant in demesne; if the terminology of high feudalism may for a moment illustrate the relationships of tenure without doing violence to them. On the lower rung of the tenurial ladder are the working tenantry or *coloni*. These are spoken of, it will be remembered, in the Theodosian Code in a reference to Britain. All that can be read into the reference is the existence of a peasantry of some order; whether the reference was to husbandmen of the Romano-Celtic villa-system or to Celtic workers on the square-fields none can tell. Again, the great villas of Britain may mean the presence of *latifundia*, and the grouping of small ones evidence of *fundi*.[116] All speculation vaporizes in the fact that the occupants of the villas were Celts and not Romans.

[114] Frank: op. cit. (Vol. V), p. 103.   [115] Op. cit. (Vol. III), pp. 363-367.
[116] Op. cit. (Vol. III), p. 80.

The testimony from inference. In addition to the above contributions from written and epigraphic evidence the physical
features of the square-field culture and the rural villas, and the
siting of property in urban areas have something to give. Evidence
is exceedingly enigmatical and desperately thin, but the addition
nonetheless worth giving.

A suggestion was made earlier[117] that the grid pattern of the
square-field husbandry was not fortuitous; someone, with deliber-
ation and rational intent, set each square and rectangle in its place;
the lynchets are boundaries of proprietary significance. Behind the
grid-pattern lies a secret of ownership and tenure. Little more than
that can be inferred. It is not beyond probability, however, that
the semblance of definite proportions between the widths of the
chains is due to a division among heirs. If differences in lynchet
depths were measured and correlated with width variations the
hypothesis might be tested; the lynchets of the original allotments would be deeper than those of the later subdivisions.

The separation of square-fields and villas supports the idea that
the custom or law behind the square-fields in Roman times remained fundamentally Celtic. In the Fens square-fields have been found
upon land drained extensively by Roman land drains. The drainage works are not in the proximity of villa sites and their association with the square-fields may represent a superior private
ownership dominating and controlling an emphyteutic tenantry[118]
It is unlikely. The theory is contrary to the bulk of evidence for
the square-fields and the villa-system and there is nothing to support a case for emphyteutic tenure. The great villas can house
with comfort a domiciled tenantry but lack of evidence for land
division, and the centrality and extent of the homesteads suggest
an unlaminated ownership. On the smaller villas there is even less
cause to assume the existence of a tenurial system of landlords
and tenants. Residential ownership seems to be the vogue among
the villas.

Country air always circulates through the towns. Silchester has
urban houses blessed by extensive gardens, nearby open
spaces and a carefree reaction towards town-planning.
The rigidity of town-plans generally and the endeavours at Silchester and elsewhere to align public buildings with new streets
points to serious intention in the minds of the responsible
authorities to control the development of the Romano-Celtic towns.
But nevertheless there is a healthy regard for private property.

[117] p. 25 ante.   [118] Frank : op. cit. (Vol. III), p. 86.

Only public buildings are squeezed and twisted. The town-plan cannot have been of great moment to private owners. Later alignments of domestic buildings were probably an expression of compulsory planning, but could just as well be the result of voluntary siting following logically upon a deposited plan. The inability to control future development at the perimeter shows considerable laxity in planning control and yet some authority has the power to project chess-board streets across the interlacery of private boundaries, and to design, erect and finance the building of city walls. If the civic authority owns the land, a simultaneous falling in of leases would ease the planning problem and facilitate re-planning. But this cannot have been the heart of the matter. Whatever authority the civic powers had and the extent to which ownership was affected by it remains an enigma.

It is clear that the military men who planned and engineered the forts and the great road arteries had powers and intentions which disregarded private considerations. The road system in the first place was a military stratagem and doubtless most of it was of military construction. Miles of construction were forced through virgin forest and across open moor and fen. Apart from the village field areas, it is questionable whether in the days of pioneer road construction ownership over open tribal land was vital enough to react to the incision of the roads. Tribal interests would be adversely affected when the roads laid open closely defended country, by cutting gaps through protecting woodland, widening mountain passes and bridging rivers. Extraction of gravel, stones and other road-metal would hardly affect a people whose cities and villages at best were timber built. The road construction in later days would be of greater consequence and in the civil zone it cannot be imagined without the protection of civil law and compensation. However that may be, the good that came with the Roman roads has endured the ages. Generations have benefited. Of all the glories of Roman Britain the roads remain useful.

CHAPTER II

SELECT   BIBLIOGRAPHY

Barger, Evert: *The Present Position of Studies in English Field-Systems*. (English Historical Review, Vol. LIII, July 1938).
Berry, C. A. F.: *The Dating of Romano-British Houses* (Journal of Roman Studies, Vol. XLI, 1951).
Childe, V. Gordon: *Prehistoric Communities of the British Isles* (3rd Ed., 1949).
Collingwood, R. G.: *Town and Country in Roman Britain* (Antiquity, Vol. III, September 1929).
Collingwood, R. G.: *The Archaeology of Roman Britain* (1930).
Collingwood, R. G.: *Roman Britain* (1945).
Collingwood, R. G. and Myres, J. N. L.: *Roman Britain and the English Settlements* (2nd Ed., 1937).
Curwen, E. Cecil: *Prehistoric Agriculture in Britain* (Antiquity Vol. I, September 1927).
Curwen, E. Cecil: *Air-Photography and the Evolution of the Corn-field* (2nd Ed., 1938).
Daniel, G. E.; Clark, J. G. D.; et al.: *The Heritage of Early Britain* (1952).
Fox, Aileen: *The Early Plan and Town Houses of Silchester*. (Antiquity, Vol. XXII, December 1948).
Fox, Sir Cyril: *The Personality of Britain* (4th Ed., 1943).
Frank, Tenney (ed.): *An Economic Survey of Ancient Rome*, Vols. I, II, III and V (1933-1940).
Gilbert, E. W.: *The Human Geography of Roman Britain*. (Historical Geography of England, ed. H. C. Darby, 1948).
Haverfield, F. (revised George Macdonald): *The Romanisation of Roman Britain* (4th Ed., 1923).
Haverfield, F. (revised George Macdonald): *The Roman Occupation of Britain* (1924).
Haverfield, F.: *Ancient Town Planning* (1913).
Hawkes, C. F. C., and Hull, M.R.: *Camulodunum*. Report of the Research Committee of the Society of Antiquaries No. 14 (1947).
Hawkes, Jacquetta, and Hawkes, Christopher: *Prehistoric Britain* (1947).
Holleyman, G. A.: *The Celtic Field-System in South Britain* (Antiquity Vol IX, December 1935).
Hunter Blair, P.: *An Introduction to Anglo-Saxon England* (1956).

Raistrick, A., and Chapman, S. E.: *The Lynchet Groups of Upper Wharfedale, Yorkshire*. (Antiquity Vol. III, June 1929).

Randall, H. J.: *Population and Agriculture in Roman Britain* (Antiquity Vol. IV, March 1930).

Richmond, I. A.: *Roman Britain*. The Pelican History of England, Vol. I (1955).

Richmond, I. A.: *Ancient Rome and Northern England* (Antiquity Vol. XIV, September 1940).

Seebohm, Frederic: *The English Village Community* (4th Ed. rep. 1926).

Seebohm, Frederic: *The Tribal System in Wales* (1895).

Stevens, C. E.: *A Possible Conflict of Laws in Roman Britain* (Journal of Roman Studies, XXXVII, 1947).

Vinogradoff, Sir Paul: *The Growth of the Manor* (3rd Ed., 1920).

Wheeler, Sir Mortimer, and Wheeler, T. V.: *Verulamium: A Belgic and Two Roman Cities*. Report of the Research Committee of the Society of Antiquaries No. 11 (1936).

Wheeler, Sir Mortimer: *London in Roman Times* (1930).

Wheeler, Sir Mortimer: *Belgic Cities of Britain* (Antiquity Vol. VII, March 1933).

Wheeler, Sir Mortimer: *Prehistoric and Roman Wales* (1925).

Ward Perkins, J. B.: *Roman Villa, Lockleys, Welwyn* (Antiquity Vol. XIV, September 1940).

Ordnance Survey Map of Roman Britain (2nd Ed., 1931).

CHAPTER THREE

OLD ENGLAND

DIPLOMATIC AND OTHER EVIDENCE

Land charters and law codes. The history of landownership
in Old England is greatly dependent upon the contents of land
charters and similar *diplomata*. Together with the written law
codes these present a considerable body of evidence. The evidence
is by no means unequivocable. The salient features of the land
story are not written plainly on the face of the documents. However brilliant translation may be it is only the beginning of sorrows
for one who would wrest secrets from land charter and law code.
Great difficulties are inherent in the very nature of the documents.
What appears to be a statute is likely to be nothing more than a
custumral, or a capitation of ancient customs, or partly customs
and partly innovatory law — "new resolves are mixed up with
statements of old custom in these Leges Barbarorum".[1] Moreover,
the run of the earliest laws is limited by the bounds of the petty
kingdoms, despite the fact that a local royal legislator might
call himself overlord of the English. Even in the latter days, when
the small kingdoms have been caught up in a supreme monarchy a
unified law code does not prevail; local laws and customs continue,
notably in the Danelaw.[2] Added to this is the complication of time.
Four centuries divide the promulgation of the first written laws
under King Æthelberht of Kent in the opening years of the
seventh century from the great dooms of King Cnut in the
eleventh century. Technical expressions are another difficulty,
common alike to the laws and the diplomata. Words are used
which have no equivalent in modern usage : what light would
break if only the true meaning of *hide* were known! Diplomata on the other hand, harbour obscurities peculiar to themselves. The documents may be dispositive in character or nothing
more than documents of evidence;[3] often it is difficult
to tell which is which.[4] Precise law is not known. Whether a
document is a contract, conveyance or unilateral gift, or lies
within more than one of these categories is by no means always

---

[1] Pollock and Maitland : *History of English Law before the Time of
Edward I*, Vol. I, p. 12.
[2] Stenton : *Anglo-Saxon England* (2nd Ed.), p. 499.
[3] Robertson : *Anglo-Saxon Charters*, p. xv.
[4] Whitelock : *Anglo-Saxon Wills*, p. xxxiv.

apparent.[5] Wide, simple words are used to cover a great variety
of actions; royal sovreignties over land are given away in
terms which appear to pass the land itself in absolute ownership.[6]
Added to all the confusion is the subtle deceit of forgeries and
subsequent tamperings with original writings. Nevertheless, it is
these written laws and diplomas that make the greatest contribution to the land narrative.

Other literary evidence. Lesser contributions are found in other
writings, some of ageless literary merit. Bede, peerless historian
and scholar, offers here and there things of consequence, although
his references conflict with other sources of information where he
has relied too much upon hearsay evidence.[7] The Anglo-Saxon
Chronicle, laconic and less erudite, is likewise relevant in places,
although contradictory in some measure even among its own
versions. And so it is with other writings of a private nature.
Entirely different in character are the three strange yet significant
schedules of hidage, known as the Tribal Hidage, the Burghal
Hidage and the County Hidage.[8]

The nature of the facts. Alongside the obscurities, between the
contradictions and behind the technicalities scholars have identified a wealth of fact, but nowhere is the picture complete.
Some facts shine in their own light : landbooks, writs and wills are
evidence of land transactions, of the variety of the transactions,
and of different types of land proprietorship; and written laws
dealing with land matters cannot deny themselves. Other facts,
however, are only clear by a light which each borrows from the
other : the earliest administrative divisions of the land (*regiones*)
are discerned from the dual witness of historical writings and land
charters.[9] Also there are facts readily inferred : laws and custumals
defining obligations and liberties between occupiers of land and
others with proprietary rights inadvertently throw light on social
institutions and features of the social order of relevance and
importance to land affairs. In other places inferred facts may
be less certain : Maitland[10] thought he saw in the granting of
Old English immunities the germination of seignorial justice;
odd words and phrases peppered among charters, laws and
writings allude to the existence of open-field husbandry;

[5] Op. cit., p. xi.
[6] Maitland : *Domesday Book and Beyond*, p. 241.
[7] Maitland : op. cit., p. 512.   [9] Stenton : op. cit., p. 291.
[8] Op. cit., p. 455.   [10] Maitland : op. cit., p. 276.

four uses of the word 'folkland' in law and charter have prompted
the theory that folcright was a major criterion of land-holding;
an incident in a biography of St Cuthbert suggests the layout
pattern of an Old English village;[11] and so on.

Archaeology and toponymy. When all that is extant is
sifted much remains unrevealed. It is just at such a point that
archaeology and toponymy have carried knowledge of the period
a little further. Surveys of place-names are reaping great rewards,
in especial, by locating the bounds of the ancient Danelaw:
"The Scandinavian place-names which are scattered over the Danelaw, and concentrated in certain parts of it are the most obviously
significant of all the materials for its history."[12] Boundaries of
other political divisions and the marches of earlier folk settlements
have likewise been identified. By similar study an Anglo-Saxon
foundation has been discovered for most village sites in the
English shires.[13] Place-names and archaeological evidence have
been used to discover how the early Saxon settlements were made;
in East Anglia, Sir Cyril Fox[14] identifies by means of archaeological
evidence areas of primary and secondary settlement. Archaeology
has also established the fact that there was a marked settlement
and development of land after the coming of the Christian Church.
And to that science again must be attributed the suggestion that
the scanty population of the earlier East Angles could not man the
ancient earthworks, and so the Fleam Dyke was cut to shorten the
defences of their south western boundary.[15]

Fresh knowledge has been gained by toponymy and archaeology
in these and many other directions. But archaeology has a solo
role to play: theories deduced from exiguous written
matter are supported or challenged by what the spade reveals.
The rude chronologies of Anglo-Saxon tradition are a case in
point; they have not escaped suspicion in the light of recent
archaeological findings.[16] On the other hand, archaeological
evidence[17] tends to endorse the theory that the English settlers were
two, not three, different peoples.[17a] Discovery of what appear to be
isolated farmstead sites in the Danelaw country has led to the belief[18] that in those locations are to be identified the homes of the

[11] Stenton: op. cit., p. 284, n.   [12] Op. cit., p. 513.
[13] Clapham: *A Concise Economic History of Britain*, p. 43.
[14] Fox: *Archaeology of the Cambridge Region*, p. 307.
[15] Op. cit., pp. 293-297.   [16] Stenton: op. cit., p. 24.
[17] Fox: op. cit., p. 238.
[17a] Hodgkin: *A History of the Anglo-Saxons*, Vol. I, pp. 154-161.
[18] Fox: op. cit., p. 303.

free *sochemanni* of Domesday Book who strut in grand hauteur over the fens and dales of Danelaw. These are random instances, where the spade either endorses or contradicts literary evidence. There are numerous others.

THE SOCIAL ORDERS

Cabbages and kings! Old English writings speak of many things: nothing of shoes, but much of ships and sealing wax, of cabbages and kings. At first cabbages and kings were things apart. But between the settled England of the sixth century and modern times there runs a long period in which English society, from king to humblest subject, is wedded to the land. The affiance began in Old England, and Norman feudalism perfected the nuptial. Social orders, therefore, have an important place in the land story of Old England.

Free ceorls. The Romanesque theory of Saxon beginnings lost countenance before Maitland's attacks;[19] but has not been completely worsted.[20] Maitland wanted a free fighting peasantry as the axis about which earliest English society turned, and subsequent opinion largely followed him. The first trustworthy glimpse of society after the English settlement, the laws of Æthelberht, king of Kent, introduces the *ceorl* as one whose freedom, popularity and convenience of social position — between the nobility and the lowest social orders — qualify him to meet Maitland's requirement. He is a Kentish ceorl. Westward lives his counterpart. The laws of King Ine of Wessex, admittedly almost a century later than those of Æthelberht, are in fullness of reference richer evidence. What is written in Wessex law leads to the impression that the Kentish ceorl stands more worthily among society than his western brother; he is "dearer born" for the wergild he attracts is higher.[20a] In any event ceorls are ubiquitous. The appellation covers a wide variety of folk not only in Wessex and Kent but also in Mercia and Northumbria,[21] where the ceorl seems to have been socially equal with the ceorl of Wessex.[21a]

The laws of Ine appear to contradict those of the Kentish king in another particular: a shadow of lordship falls across them.

[19] Maitland : op. cit., p. 222.
[20] cf. Barger : *The Present Position of Studies in English Field-Systems*, E. H. Rev., Vol. LIII, 1938.
[20a] Hunter Blair : *An Introduction to Anglo-Saxon England*, p. 260.
[21] Stenton : op. cit., p. 275, n.
[21a] Whitelock : *The Beginnings of English Society*, p. 84.

The shadow comes from two different directions. A noble class, the *gesithcundmen*, in the interests of husbandry and social wellbeing were required to ensure that at least a specified proportion of their land was *gesettland*; a term connoting settlement by a colonising peasantry. Elsewhere, the laws provide that "if a man take a yardland at an agreed gafol and plough it, and the lord later wishes to establish an obligation of labour as well as gafol, that man need not submit unless his lord has provided him with a homestead as well as the land".[22] Do these passages mean that the ceorl of Wessex was in the days of Ine more of a bondman than his counterpart under Æthelberht? They have been read that way. The ceorl is seen here as the coloniser of gesettland under the gesithcundmen. He is a *gafolgelda*, one who renders *gafol* to a lord. He may be less worthy and render gafol and labour.[23] Later, in the peace terms drawn between King Ælfred and Guthrum, the Dane, reference is made to the ceorl "who occupies rented land". Here again the weight of modern opinion[24] sees a nascent lordship rising above the free peasant.

Vinogradoff[25] has argued the contrary. For him the reference to gafol does not imply lordship and vassalage but payment of tribute to the king by an essentially free man. The ceorl has no lord betwixt himself and his sovereign. Some of his kind (*franklins*) may be more encumbered than others but in no way do they approach the bondage which in later, darker days becomes villeinage.[26] Freedom after all is relative. Those who see lordship rising over the ceorl of Ine's day do not say he loses his freedom. Some go further than others. But this without cavil must be admitted: by the eleventh century there emerge two distinct social classes among the peasantry—the *geneatas* and the *geburas*. Between the two, the line that divides freedom from bondage can be drawn with a surer hand.

Geneat and gebur. Neither geneat nor gebur had ceorl ancestry in every case. It is probable that geneatas were known whose forebears were nobly born. Gesithcundmen, king's companions of past days, lost all social identity after Athelstan's day, either in the heights of the new thegnly orders or in the depths among the king's lesser servants[27] where they were in danger of passing into

---

[22] Jolliffe : *The Constitutional History of Medieval England* (2nd Ed.) p. 21.
[23] Op. cit., pp. 20, 21.   [24] Stenton : op. cit., p. 259, n.
[25] Vinogradoff : *The Growth of the Manor*, p. 240.
[26] Vinogradoff : *English Society in the Eleventh Century*, p. 429.
[27] Stubbs : *The Constitutional History of England* (5th Ed.). p. 173.

the ranks of the geneat peasantry. Geburas could claim no grander origin than the ceorls, often nothing so worthy. Many are the children of manumitted slaves — the *coliberti* of the Domesday Survey. For them the new status meant freedom; but a relative freedom. In the latter days of Old England the line that divided the free from the bond cleft gebur from geneat, and left the gebur bound.

Both gebur and geneat were peasants. To the one life must have been at its best parochial, hide-bound, monotonous; but the other rode into wide horizons, at times under the oriflamme of a thegnly master. Whatever the genealogy of particular geburs may have been, many authorities see the class as the social successors of the landless ceorls of Ine's law. At all events they were in "a very dependent position"[28] under their lords; arduous agricultural tasks had to be performed on the lord's land, the lord's fold had to be watched, the lord's hounds fed, and heavy payments in kind and money paid to the lord in addition to the irony of the free householder's hearth-penny payable to the church. The geneat does not appear in Ine's law. It has been suggested[29] that the Wessex gafolgelda, the freeman who pays gafol but gives no labour to his lord, was a prototype. The geneat holds land and for the privilege renders *land-gafol* and other dues, but unlike the gebur there is a professional élan about him; he is the lord's fellow, more frequently in the saddle than behind the plough; he rides far and near on the lord's business; he builds the burh, the roads and bridges; his duties are many and various but always they become his status.

Other peasants. Although the gebur of the eleventh century cannot claim to be the peer of the geneat, his is not the lowest rung on the social ladder. Essentially he is a husbandman in his own right, and in this he differs from the *kotsetla*.[30] This lowly peasant, it is true, had a small share in the open arable fields but at most it was five acres. From him life demanded constant labour. To the peasant classes also belonged many village functionaries. Pigs were not led in ones and twos by proud owners to the pannage grounds; the swineherd of the tun community herded them thither. Other common needs were met in similar fashion: bees were with the bee-keeper, seed with the sower, oxen with the ox-herd, sheep with the shepherd and the woodlands

[28] Maitland : op. cit., p. 329.
[29] Chadwick : *Studies on Anglo-Saxon Institutions*, p. 87.
[30] Stenton : op. cit., p. 466.

were the care of the wood-ward and the meadows of the hayward. All are peasants. And so is the lord's own reeve who has oversight of man and maid. Only the slaves are classless, landless, rightless.

The thegns. At the other extreme, immediately superior to the aristocratic peasantry were the military orders of the later days, the thegnly class. Thegns were noble by blood and inheritance. "The distinction between the thegn and the peasant", writes Stenton,[31] "was the fundamental line of cleavage in Old English society." Thegns normally were well-to-do. Some were inordinately rich, others economically less endowed than prosperous geneats but always clear between them rose "the pale spectrum of the salt." A thegn was never a peasant. That did not mean an insurmountable bar dividing peasantry from thegnhood; a peasant could always thrive to thegnright. And yet thegnhood is rather a vocation than a status. Greatest among the thegns are the "king's thegns" who serve the king. Lesser men are thegns of lesser lords by commendation. Thegnly rank from earliest days reflects the prestige of the liege lord to whom the thegn is in homage bound.[32] Thegns are the vassals of kings and earls and dignitaries. But in turn the thegn is the lord of the peasantry, of the geneats who follow in his retinue and the geburs who till his gesettland. In early Wessex the ruck of nobility of thegnly station other than the king's thegns were *gesithcundmen* or *gesiths.* Terminology in Northumbria was different but the social pattern the same; the gesiths stood where in Wessex the king's thegns stood and the king's thegn was a young nobleman in personal attendance on the king. After the days of Ælfred *thegn* became generic and *gesith* passed into history.

The ealdormen. Gesith is the Anglo-Saxon rendering of the word "comes" of the earliest Latin texts.[33] Later the Latin word denotes a more specialised ranking[34] and in English was translated *ealdorman.* Ealdormen ranked next to the throne among the secular classes. As a general rule in later days and from earliest times in Northumbria and other places, the title and rank came by appointment rather than inheritance[35] and were marks of service and kingly favour. But "the ealdorman has the best claim of any Saxon official to an origin independent of the crown";[36] and it is

---

[31] Stenton : op. cit., p. 481.   [32] Chadwick : op. cit., p. 85.
[33] Pollock and Maitland : op. cit., p. 33.
[34] Chadwick : op. cit., pp. 164, 165.   [35] Stenton. op. cit., p. 302.
[36] Jolliffe : op. cit., p. 38.

probable that in Mercia the rank originated within the blood-tie
and that inheritance was a factor in the case where petty kings,
heirs of dynasties, forwent kingly rank and adopted the humbler
title.[37] The old Kentish law codes know nothing of ealdormen.
Above the aristocratic ceorls of that unique kingdom stand *eorls*,
superior by birth and not service. Yet time tells, even in Kent, and
by the tenth century eorls were king's companions, not great
aristocrats independent of the crown. They were becoming one
with the general class of ealdormen throughout England.

The social significance of the ealdormen was always military
and political. Politically they presided over judiciary assemblies,
executed the law, exacted the penalties of justice, championed the
weak; in short ruled the provinces under the king.[37a] The extent of
an ealdorman's jurisdiction, the *ealdormanory*, is uncertain. It
can be presumed with a fair degree of assurance that originally it
was a shire in Southern England. How the boundaries ran in the
Midlands is more obscure.[38] Later, about the beginning of the tenth
century, the smaller ealdormanories gave place to extensive
provinces co-terminous for the most part with the traditional
kingdoms of Old England.[39]

The earls. Under Danish influence the *earl* replaced the ealdorman
and the *earldom* the ealdormanory. Earldoms were essentially innovatory, artificial creations whose boundaries disregarded local traditions.[40] Within them the responsibilities of
the earl differed little from those of the erstwhile ealdorman
but the earldom was never an administrative unit. The administrative land divisions were something new. The ancient, comfort-
able administrative ealdormanories were replaced in the reign
of Eadgar by counties or shires each governed by a shireman
or shire reeve.[41] Under Cnut these officials attracted the title of
sheriffs. The sheriff was always the king's servant and of thegnly
status. Unlike the earl he did not tower towards majesty above
his fellow nobility.

The king. The passing of the smaller ealdormanories was not
an event in isolation. Great earldoms bespeak great kingdoms.
The advent of a universal monarchy in Ælfred marks a turning
point in the constitutional history of England. Kings had adopted

[37] Stenton : op. cit., p. 301.
[38] cf. Whitelock : op. cit., p. 78.
[39] Jolliffe : op. cit., p. 123.
[41] Jolliffe : op. cit., p. 124.

[37a] Chadwick : op. cit., p. 169.

[40] Stenton : op. cit., p. 408.

the title *rex Britanniae* and *rex Anglorum* a century or more
before Ælfred reigned.[42] But they were kings of Mercia and their
titles only reflections of a conqueror's overlordship, a pre-
eminence in their persons born of homage paid them by victims
of conquest or power politics rather than the popular acclaim
which supported Ælfred. There is, however, nothing of a nascent
democratic, elective impulse in the fact that "all the English
people submitted to Ælfred."

Before Ælfred, kingship of the petty kingdoms was more akin
to lordship over personally sworn men, than hereditary and
autocratic monarchy; the king was first *hlaford*, lord of men, and
only secondarily *cyning*. Paying homage beneath him and alongside him were sub-kings and joint-kings. At death the king's vassals
sought another lord. Only in this might be seen an element of
election.

Ælfred reigned in days of constitutional night. All men looked
to the king. To some he was commended lord but to all he was
guardian of the folcright and every individual and common interest
that pertained thereto. He was not supreme legislator or executive
or royal advocate.[43] Only as the light of a stabilised and authoritative monarchy dawned over the thrones that linked Edward the
Elder with Edward Confessor did the truer elements of kingship
develop. In them was something finer than Ælfred ever knew. The
first monarchs of all England had "access to reserves of loyalty
and affection not to be explained by the legal rights of the
crown." And, what is more, there was nothing of the "obligatory,
lasting bond of homage riveted into the land by the material
interest of tenure".[44] The supreme kings of Old England were not
paramount lords of every acre.

Men of the Danelaw. Diverse laws were reconciled under the
supreme monarchs. But no attempt was made in the east to check
the run of Danish law in the Danelaw, although the king's
franchise was honoured there. Socially the toleration left its mark.
Elsewhere the ceorl is losing freedom and status to the thegn and
higher classes who are *hlaford* over him. In Danelaw there is an
enigmatic freedom. Peasant proprietors stand out in strange contrast to the ceorls of other parts of England. Two names are used
in Domesday to describe them: *sochemanni* or *socmen*, and
liberi homines.[45] Just what distinguishes one from the other or
the two jointly from other classes is not known, but they are

---

[42] Stenton : op. cit., pp. 202, 210.   [44] Op. cit., pp. 136, 137.
[43] Jolliffe : op. cit., p. 54.   [45] Stenton : op. cit., pp. 508, 509.

unquestionably freer than the gebur or geneat; if indeed there was ever any correspondence between the old and new orders. All are commended to a lord, and services of a very light nature are required of them. In the case of the socman attendance at the lord's court may have been imperative but it is possible that the *liberi homines* do not even have this obligation imposed upon them.[46] Another Danelaw anomaly is the appearance of the word *hold* in Northumbria. The term was applied to the king's high reeves, men of singular eminence who from earliest days were the mainstay of the nobility, between ealdormen and gesiths.[47]

The hierarchy. Northumbrian law (the *Northleoda Laga*) is important and relevant not only for the testimony it bears to the existence and dignity of the hold but also for the clarity in which it depicts the dichotomy that divided all social orders in Old England into religious and secular. The graduations of secular society were reflected, order by order, among the hierarchy. Supreme and alone was the king; then the archbishop equated with the aetheling (the king's son); afterwards the bishop with the ealdorman; and the thegn with the lesser clergy (mass thegns). It is not suggested that this statement in the northern law is exhaustive of social gradings throughout Old England, but it is approximate enough for a broad outline.

Apart from the above elemental social classes and orders, there were differences of function which in themselves made for social distinctions. Certain of them were linked with land occupation and ownership and references to them are more appropriate in a later context.

THE LAND BURDENS

When attention is turned from the society of Old England to the land it occupied and owned, two main factors become at once apparent. On the one hand, were the land burdens in great variety and on the other the changing pattern of land settlement. The latter was in some measure dependent upon the former and the land burdens will be dealt with first.

Four main classes of land burdens. The nature and number of land burdens were not constant through the six centuries of Old England. The many variants gather into four main classifications. Remotest in time and longest in continuity were burdens whose

---

[46] Stenton : op. cit., p. 520,   [47] Op. cit., p. 501,

provenance lay deep in tribal days; of such were the obligations of feorm, fighting and frankpledge. Another class consisted of the secular burdens of royal and territorial administration. The Church was responsible for the third. And the Danes, the scourge of later days, the cause of the fourth.

Feorm. Until the imposition of geld by the Danes there was no land taxation in England. Much of the royal revenue came from the king's *feorm*. To say there was no element of taxation in this contribution may be going too far. From its very nature the charge lay within the shadow of the kingly, and yet it was no arbitrary creation of royal sovreignty. Scholars have endeavoured to trace its origin to the feasting rights of tribal chieftains itinerating among their subjects. Some authorities are more certain than others.[48] The question, however, remains open. When it is realised that there is no concensus of opinion upon the ultimate incidence of the feorm it is not surprising that uncertainty attends its origins. The incidence, in the opinion of one scholar,[49] fell only upon crown land, the *terra regis*; for another[50] feorm was a public burden and the incidence common to all land; a third opinion[51] suggests that at all events the king's own land was free. The problem is interlocked with the obscurity of land tenure and only as greater light falls in that direction will thoughts become clearer.

There is some certain ground. Neither the fact that the feorm issued from the land, and in that sense can be regarded as a food-rent, nor that it was revenue of the crown can be gainsaid. The amount rendered was often expressed as "one night's farm" (*firma unius noctis*); an expression strikingly reminiscent of a king abiding the night under the roof-tree of his subjects. In other cases the amount was one or two days' farm, or two nights' farm. Nowhere in the English texts are details given of the quota of provisions involved in providing *firma unius noctis*. When many of the ancient dues were commuted to money payments the firma of Wiltshire and Somerset averaged about £105.[52] Whether rendered in cash or in kind the feorm was too great a burden for the average settled tun and village community to carry. Communities were grouped for the purpose and each community rendered its feorm to a king's tun (*feorm ham*) over which the royal hand

---

[48] Seebohm : *Tribal Custom in Anglo-Saxon Law*, p. 41.
[49] Jolliffe : op. cit., pp. 128, 129.
[50] Stenton : op. cit., p. 284.
[51] Chadwick : op. cit., p. 372.
[52] Round : *Feudal England*, p. 112.

appointed a reeve;[53] an arrangement which may be responsible for the notion that only royal lands were liable to the feorm.

Military burdens. The burden of the feorm was essentially one which fell directly upon the land. In this it differed from the ancient obligation to fight in the national levy, known as the host or *fyrd*. Duty to fight in the host, coupled with work upon bridges and fastnesses,[54] was an obligation unquestioned and accepted from primitive times. The constitution of the fyrd remains a mystery. It cannot be said with confidence that the obligation to serve was rooted in the soil. The military man of the documents is always the fully caparisoned noble. Archaeology goes further and dresses the ceorl in target and greaves and moves "contingents of peasants dimly behind the aristocratic foreground."[54a] Even so the mystery is not solved, for the common freeman of England were not all ceorls or even peasants, and it is questionable if all were armed to the host.[55] What is clear is the use of land as a broadcloth upon which the fyrd is patterned. Men are summoned to the host, to bridge work and fastness bettering from the hides, the hundreds and the shires. The land in this sense measures and marshals the might of the kingdom. Military service determined according to land measure tended in later days to create a close association between the land and military obligation, so much so, that by the time of the Domesday Survey lords were freeing land from military duty by paying compositions.[56]

Frankpledge and suit of court. Historically, the relation of frankpledge to the land is similar to the story of military obligation. Origins lie remote in tribal days and the obligation is later woven into the pattern of land settlement. The idea of frankpledge is a difficult notion for modern minds. Within the tribe, each man became law-worthy by virtue of the *mund*, or bond of kin. Later a parallel bond arose between lord and man, between patron and the man who sought his protection by commendation. The mund of the tribe was forsaken and "the mund of lordship, originating in the place of the house-father over his sons and men, spreads itself over that wider family of protected and com-

[53] Stenton : op. cit., p. 284.
[54] Many authorities refer to these three cognate obligations as the "trinoda necessitas", a term in the opinion of Professor Stenton deriving from a misreading of the phrase "trimoda necessitas" (Op. cit., p. 286).
[54a] Stenton : op. cit., p. 287.
[55] Hodgkin : op. cit., p. 595.
[56] Jolliffe : op. cit., p. 221.

mended dependants to whom the mundbora is not father, but
lord".[57] Constitutionally, the mantel of the lord's mund was a
livery of mutual pledges. He whom the lord protected, upheld
(maintained) his lord in action and property, and was himself
the subject of the lord's guarantee of worthiness and of the lordly
pledge to the community at large that the man would answer
with his presence in the public courts of law. A man's appearance
in court was necessary not only as suitor or defendant but inevitably as doomsman. Freemen were judge and jury. Without them
a court could not be, and suit to the *popularia concilia* was a
common obligation from earliest days.[58] In these two forms,
responsibility to be in frankpledge (*frithburgh*) and obligation to
do suit of court, the burden of jurisdiction developed in Old
England and eventually became territorialized, although the administrative units were not the same in each case. Territorialization
meant a gradual forsaking of the lord's mund, as the tribal mund
has been forsaken in the past, for social associations of another
order. All men had to be in frankpledge and tithing if they had
left the mund of their lord. The tithing was either an arbitrary
grouping of persons into tens (*decenna*) for the purpose of
frankpledge, or the tun community itself: "the township discharges its duty of having all its members in frankpledge."[59]
Obligation to do suit of court was woven into the land pattern
by the coming of the hundreds and shires. For the most part the
men of the hundred answered to the hundred-moot and the men
of shire to the shire moot, but it was too early to regard these
obligations as in a strict sense predial.

Other burdens. The movement landwards, which showed itself
in whatever evolved from the ancient tribal obligations being found
in the soil, was expressive of radical change in the social order.
Society was becoming increasingly sedentary. Customs localized.
The three salient types of tribal obligation can be identified in
most areas but they vary in form and content according to
locality. For example, military duty may in one place include the
building of royal villages, and the king's feorm involve the feeding
of the royal horses. Local custom, moreover, was responsible for
burdens and services that had no common roots within the three
categories of tribal dues. The king commands riding services,
other than military, from the land; sporting services; building
reparations; and coastguard duty. Doubtless whatever was need-

[57] Jolliffe : op. cit., p. 17.   [58] Stenton : op. cit., p. 294.
[59] Pollock and Maitland : op. cit., p. 569.

ful in the economy of kingship is found in the land. The land charters use wide, omnibus phrases to describe the gamut of burdens: "all earthly hardships, known and unknown"; "all tribute of secular payments, labours and burdens"; "all public tribute, purveyance, royal works, military service".[60] These words are used in charters granting blessings of immunity from local burdens. Kings were more liberal with some immunities than with others. Only on rarest occasions was the land freed from fighting duty and bridge and borough work; so extreme a favour was only extended to a church or saint or other ecclesiastical donee.

Church-scot and tithe. Apart from grants of immunities, the Church had church-scot and tithe in her own right. Both fell as additional burdens on land. Church-scot and tithe were originally voluntary, but each became the subject of secular law; church-scot first by Ine's laws, and two centuries later tithe.[61] The burdens are not one and the same, nor was one the precursor of the other. For a period both were imposed together, but tithe eventually outplaced church-scot as the foundation revenue of general church finance. Usually church-scot was rendered in kind; a horse-load (*summa*) of the best corn from each hide or some other contribution related to land-area.[62]

Tithe did not fall entirely upon the land because other property was titheable. But in a day when land was the staple of wealth, the burden had peculiar significance for landed interests. As the Old English period advanced tithe, which in earlier days had gravitated to what were then the pioneer churches, remained with the *old minsters*, but at the instance of the land proprietor sharing was permissible between old and new churches, where the latter had to support a grave-yard. Noteworthy among other land burdens in favour of the church were plough-penny and hearth-penny, payments made at Eastertide in respect of plough-teams and the households of freemen.

Danegeld. Although the secular arm of the State imposed the church dues it did not change their nature, always they were church dues, never Exchequer taxes. Throughout the wide range of land burdens nothing can be spoken of as land taxation until the imposition of the Danegeld in the last decade of the tenth

[60] Maitland: op. cit., p. 235.
[61] Stenton: op. cit., pp. 153, 156.
[62] This relationship was a feature only of the earlier days. (Cf. Stenton: op. cit, p. 153.)

E

century. Danegeld was the only direct taxation of land known in Old England.[63] No Englishman of pre-Conquest days would have recognised it by that name; Danegeld is a Norman designation.

In Old England the imposition was the geld, levied to fight and bribe the Danes, and every Englishman felt its weight and ignominy. Originated by Æthelred the Unready to buy peace from a Danish raiding force, the levy in the days of Cnut and his pre-Conquest successors had become army-geld and ship-geld, crushing taxes exacted from the land to maintain a standing royal army and navy. The impost was never an annual tax; the king levied it whenever occasion required. Its cumulative weight was so formidable that the social pattern changed under the pressure. The English peasant lost his freedom to his commended lord (hlaford) who was ready to discharge the tax burden in exchange for greater service. Men were ground into the soil. And the hide which in sunnier days held the spell of home and family in its mystery became a sinister unit of geld assessment.

LAND SETTLEMENT PATTERN

The marshalling of land for the discharge of land burdens is reflected in the land settlement pattern as units of assessment and incidence, but of equal consequence are political considerations, military needs, social groupings, economic activity, tenure and ownership and the advance of agriculture against virgin land. These influences fall into two classes; those which affect topography and in that sense are visual, and those which are invisible and ghostly, a web of boundary lines and abstract ideas.

Saxon open-fields and other field-systems. The establishment and practice of agriculture are important among the visual class. Although no precise, well-featured picture can be drawn of husbandry in Old England, much has been conjectured. There is no doubt that the Saxons ploughed their land in elongated, sinuous ploughlands, high-ridged and parallel with each other in compact blocks. Whether they introduced the system into Britain is another question. The heavy plough so necessary for this kind of work may have come with the Belgae of pre-Roman times;[64] it has been suggested that what appear to be typical Saxon

[63] Jolliffe: op. cit., p. 127.
[64] cf. p. 24 ante.

terraced lynchets among the chalk escarpments of Cambridge-shire are workings of pre-Saxon origin.[65]

Lack of evidence for the use of the heavy plough in the Celtic fringes of the west is no argument in favour of Saxon introduction. The small, squared fields of the west bring to mind the system which has been identified as Celtic on the light-soiled uplands of the south and east. Sitings of all Celtic square-fields suggest that the terrain was the formative factor which determined their layout[65a] and not a limitation of plough types. The eight-oxen plough would be quite unsuitable, either for the light soils of the Down-land or the cramped, ploughable pockets of the mountainous west. It appears to have been used in the first instance for opening up heavy, natural scrub and woodland.[66] The preservation of the workings of the Celtic field-system is indicative of a Saxon preference for the lowlands, but cannot be interpreted to support the theory that Romano-Britains had no heavy plough with which to work the deep valley soils. The villa sites show that the cultivated land of Roman Britain was not confined to the uplands, and even on the hills themselves the tendency was valleywards. Heavy ploughed fields, opening up the valleys, would for the most part be indistinguishable from later Saxon workings.[67] Continuity between Roman and Saxon sites is difficult to establish as a general principle, but archaeology makes it plain, at least in the south-eastern midlands, that the Saxons settled first along the river valleys, that is to say, in those areas pre-viously settled by Britons and Romans.[68] From these primary sites a secondary phase developed; the settlers scattered sporadic colonies against the green-velvet background of the natural woodlands. The rate of progress was greatly accelerated after the advent of the Christian Church,[69] and by the eighth century Saxon settlements adumbrate to a remarkable degree the village locations of modern times.[70]

The study of place-names and archaeological evidence are respon-sible for this information; but these sciences can tell little, if anything, of the methods and systems of agriculture. The law

[65] Fox : op. cit., p. 306.
[65a] Sayles : The Medieval Foundations of England (2nd Ed.), p. 118.
[66] Clapham : op. cit., p. 47.
[67] Based upon the same principle, an argument has recently been mooted to establish the view that the observable ridge and furrow of modern times does not represent Saxon original open-fields but nineteenth century ploughings. [cf. Kerridge : Ridge and Furrow and Agrarian History Econ. H. Rev., Vol. IV, No. 1, 1951.]
[68] Fox. op. cit., p. 307.   [69] Op. cit, p. 307.
[70] Clapham : op. cit., p. 43.

codes tell something. Ine's laws make express reference to common-grazing rights over meadowland divided into shares among many owners.[70a] Certain charters identify boundaries by making mention of topographical landmarks among which hints of husbandry practice (e.g. headlands) may be recognised. Oblique references to intermixed holdings are also found in land charters.[71] Kentish diplomata refer to sulungs and use specific names,[72] thereby indicating a difference between the agricultural system of Kent and the system frequently found over the rest of the kingdom.

Documentary and other evidence is insufficient to support Dr. Gray's thesis that the detailed land records of the thirteenth and later centuries are trustworthy sources from which to deduce the nature and distribution of field-systems in Old England. On the assumption that they are so, he discovers seven different field-systems.[73] In the heart of Old England, the Saxons pursued the traditional Germanic open-field system; it is not proposed to look at this more closely until it features in the land story of the late medieval period. Kent is distinguished by a unique system of enclosed lands. Essex also shows a reluctance to practise open-field husbandry and likewise East Anglia. Gray thought these south-eastern departures were the outcome of Roman influence. This may be so, but probably only indirectly through contemporary Continental inspiration. To the extreme west the land was subject to a true Celtic system adapted to the high hills and valleys. On the marches between Old England and Celtic Britain three hybrid systems evolved; one in the centre about Hereford-shire, another to the north and west, and a third in the southwest.

The Celtic system of the West did not evince the settled agri-culture and rotational cropping which the Celtic fields of Roman Britain suggest.[74] The nature of the hill country is not conducive to early settlement. In days when natural grazing was comparat-ively plentiful the Celts appear to have focussed their activities upon small *inland* permanent plots and to have broken as need required either virgin soil or erstwhile ploughland, long abandoned to fallow. The system petrified in time and holdings are found scattered in pieces, as was the case with the traditional open-field system; but there is no evidence of rotational agriculture. This system was widely known in Scotland as rundale or run-rig.

[70a] Hodgkin : op. cit., p. 205.
[71] Maitland : op. cit., p. 361.
[72] Stenton : op. cit., p. 279.
[73] Gray : *English Field Systems*, pp. 411-418.
[74] cf. p. 25 ante.

Tuns and hamlets. Topography of the west encouraged hamlet foundation rather than large, tight-clustered tuns. An earlier theory supposes the characteristic scattering of dwellings in the west to be the outcome of Celtic agricultural practice, but the colonising hamlets among the eastern woodlands and the discovery of clustered villages associated with Celtic fields have undermined its cogency. Both hamlet and clustered village in Old England maintain an aloof indifference to the system of Roman roads.[75] Doubtless these hatchments of a dead civilization, together with the traditional open ways of prehistoric times were the arteries of traffic. They certainly proved useful landmarks for identifying the boundaries of private ownership,[76] and probably the boundaries of kingdoms, but settlement sites were not ribboned along them. Settlements were essentially agricultural, and even to-day the ancient wisdom of their locations is evident by the balance of natural resources in the sites chosen.[77]

The burhs.[78] The Saxons eschewed urban ways. With the exception of London and a few other revivals of Roman days no development other than the essentially agricultural tun and isolated holding patterned the land until the coming of the Ælfredian and Danish burhs. Burhs were fortified places. Not all burhs attracted urban development but it was under the protective shadow of fortifications and defences, especially those which extended the defence policy of Ælfred against the Danes, that markets and mints and all that might in Old England be termed urban, burgeoned and blossomed. Militants, merchants and moneyers contested the ground within the burhs. Where competition was exceptional the *hagan*, as the plots of houses and other buildings were termed, were tightly packed together,[79] but at heart the burh was always rural. Fields and commons were never far from any burgess. In later times according to one theory the county borough became a microcosm of the landownership pattern of the county, not the visual, but the ghostly pattern.

The hide. Between the visual and invisible land pattern there was one common factor — the hide. Historically it

[75] Fox: op. cit., p. 311.
[76] A grant of land by King Edred defines the property conveyed by stipulating that "the estate at Alwalton consists of five hides and these are the boundaries: the posts on Ermine Street, then north along the streets to the dyke as far as the Chesterton boundary . . ." (Robertson: op. cit., p. 57).
[77] Orwin and Orwin: *The Open Fields*, p. 24.
[78] cf. Chap. VII.   [79] Stenton: op. cit., p 519.

is the great enigma of the period, a keyhole without a key at which learned eyes have grown weary with watching. Maitland lingered long: he thought he had found a key. The hide was a land measure! No one quarrelled with that. But when he maintained that the true, original hide was 120 acres of arable land,[80] voices were raised to contradict him. There is no evidence for a stable content of acres, the visual hide varies in acreage. What is certain is the antiquity of its origin. From the beginning it is there; not a precise land measure expressible by the finesse of fractions but certainly the basic, indeed the only, unit of land division. It is the family holding of the earliest Saxon settlers, the *terra unius familiae* of the first Saxon documents. So close is the word connected with family, that Bede and other contemporary writers use each word as a metonym of the other.[81] The family is the hide; the hide is the family. Land is measured in families because the family holds a hide. There was nothing constant in its structure and content because the demands of the elemental family of Old England were not uniform. Variation in fertility also influenced the physical dimension of the family holding; a family would require a wider acreage of poor land than of rich land for the production of its sustenance.[81a] Hides expressible in terms of acres were Norman units of mensuration[82] and probably were never more than the calibrations of an advanced taxation technique.

The hide as a unit of assessment was certainly not of Norman origin. The manner in which the folk of earliest England stood to discharge their land burdens was determined by the hidation of the land. One man from each hide for the bettering of the burhs was a common formula.[82a] That which was *terra unius familae* was also *terra unius tributarii*. One of the most ancient extants is a document known as the Tribal Hidage. It assesses to tribute the subject provinces of the Mercian kings. The assessments are all round numbers of hundreds or thousands, a characteristic feature of the hide as a taxation tally, and indeed of the hide as a land measure. The rounded figures of the land books approximate to what appears to the nearest five-hide unit.[83] Villages, woodlands and valuable waters are referred to as five, ten, twenty, or more hides and nowhere are the multiples of the hidage less than five. The fact that the king was giving away sovereign rights to tribute and other burdens may account for the crude assessments;

[80] Maitland : op. cit., pp. 490-520.   [81] Op. cit., p. 358.
[81a] Hunter Blair : op. cit., p. 268.   [82] Stenton : op. cit., p. 276.
[82a] Whitelock : op. cit., p. 76.   [83] Stenton : op. cit., p. 284.

if so, the hide of the documents may well have had no significance apart from its role as assessment unit. As such, it is always un-baked clay in the hands of the royal assessors; they mould it and dispense it as best suits their purpose. By the days of Edward the Confessor the hide is the unit which in neat parcels of a hundred underlies assessment to the Danegeld and perhaps the structure of the hundreds, those basic administrative land divisions of immed-iate pre-Conquest England.[84]

The hundred. Like the hide the hundred is one of the great riddles of history. What it became is no mystery. But of its beginnings and in that sense its true nature conjecture counters conjecture. At the end of the Old English period it is a land division pivoted about the hundred-moot. The lands of the hundred discharge their land burdens in the name of the hundred; the hundred is liable for geld, for fyrd-service, for tribute; and suit of court is owed to the hundred court by the freemen of the hundred.

The administrative pattern came late in time and makes the inability to fathom the mystery of the genesis of the hundred the more irritating. Lately an argument has been propounded[85] which sees the hundred as a voluntary expression of the inchoate society of the tenth century, making for peace and order; a voluntary binding of guildsmen into tithings and thence into larger groups, *hyndenne*, for the sanctity of the frith or peace bond, mainly concerned with raising hue and cry against thieves. Under royal patronage the hundreds are eventually made compulsory and their courts judgment seats in folkright. To these divisions, with their judicial centres, is assigned responsibility for the effective discharge of land burdens. On the other hand the obligation of the land to meet the king's feorm or tribute may well have been the origin of the hundred.[86] The Tribal Hidage with its rounded hund-reds of hides is pertinent evidence. Authorities find no difficulty in agreeing that as a minor division of the shire the hundred was in the first place an institution of Wessex and was exported from the western kingdom in the days of its hegemony.

The Shire. The earliest Wessex shires or *scira* over which an ealdorman exercised administrative authority were the small

---

[84] The Northern Danelaw was not hidated. The unit of measure and assess-ment which corresponded to the English hide was the Danish "ploges-land" or carucate, arranged in combinations of sixes and twelves, instead of fives and tens.
[85] Jolliffe: op. cit., pp. 116-123.   [86] Stenton: op. cit., p. 295.

Wessex ealdormanories. Through the rest of England there was much variety. Westward and northward where Celtic influence was felt the administrative unit was the scir, an area often corresponding, as in Wessex, to the jurisdiction of the ealdorman. In Kent the divisions were *lathes*; and in Sussex *rapes*. In the east and parts of Mercia the nomenclature of the local administrative units is unknown.

Behind these land divisions and perhaps behind certain groupings of hundreds[87] are ranged in a diffused remoteness *regiones* and *provinciae*, a nebulous land pattern which the Saxon word *maegth* (often used when Latin is rendered in English) suggests had some affinity with the original tribal settlements.[88] The Danes not only broke up the administrative pattern, especially in the east and the midlands, but added their own ridings and wapentakes to the complex. And yet it was perhaps the Danish influence that paradoxically inspired Ælfred and the later kings of Wessex to fashion a universal administration of shires based upon defence points, the burhs, over the entire kingdom. Where the ancient ealdormanories and other land divisions had remained more or less intact, the new scheme of things reflected the old. But in those areas given to the Danish wars the new county boundaries, arranged neatly around burhs, were impatient of ancient marches. They patterned the eastern and midland shires into an administrative design, clearly a work of forethought and military planning, which has left an indelible mark upon the great midland plains.

LANDOWNERSHIP

Lack of precise written evidence. Although the land history of Old England is in most respects true history, the documentary evidence contains no comprehensive written land law. Points occur in the law codes where something can be seen of the features of ownership and land tenure. The land charters and writs are perhaps more eloquent. But nowhere is there trace of the pellucid thought and precise expression of the jurist. What is written is uncertain, shallow, scattered, patches of phosphorescent light on the surface of a mysterious folkright; and in its deeps the true law lies hidden. One of the most comprehensive statements, the Rectitudines of the eleventh century, is late in time and is nothing more than a written expression of contemporary

[87] Cam :*Liberties and Communities in Medieval England*, pp. 91-105.
[88] Stenton : op. cit., p. 290.

custom. The absolutism of the statute is not there. Little, therefore, can be written with certitude. Inference and conjecture play
important roles. A number of departure points suggest themselves,
and the royal hand that gave so freely by land charter and writ is
perhaps the most promising.

Royal gifts of land. From the early days of the seventh
century kings are granting tracts of land to bishops and
other church dignitaries; later they make similar dispositions in
favour of laymen. The nature of the gifts, as they appear on the
face of the documents, conveys the impression that the royal
donor is absolute owner in possession of the land; especially is this
so with the earlier charters. The king has personal ownership; he is
conveying *terra mea, terra juris mei.* Transactions of this nature
in themselves do not rouse curiosity but the extravagant dimensions
of the gifts prompt the question : What was given? When, for
example, Edgar grants to Kenneth, King of Scots, all the land of
Lothian that lay betwixt Tweed and Forth,[89] must it be concluded
that no free ceorls were landsitting in all that fair province? And
must like conclusions be drawn in respect of the vast ranges of
land that passed from the royal hand to the keeping of church
and nobles throughout the long years of Old England? Inhabitants
there must have been. Grants of barren waste would be poor
exchange for an *entente cordiale* and more sinful than the greed of
Ananias if offered to God and His Church. If the king's proprietorship were absolute, the men of the land can have been little more
than slaves, at best serfs. Where, then, were the free ceorls of
England? If the land that is given is the investment and pride of
a free peasantry, of what nature is the royal right? These are big
questions. Modern scholarship inclines to the view that, at all
events in the earlier years, the elementary proprietor of the soil was
the free ceorl and that the words of the land charters and the
legal thought of the time no more attempted to refer to the rights
of ownership vesting in the peasants than modern conveyances of
freehold reversions are concerned with the leasehold interests upon
which they are dependent. The king's interest in particular parcels
of land would not be identical in each case, time and other factors
would make for change, but whatever the interest in the land may
have been it was sufficient for the thought of the time to allow the
king to speak of *terra mea.* That phrase, therefore, covers many
variants from near absolute ownership to a mere prerogative in
royal dues.

[89] Stenton : op. cit., p 365.

For the most part what the king gives in the prodigal charters is the kingly right, the regality, to the land burdens issuing from the lands given. "Many of the landbooks even of the earliest period, despite their language, convey not the ownership of land, but a 'superiority' over land and over free men".[90] As the years pass intention to give freedom from royal dues becomes more precisely expressed. It is well illustrated in a charter of King Æthelbert of Wessex, dated 884:[91] "With the advice, covenant and leave of my bishops and earls and likewise of my brothers . . . I openly grant this freedom on my own behalf and for my dearest friends, and likewise in honour of the souls of Æthelwulf, my father, and Æthelbald, my brother, to the holy foundation at Sherborne . . . . that it be firmly and immutably and eternally freed from all royal and judicial services, including the arrest of thieves and all the irksomeness of secular labour, with the exception of military service and the construction of bridges."

Bookland and folkland. Immunity from land burdens is a characteristic of land conveyed by land charter, or *bookland* as it came to be called. Bookland stood over against folkland. The differences between them are not known with exactitude. Greater knowledge of the meaning of *folkland* would doubtless illumine the darkness that shrouds bookland. An earlier view sees folkland as the land of the people; but this has been discarded for more reasons than one. There seems little doubt among historians to-day that folkland was land held according to the traditional, verbal folkright, while bookland derived its meaning from the books or land charters that created it. Bookland in most instances meant, in favour of its holder, an immunity from certain land burdens. In this it differed from folkland and the difference may be the whole substance of the matter,[92] although probably the contrast had other features. Power of alienation and testamentary disposition seem to have been common to both types of land holding; the fact that these powers were expressly given by the land charters does not infer that folkright knew nothing of them. On the other hand there are strong grounds for seeing a difference in the matter of title; folkland was recognised and pleas were heard in respect of it wherever the folkmoots met, but bookland titles were secure in all circumstances unless disturbed by an adverse decision of the king's witenagemot.[93]

To accept the fact that a more precise meaning cannot be

[90] Maitland : op. cit., p. 232.   [91] Robertson : op. cit., pp. 17, 19.
[92] Stenton : op. cit., p. 308.   [93] Jolliffe : op. cit., p. 74.

assigned to folkland than that which defines it as land the ownership of which is fashioned within the folkright, opens the door to
many variegations of ownership reflecting the tones and colourings
of the folkright. If the folkright sanctioned alienation, it follows
that kings and other landowners could make grants of land
without creating bookland. There would be no solemn charter
signed and witnessed by the king's wisemen and upheld by threat
of the curse of God. Folkright may well have had its formulae of
gift and grant long before the use of the land book which, after
all, was a Latin thing coming in the wake of the Augustinian
missionaries. It has been cogently argued[94] that the distribution
of land at the hands of military chiefs followed the Saxon
invasions. Land passing in this manner would go first to the
great advisors, the gesiths, and from them to lesser men, the *gesithcundmen landagende*, and thus, with the passage of time, folkland
would become divided into a king's folkland and folkland in the
ownership of his subjects; the king's folkland being of the nature
of a residuum remaining in the royal hand.

From the king's folkland, land grants held at the royal will
would be made to support the king's thegns. What is then given
is something of greater substance than the sovereign rights which
the king holds in a general way over all land. The ownership approximates to absolutism but the range of the grants in terms of
physical dimensions, in most cases, is a moderate number of hides.
How far the royal will was autonomous in making grants of
folkland cannot be known. Folkland seems to have been an
appurtenance of public office in the case of ealdormen and
princes.[95]

Where the king is in possession of folkland and thus
has greater personal rights over the land than his universal sovereignties, he may convey his greater rights by the
device of a book and thus create a different form of bookland.
Whatever may have been the nature and variety of alienation
within the sanctions of the folkright, there seems little doubt that
bookland grants under the hand of the king came nigh to being
constitutional actions, expressions of the kingly will, with the
approval, if not consent, of the king's witan.[96] Where the king
stood the bookland holder by virtue of the book came to stand,
and the feorm and other dues were his. The dues were rendered to
bookland grantees by virtue of the folkright and, therefore, the self-
same land which to the bookland grantee was bookland remained

[94] Chadwick : op. cit., pp. 367-377.   [95] Maitland : op. cit., p. 254.
[96] Stenton : op. cit., p. 308.

folkland from the point of view of the land-dwellers responsible for the dues. Even so, it cannot be said that those who held folkland in these circumstances held it "of" the bookland owner; they may perhaps have held it "under" him but not "of" him. Nothing approaching feudal tenure is established.[97]

Bookland in the earliest days was created only by kingly gift. Later on the king's subjects make analogous gifts among themselves. Such gifts would convey to the grantee whatever rights the grantor had in the land by virtue of the folkright. Whereas the king when making gifts of bookland normally sought the consent of his witan and other advisers, his subjects when making express grants of land would, if they were wise, seek the acquiescence of the kindred or heirs to the transaction.[97a]

Laenland.   Although the privilege of immunity enjoyed by bookland could be given away, alienation by bookland owners did not create a lord and vassal bond linked point by point to a lord and tenant relationship. Bookland holders were for the most part free to alienate their land, but a conveyance would have an absolutism about it that would render it useless as an instrument for securing future service from the grantee. For this reason, ecclesiastical institutions and churchmen in their persons endowed with land were sometimes prohibited from alienating an essential core or *firma* of their property.

The prohibition created difficulties. Land was often the only consideration which could be offered in exchange for administrative services. A device was formulated to overcome the impasse by loaning the land and thereby creating *laenland*.[98] The transaction was not out and out alienation. The laenland holder merely acquired the benefits of landright for the duration of the loan on conditions of service or otherwise. Laenland titles were eventually the substance of writs. The written document apparently brought laenland within the beneficent purlieus of book-right and laenland became in a mannner of speaking quasi-bookland. The loans and relationships so created were expressive of an age that was groping after the *feudum*. Bookland, traditional and orthodox, shone in its own light but the loan was essentially something derivative and dependent. Maitland[99] endeavoured to see in it the origin of derivative and dependent tenure, the coming of the feudum in all but name. His view has been challenged,[100] but the fact

[97] Jolliffe : op. cit., p. 74.
[98] Jolliffe : op. cit., pp. 74-78.
[100] Jolliffe : op. cit., p. 77.

[97a] cf. D. Whitelock : op. cit., p. 153.
[99] Maitland : op. cit., p. 318.

cannot be escaped that while the essential genius of the Norman *feudum*, its inheritability, was no feature of the loan, the Saxon form of landholding was making towards a servitude beyond the confines of the folkright. He who granted the loan could enforce the one who took it to submit to oaths of obedience and render services unknown among the royal dues and other obligations of folkright. In consequence peculiar conditions of tenure developed. It is found for example that the conditions which governed the loans of St. Oswald of Worcester created a corpus of local law. The three hundred hides of the Saint were the land of Oswaldslaw and so sure a foundation was laid that although in the days of Oswald feudalism in its true nature was not known, the riding services which were among the conditions of the laenland were clearly seen in the feudal obligations of the radknights who inhabited the three hundreds in the twelfth century.[101]

Tenurial customs. Local customs grew up in this way. They were not all codes governing land loans in the strict sense. Peasants holding land by folkright under owners of bookland often acquired their land by commending themselves as vassals of the bookland owners. The lord and vassal relationship was a personal affair stemming from the hold-oath, but even so where the peasant took his land from the lord's hand, or "went with the land to his lord" a greater degree of domination resulted. The lord could and did demand rents and services beyond the folkright dues, so much so, that a provision in Ine's code limits the powers of the lord; where land only is offered, that is land without a house, the ceorl is not obliged to do service as well as pay rent although the lord may demand both. And in this way local customs of tenure were also established. The totality of obligation of the ceorl who sat on gafol-land came thus to depend upon the principles of the folkright and the requirements of custom, tempered here and there by the written codes of kings.

The Rectitudines. The customs are those that appear in the custumals of the age. The most famous and exhaustive are the *Rectitudines Singularum Personarum*. The Rectitudines divide the peasantry of eleventh century England into the three social classes already referred to—geneatas, geburas and kotsetlan. The custumal in its second part (*Gerefa*) outlines the duties of the lord's reeve or landmanager.[102] Of the three types of peasant the geneat comes nearest to freedom in landownership. His services are those of free

---

[101] Maitland : op. cit., p. 309.   [102] Stenton : op. cit., p 465.

status: specific agricultural duties at harvest time, personal duties including riding and escort service and obligations concerned with the lord's hunting, payment of gafol and an obligation to render a swine in return for pasture rights. The gebur holds a typical holding — the yardland or quarter hide. His service is onerous: nothing is determined, the work varies according to the orders of the reeve but is limited to two days a week and more at harvest and other special seasons, and includes ploughing an acre of land a week, fetching and sowing the seed, extra ploughing as boon-work and more in return for pasture rights and as rent service; in addition there are certain payments to be made to the lord, seed to be found for the three acres of ploughing done as service, and watching duties to be performed at the lord's fold; on the other hand, on entry, the lord usually provides initial stock and equipment — two oxen, a cow, six sheep, seven acres of sown land, implements and household furniture. Beneath the gebur the Rectitudines place the kotsetla. However humble his station he is in a sense a freeman because he has little to bind him to the soil. By analogy he comes nearest to an agricultural worker of modern times. No rent is paid. For his small holding in the open village fields he gives onerous agricultural service and discharges a variety of other duties varying in nature from place to place.

CHAPTER III

SELECT BIBLIOGRAPHY

Barger, Evert: *The Present Position of Studies in English Field-Systems* (English Historical Review, Vol. LIII, July 1938).

Cam, H. M.: *Liberties and Communities in Medieval England: Collected studies in local administration and topography* (1944).

Chadwick, H. M.: *Studies on Anglo-Saxon Institutions* (1905).

Clapham, Sir John: *A Concise Economic History of Britain from the Earliest Times to 1750* (1949).

Fox, Sir Cyril F.: *Archaeology of the Cambridge Region* (1923) (reissued with Appendix IV 1948).

Gray, H. L.: *English Field Systems* (1915).

Hodgkin, R. H.: *A History of the Anglo-Saxons*. Vols. I, II (3rd Ed., 1952).

Hunter Blair, P.: *An Introduction to Anglo-Saxon England* (1956).

Jolliffe, J. E. A.: *The Constitutional History of Medieval England from the English Settlement to 1485*. (3rd Ed., 1954).

Kerridge, Eric: *Ridge and Furrow and Agrarian History* (Economic History Review, Vol. IV, No. 1, 1951).

Maitland, Sir Frederic: *Domesday Book and Beyond. Three Essays in the Early History of England* (1907).

Orwin, C. S., and Orwin, C. S.: *The Open Fields* (2nd Ed., 1954).

Pollock, Sir Frederick, Maitland, Sir Frederic: *The History of English Law before the time of Edward I*. Vols. I and II. (2nd Ed., rep. 1952).

Robertson, A. J.: *Anglo-Saxon Charters*. (Cambridge Studies on English Legal History, 1939).

Round, J. H.: *Feudal England. Historical Studies on the XIth and XIIth Centuries* (1895).

Sayles, G. O.: *The Medieval Foundations of England* (2nd Ed., 1950).

Seebohm, Frederic: *The English Village Community* (4th Ed., rep. 1926).

Seebohm, Frederic: *Tribal Custom in Anglo-Saxon Law* (1902).

Stenton, Sir Frank: *Anglo-Saxon England* (2nd Ed., 1947).

Stubbs, William: *The Constitutional History of England in its Origin and Development* (Vol. I, 6th Ed. 1897, Vol. II, 3rd Ed. 1887, Vol. III, 4th Ed. 1887).

Vinogradoff, Sir Paul: *English Society in the Eleventh Century. Essays in English Medieval History* (1908).

Vinogradoff, Sir Paul : *The Growth of the Manor* (3rd Ed., 1920).
Whitelock, Dorothy : *Anglo-Saxon Wills* (Cambridge Studies in English Legal History, 1930).
Whitelock, Dorothy : *The Beginnings of English Society (The Anglo-Saxon Period)*. The Pelican History of England, Vol. 2 (1952).

CHAPTER FOUR

UNDER THE NORMAN KINGS

THE DOMESDAY INQUEST

Domesday Survey — a unique record. The conquest of England in 1066 by William, Duke of Normandy, established a dynasty of Norman kings that ended with the death of Stephen. The Norman rule brought changes, political, constitutional, social, economic and cultural; not all were immediate; some reached further than others; but in one form or another the influence of them can be traced through all subsequent centuries. No episode is of greater moment in the land story. The change of fortune and circumstance is poorly documented, save for one classical exception — the Domesday Survey of 1086.[1] This great *descriptio* stands alone. Nothing of equal weight and grandeur appears for at least a century. The Norman period has its royal and baronial writs, its charters, geld inquests, cartularies and an important Pipe Roll of 1130, and certain writings coming afterwards throw light in retrospect, but compared with the later centuries of Old England the period lies in darkness. The Norman came with strange, strong views, concepts of a rigid feudalism but he brought no written laws in the keels of his boats. William and his sons sought to uphold the laws of King Edward and the lawbooks of the period are mostly attempts to cast back to the Saxon dooms.[2] The result is unsatisfactory. Saxon laws were foreign to the Norman invaders and too brittle with age for practical manipulation. What is known of the social and economic changes under the Norman kings rests almost entirely upon the testimony of the Domesday Survey.

Difficulties of Interpretation. Mighty though that work is and comprehensive and efficient its undertaking, interpretation is burdened with difficulties. In the first place, the Survey was inspired and produced by Frenchmen. The very procedure of its compilation is exotic,[3] an import from across the Channel. Sworn panels of barons, the sheriff of the county and *juratores* from the

---

[1] Stenton: *The First Century of English Feudalism, 1066-1166,* pp. 8-10.
[2] Pollock and Maitland: *The History of English Law before the Time of Edward I* (Vol. I), pp. 97-104.
[3] Jolliffe: *The Constitutional History of Medieval England* (3rd Ed.), p. 199.

73   F

hundreds and vills[4] answer on oath to questions put to them by special commissioners (*barones regis*) appointed by William, the King. It is this use of the Frankish inquest that has earned for the *descriptio* the title of the Domesday Inquest.[5]

English voices were not altogether silent. Round[6] suggests that the panels of juratores were a combination of the Old English deputations from the vills to the hundred court and the newcomers to the hundred, the *francigenae*. He concludes that the testimony of one had equal weight with that of the other. Nonetheless, the Inquest is an exhaustive enquiry into English social institutions, land economy and agrarian order, made by men who thought in Norman concepts and wrote in Norman idioms. Further obscurity derives from the element of Procrustean method common to every wide census or statistical enquiry. Standard questions were put by the commissioners to tenants and doomsmen in all parts of the realm. No allowance was made for the diversities of custom, law and economic and social order still peculiar to local regions, the once separate kingdoms of the English and the lands of the Danelaw.

Nine months had been given for the gigantic task. The time was short and prevented one body of commissioners presiding over each and every local inquest. Lack of centralization militated against a rigid standardisation. Each panel of commissioners read the questions as they thought best and returned answers accordingly. Differences in the results are so apparent that scholars have attempted to determine from them the geographical circuits of the several panels of commissioners. The different readings and methods of treatment make the task of interpretation the more irksome, added to which the compilers of Domesday make no attempt at precise definition.[7] What is meant by many of the terms can only be known by careful comparison with other texts and deduction from the connection between an unknown term (e.g., *manerium*) and a known term (e.g., *vill*). Confusion is the more confounded by the absence of written law; the notions of law that guided the thought of the inquisitors remain hidden. Finally, the instructions given to the commissioners were charged with the false assumption that the social and economic conditions of the day Edward Confessor was quick and dead (*tempore Regis Edwardi*) had remained unaffected by the twenty years of Norman conquest, violence and upheaval. As a consequence the record of the state of affairs in

---

[4] The "vill" was the Norman equivalent of the Saxon tun.
[5] Ballard : *The Domesday Inquest*, p. 13.
[6] Round : *Feudal England*, p. 120.
[7] Vinogradoff : *English Society in the Eleventh Century*, p. 161.

Edward's day tends erroneously to approximate the conditions at the time of the Inquest.[8]

Comprehensive transcription of original returns. Apart from these difficulties arising out of the principles which governed the interrogations, Domesday Book is not a straightforward record of the answers to the questions. Vital features of early Norman land economy, familiar and testified to before the commissioners of Domesday, do not appear on the face of the Survey because the original returns suffered a comprehensive transcription and recasting.[9] The format of Domesday Book is not the form in which the evidence was originally written. A document known to antiquaries as the Inquisitio Comitatus Cantabrigiensis has been identified[10] as a copy of the original evidence given before the commissioners for Cambridgeshire. Therein the detailed answers to the questions are inscribed, vill by vill, hundred by hundred. Domesday Book, however, presents its facts fief by fief; it transcribes what was originally arranged geographically into a proprietary cadaster and record. The Survey is consistent in this and there is nothing to prove or indicate that the procedure adopted in Cambridgeshire was not common to every other county.

The Inquisitio Comitatus Cantabrigiensis is not the only extant document standing immediately upon the original returns of the great Inquest. A survey of the lands of the Abbey of Ely, the Inquisitio Eliensis, seems to have been partly compiled from this original source, and partly from the second volume of Domesday Book. The second volume, or Little Domesday, is not a later edition of the Domesday Book proper[11] but a record of the three counties, Essex, Suffolk and Norfolk, exceptionally rich in detail and strictly in accord with the inspiration of the main volume. These few documents, together with a survey peculiar to the southwest—the Exeter Domesday, Liber Exoniensis — comprise the Domesday MSS to which modern historians owe so much.

---

[8] Stenton : *Types of Manorial Structure in the Northern Danelaw*, p. 51.
[9] Maitland : *Domesday Book and Beyond*, pp. 10-12.
[10] Round : op. cit., p. 8.
[11] Usually referred to as Exchequer Domesday.

BEHIND DOMESDAY

Motives for the Survey are unknown. Domesday Book is a great light in a dark place. Yet, the illumination fails to reveal its own inwardness and meaning. No one can affirm without a shadow of doubt what lies behind Domesday Book. The Anglo-Saxon Chronicle is characteristically incurious. Its straight-flung words merely record that at the Gloucester gemot in the Christmas of 1085 "the King had muckle thought and deep speech with his wisemen about this land, how it was set, and with what men. Then he sent his men over all England into each shire and let them find out how many hundred hides were in that shire, and what the King had himself of land or cattle in those lands, or what rights he ought to have in the twelve month from the shire. Also he let them write how much land his archbishops had, and his bishops, and his abbots, and his earls, and, though I tell it longer, what or how much each man had, that was landsitting in England, in land or cattle, and how much it was worth. So very narrowly did he let them speir it out that there was not a hide nor a yardland nor — it is shameful to tell, though he thought it no shame to do — so much as an ox or a cow or a swine was left, that was not set down in his writ: and all these writs were brought to him afterwards." Many hypotheses and theories have been put forward claiming to explain the essential purpose of the great Inquest. The words of the Chronicler, of course, have not been overlooked. But the focus of attention has been upon the scope and framing of the questions the Commissioners asked, the structure and contents of the Domesday volumes and other MSS, and the trend of policy immediately after the completion of the Survey.

The outline of the Survey. One of the outstanding contributions that the Cambridgeshire Inquest makes to the knowledge of Domesday is its testimony to the content of the interrogation. Adolphus Ballard[12] translates the questions as:

"1.   What is the name of the mansion?
2.   Who held it in the time of King Edward?
3.   Who now holds it?
4.   How many hides are there?
5.   How many teams—in demesne—of the tenants?
6.   How many villans—cottars—slaves?
7.   How many freemen—sokemen?

[12] Ballard : op. cit., p. 14.

8. How much wood—meadow—pasture?
   How many mills? How many fisheries?
9. How much has been added or taken away?
10. How much was the whole worth?
    How much is it worth now?
11. How much has or had each freeman or sokeman there?
12. And if more can be had than is had."

Exchequer Domesday attempts to take the answers given to these questions and relate them to the Norman fiefs and tenantries. Little Domesday goes beyond the requirements of the questions. Its greater detail may point to its earlier compilation,[13] as if William had originally intended an exhaustive economic census, and experience of the magnitude of the work, in Norfolk, Suffolk and Essex where it was first begun, had modified his ambition. There is ample evidence of a general principle governing the arrangement of the subject matter in the final record; the entries for the counties north of the Thames are remarkably consistent. At the head of each description of the lands of a county appears a recitation of the burghal and county customs. This is followed by an index of the landed tenants of the shire and the main bulk of the text details the landholdings of each. In some counties the record of the lands of the king's tenants-in-capite and their sub-grantees is followed by a statement of the lands of the king's smaller tenantry, the vavassours and letter freeholders. The turn of policy immediately after the Survey is important, both as positive and negative evidence. The geld appears to have been collected after that time from the fiefs of the tenants-in-capite and not from the vills and hundreds as before. The negative evidence is the failure to re-assess the land in accordance with the hidages given in the Survey.

Theories of the motives behind Domesday. Many hypotheses and theories have been postulated to explain what lay behind the great Survey. Variety and contradiction are inevitable. Some authorities see a plurality of motives moving the Conqueror's policy, others are careful to identify and emphasise a single aim. The narrower school boasts no less a votary than Maitland.[14] For him one great purpose seems to underlie the questions and to mould both the form and substance of the Book: it is a geld-book. Vinogradoff[15]

[13] Round : op. cit., p 141.
[14] Maitland : op. cit., p. 3.
[15] Vinogradoff : *The Growth of the Manor*, p. 292.

wants this and something more. He admits the fiscal motive, advocated so forcibly by Maitland, but argues that the recasting of the Domesday evidence, as pertaining to the fiefs, was a calculated attempt to underscore in matters economic and social the personal nexus of tenure linking each and every landholder to the king as supreme lord. In another place[16] he wants Domesday also to be a record of title. In this a later historian[17] follows him, but bases his view on the boast of the Conqueror that no Englishman was unjustly deprived of his lands; the Norman tenantry must be able to recognise their English antecessors, if their land titles are to be secure and legitimate. Legitimacy of title is important not only from the view-point of the tenant of lands, but also in the eyes of a king who wishes to levy a heavy land tax upon the fiefs of England. Jolliffe[18] also sees security and determination of titles as a probable provocation of the Survey. He refers to the general use of the Inquest by the Normans to determine landed rights, and associates the great Survey with the universal oath of fealty which the Conqueror took from the tenants and their sub-tenants at Salisbury in the year 1086. Registration of fief holders would also enable the Conqueror to ascertain miscarriage among the land grants which followed upon the Conquest, and to identify the whereabouts of Englishmen still in possession of forfeited possessions. Freeman regards this as the main purpose of the Conqueror's Inquest. Galbraith[19] also supports these interpretations. Domesday Book in his view is not primarily a geld-book but "a return by manors and by tenants-in-chief" the purpose of which is to stamp upon the conquered lands feudal notions of tenure and landownership.

The view that Domesday Book was a register of title and the demarcations of personal fiefs is borne out by one Robert Fitz-Neal, Treasurer of England, writing within a century of its compilation.[19a]

Ballard[20] suggests the Conqueror desired an index of the strength of the host in England. And yet another view was taken by J. B. Phear at a Domesday Commemoration. In his opinion the main object was the provision of a deposited statement of the royal dues from county and borough as a safeguard

[16] Vinogradoff : English Society in the Eleventh Century, p. 227.
[17] Stenton : op. cit., p. 59.
[18] Jolliffe : op. cit., p. 163 n.
[19] Galbraith : The Making of Domesday Book, E. H. Rev. 1942, Vol. LVII, p. 177.
[19a] cf. Galbraith, Studies in the Public Records, pp. 103-104.
[20] Ballard : op. cit., p. 9.

against peculation. The detail of Little Domesday and of the Exeter Domesday is suggestive of a full-dress economic census. There may have been some trace of this in the original intention, but it cannot have been a predominant motive otherwise the whole project would have been abandoned when it was found that the scope of the enquiry and the volume of the returns would make the task impracticable.

Among the various probings into what lay behind the Domesday Survey, two views are of peculiar relevance to the land story. The view that sees the Survey as a geld-book, and the one which regards it as a register of fiefs and titles. The latter is of greater significance than the former for it takes count of the fundamental feudal idea of derivative and dependent tenure.

DERIVATIVE AND DEPENDENT TENURE

The king as paramount lord. Overall lordship of the king is the great idea that forever marks off landholding under the Norman kings from the proprietary notions of Old England. Therein is the heart and inspiration of Norman feudalism; there the source of the light which brings meaning to the frame and fabric of Domesday Book;[21] and there the reason why landownership for the subjects of the Crown is inevitably derivative and dependent tenure.[22]

There is reason to think that only in conquered England under the iron monarchy of William I was an outworking of so unadulterated feudalism possible.[23] The Conqueror can allot the feudal lands of the English felons who fought against him. The hard won acres come into his hand and to none other. He alone has power to exact redemption fines from the English who wish to keep their possessions. He alone can confirm a valid title where no redemption fee is taken. All men in England, conquerors and conquered alike, must look to the king before they dare call any land their own. Ownership is derived from the royal hand and is dependent upon the royal sanction. All landright is of the king. Ownership in any but the king's hand is tenure.

Mesne lordship. He who held land as tenant of the royal lord could himself become lord by granting the land to another. The primary rung in the feudal tenurial ladder was the tenant in actual

[21] Jolliffe : op. cit., p. 140.
[22] Pollock and Maitland : op. cit., p. 234.
[23] Op. cit., p. 69.

possession of the tenement, the tenant *in dominico*. The ultimate rung was the king, the one man in all the realm who was never tenant. Between the two extremes the rungs were either an ascending series of lordships or a descending series of tenures, according to the view taken. There is no land unowned in all England. Land can be without a tenant, where he who is in possession is the king; but land without a lord there cannot be — *nulle terre sans seigneur*.

Lord and vassal means lord and tenant. Lordship implies vassalage. Vassalage was known in England long before the Conquest but the essential difference between the lord and vassal relationship of Old England and that of Anglo-Norman feudalism lies in the doctrine of tenure : lord and vassal are also lord and tenant. The tie that creates the new relationship is the stygian oath of homage.[24] The feudal tenant swore to become "the man" of the lord "for the tenement he holds of him and to bear faith to him of life and members and entirely honour him against all other men save the king." In response the lord swore to "maintain his tenant in his tenement . . . to warrant his tenure in law, and to defend him against all men" The lord's interest, his *seignory*, is not absolute ownership. It is not ownership under the omnicompetent will of the lord, within the grace of which the tenant is granted sanction of occupation. The tenant's interest, his *feudum*, is truly ownership. For this reason the supreme lord, the king, was never absolute owner of every English acre. He was lord paramount of every acre; nothing more, and nothing less. Where the king is in possession of the land his proprietary interest approximates closely to absolute *dominium;* but never does it go all the way, for the royal demesne, the *terra regis*, is always the treasure of the realm.[25] And a king not in possession owns no more than the supreme seignory, and must uphold the tenant's right of formal defiance (*diffidatio*) against his own caprice.[25a]

The feudum or fee. As a general principle that which is held of the king or intermediate lord is the *feudum*. There are anomalous interests of which the most important is the *alod*. The feudum was the norm that gave name and character to the tenurial system. Like much else in the language of the Conqueror's landright, the term was confused and blurred in meaning. When, in the twelfth century, the land law is the subject of precise thinking, *feudum* is

---

[24] Jolliffe : op. cit., p. 153.   [25] Jolliffe : op. cit. (2nd Ed.), p. 183.
[25a] Sayles, *The Medieval Foundations of England*, p. 206.

broad and general, conveying nothing more articulate than the idea of an inheritance.[26] In the days of the Domesday Survey it denotes the concrete, tangible lands of a feudal tenant and the abstract idea of an interest held of a superior in exchange for services rendered. The English translation of the Latin is the word *fee*; it has been suggested[27] that the modern usage of the word as payment for services is not unrelated to the strict feudal purport. The feudal tenant held the *feudum* or fee in consideration of military or other services rendered to the lord from whom title to landright was derived.

The obligation to render service and to honour the strict oath of homage meant that although there was an element of heritability germinating and growing within the *feudum*, nonetheless there was an inherent precariousness; the risk of forfeiture for contempt of the homage bond or for commission of treason was ever present. Moreover, he who held in fee had no freedom of alienation.[28] Should a tenant desire to pass his *feudum* to another, he had to seek the confirmation of his immediate lord. Writs and charters were used to effect alienation, especially when the king granted his own demesne to another, but documents of this kind were never accepted as unequivocable evidence of the righteous cause of one dis-seised; the favourable verdict of doomsmen was necessary to uphold an action for possession.[29] What the hundred court, and the newly created feudal courts do not know they cannot endorse.[30] Alienation had to be by public, notorious act.

Villain and villain-land. Feudum is not the only word that came in with the Frenchmen. At the same time came *villanus*. The pages of Domesday are everywhere familiar with the villan who sits on *terra villanorum*. Villan for Maitland[31] conveys a meaning on all fours with the Saxon tunesman. As the tunesman is the man of the tun, so the villan is the man of the vill. Whatever the Norman villan may have been, he was certainly the forebear of the later villain whose very identity is commingled with the soil. When the land he occupies is passed from one lord to another, the lord's property in him passes with the land. So lost in the soil does he become that the term *demesne*, used of land "in hand" to the lord, embraces both land actually "in hand" and land occupied by the

---

[26] Pollock and Maitland : op. cit., p. 235.
[27] Op. cit., p. 236 n.
[28] Vinogradoff : op. cit., p. 225.
[29] Stenton : *The First Century of English Feudalism, 1066-1166*, p. 43 et seq.
[30] Ballard : op. cit., p. 70.
[31] Maitland : op. cit., p. 59.

lord's villains. In the Danelaw, if not elsewhere, this use of the word was known at the time of Domesday and employed by the Domesday commissioners.[32]

Hiring land. Although comparatively little is known of the nature of the landright enjoyed by the early Norman villan, it seems certain enough that a villan did not have a *feudum*, in the abstract sense of the word. Villan occupation approached the idea of hiring land rather than owning a *feudum* although in essence it was not exactly a hiring. Hiring land in the days of early feudalism was possible in principle because the Normans had accepted the Old English laenland; an interest in land granted and continuing for three or more lives. Domesday Book records instances of land-holders who have no powers of alienation even in King Edward's day, and it has been thought that such entries refer to laenland titles of Old England expressed in Norman idiom.

Continuity between Old England and Anglo-Norman England. Tracing continuity between land-holding traditions and practices of Old England and feudal tenures under the Norman kings is a task that has long engaged historians. Conclusions vary. There is nothing settled or certain. Vacillation is well seen in the theories which attempt to account for Norman military tenure. The earliest writers who can be numbered among the modern thinkers see William the Conqueror dividing the realm into military fiefs and enforcing foreign mutilation. Later thought contends that the change was not so cataclysmic; the inevitability of gradualness is responsible for an evolutionary process moving from English thegn-hood to Norman knighthood. Later champions led by Round[33] withstand the evolutionists. And to-day historians, while acknowledging a similitude in social relationships between the thanes and kings of Old England and the knights and monarchs of Norman days, emphasise the radical difference in the notions of tenure brought in with Norman feudalism.[33a]

The subject would have been less imponderable had society in pre-Conquestial days retained a more vital freedom. Men in Old England had lost much freedom under the unified monarchy. Social patterns began to resemble on the surface at least the lord-vassal relationship of Norman tenure. There is little wonder that the commissioners of Domesday misunderstood what they saw.

[32] Stenton : *Types of Manorial Structure in the Northern Danelaw*, pp. 7-10.
[33] Round : op. cit., p. 225 et seq.
[33a] Sayles : op. cit., pp. 199-211.

For generations the English kings had by bookgrant assigned regalities to favoured subjects; the kingly power to levy tribute and
geld had been given into private hands. While the folkright harnessed the king's prerogatives, it was not vocal in the ears of the
owner of bookland. A bookland owner might demand what
prudent kings dare not dream of; to him may be rendered land
gafol and other dues at the expense of the king's subjects who
before the grant of bookland were freemen under the royal lord.
Despite the excessive burdens private bookland owners pressed
upon the peasantry, the English ceorls remained freemen; they
would transfer their land and persons at will to other lords. This
freedom in landright was for the Norman a mystery which evaded
comprehension. Burdened men who pay land gafol and tribute or
discharge obligations, dignified or menial, to a superior are, to
the Norman mind, at best tenants *in feudo*, rendering service to
their lords to whom by tenure and homage they are bound.
Norman eyes saw tenure where there was no tenure.[33b] At the time
of the Conquest the people of the Danelaw are to all appearances
living in a sturdy freedom; *sokemen* and *liberi homines* are found
in telling numbers. And it is in respect of the Danelaw that
Stenton[34] sees so clearly the assumptions of the Domesday commissioners covering a remarkably transparent fiction of continuity
of tenure and type between the day of Edward Confessor and
1085. What was, in King Edward's time, merely sokeland becomes
in the magic of Domesday ink tenurial, a seignory of a lord to
whom the freemen of the soke are bound.

The Norman surveyors were not wholly oblivious of the strain
that the rigid feudal formulae imposed upon their power of
expression. They were conscious of anomaly. A noteworthy example is the introduction of the *alod* as a principle of landholding
over against the *feudum*. Whether the cause of this aberration was
Old English bookland, as Vinogradoff[35] thought, or folkland, as
Ballard[36] thought, none can tell. The alod and other anomalies
were doubtless inevitable. The essence and true nature of the new
order is derivative and dependent tenure. This tenure is the fulcrum
around which all policies pivot and by which the long future of
landownership is influenced. It came with the Conqueror and, like
William, it came to stay.

[33b] Barlow : *The Feudal Kingdom of England*, 1042-1216, p. 120.
[34] Stenton : op. cit., p. 51.
[35] Vinogradoff : op. cit., p. 255.
[36] Ballard : op. cit., p. 143.

DIFFERENCES OF TENURE

Land tenure for the Normans meant something more than the basic dogma of landright. It is the medium in which and by which social status and order are expressed. The day is not far distant when the Latin *status* will be appropriated to fashion the word *estate*;[37] a generic noun descriptive of a man's landed interest, whether feudum or something less. Because tenure was woven so closely into the texture of society it began to reflect in a multiplicity of ways the status of all sorts and conditions of men. Two hundred years on from the Conquest the great law codifiers will identify the niceties that mark one tenure from another, arrive at concise definitions and set the entire array under accepted captions. There is great danger lest their neat work and phrases should be mistaken for the thought and language of the day when men of action are laying the foundations of tenure as practical working arrangements. In those early days it is possible to detect the beginnings of the differentia which the later lawyers will use to distinguish one tenure from another, but the nuances of their mature thought must not be expected.

Tenure by knight's service. Among the accepted captions of later days the one above all others that brings most vividly to the lawyers' dull formulae the colour and glitter of Norman chivalry is tenure by knight's service. Domesday Book does not know this tenure by name. But two contemporary charters refer to tenants who serve king and lord by providing knights and rendering knight's service.[38] The evidence is exiguous in the extreme, but sufficient to advance by a century Round's[39] "earliest glimpse of the organisation of that purely feudal host among whom our lands had been parcelled out to be held . . . by military tenure"

Even so it cannot be said that tenure by knight's service in the first century of feudalism was the same at every point as the thing it later became. The Angevins speak of *feudum unius militis* but their Norman forbears seem never to arrive at a formula for a knight's fee or *feudum*.[40] The Conqueror and his sons have no uniform standard. Great honours and baronies were carved out of the forfeited lands and charged with the burden of providing equipped knights to the fyrd and later for guard duty at the

---

[37] Pollock and Maitland : op. cit. (Vol. II), p. 11.
[38] Stenton : *The First Century of English Feudalism, 1066-1166*, p. 153.
[39] Round : op. cit., p. 236.   [40] Stenton : op. cit., p. 157.

castles. Nowhere is there any evidence that the military burden
is equated to the extent of the lands granted. The charge, the
servitium debitum, was usually expressed in multiples of five or
ten knights,[41] but the areas and values of the knight's
feuda do not reflect these neat assessments. Another feature
that distinguishes the earlier period of grants by knight's service
from later times is the extent to which oral testimony and tradition
are relied upon as evidence of the *servitia debita* pertaining to the
lands of enfeoffed knights. Documentary records of land grants
only became common practice towards the end of the Norman
period.[42] Vinogradoff[43] endeavours to find early traces of a knight's
fee in the five-hide unit among the hidated shires of southern
England. His advocacy is not prolonged; he admits an extensive
obscurity, especially in the evidence of Domesday. He shows,
however, that the Survey assigns a considerable total hidage to a
wide-ranging class of military tenants *(milites)*. The landholdings
of some of these military men are relatively quite small; holdings
of four, two and one virgate. Doubtless many of them are fractions of large knightly holdings scattered among the manorial
units of great honours, but some must represent the landholdings
of knights quartered in the household of a lord and, therefore, not
dependent for total sustenance upon their own land resources.
Others of these holdings are not knights' land at all, but the
holdings of retainers, men-at-arms, a multitude of lesser military
folk. The word *milites* is wide enough to embrace these and the
servientes, the *francigenae*, the vavassours and later sergeants.

Tenure in sergeanty. Perhaps it is not going too far to say that
among the lesser military men who held land in 1086 is to be
found a nascent tenure in sergeanty. Tenure in sergeanty as it
eventually developed was comprehensive of many social differences. A dichotomy divided the true military tenants, who were
said to hold land in grand sergeanty, from other sergeants who,
rendering personal services of great variety, held land in petty sergeanty. The divide is discernible among some of the earlier
documentary evidence before the nomenclature was perfected.
Military duties are linked with those of hunting service and
overseer's responsibility, in a Durham tenure known as *dren-
gage*.[44] *Radknights* are another species whose duties were
agricultural work and riding service. Of an entirely different

[41] Round : op. cit., p. 259.   [42] Stenton : op. cit., p. 152.
[43] Vinogradoff : op. cit., p. 55.
[44] Op. cit., p. 63.

order, and yet surely among the foundations of sergeanty are the tenants of Toresbi and Revesby[45] who in 1142 are holding two ploughlands by "the service of the bakery"; later the same tenants hold an equivalent fee for "the half of a knight's service." This early division of knight's service into fractions is probably one of the nodal points, on the lower stems of knight's service tenure, from which tenure in sergeanty budded. Undoubtedly the correspondence was real in later days and is expressed by the equation *duo servientes* = *unus miles*.[46]

The fruits of chivalry. Inherent in military tenures were elements which the thought of a coming age will regard as the paramount benefits of military tenure. These, the seven fruits of chivalry, were aids, wardship, marriage rights, reliefs, fines, primer seisin and escheat. These fruits are the cause that make tenure in chivalry so burdensome to the tenant and so attractive to the lord; especially to the royal, supreme lord. Nothing is very clear in the beginning. Norman thought is characteristically vague.[47] The Leis Willelme make definite reference to the vavassour's relief of one hundred shillings,[48] and the great Pipe Roll of 1130 witnesses to Henry I trafficking in reliefs, wardships, marriage rights and escheats. The incidents were, nevertheless, still collateral to the main purpose of military tenure and consideration of their meaning and significance may well remain until the time comes to consider the centuries when these fruits will have become the pivot of state policy.

Spiritual tenures. Within two generations of the Conquest clerks are drafting charters of enfeoffment in knight's service and introducing conventional formulae and phrases.[49] It is then that charters passing land in perpetual or free alms display individuality and excite the minds of diplomatists. Domesday Book and certain early charters employ the word *elemosina* to cover land grants made in charity.[50] Grants in alms were not in every case made to God, the saints or the Church; the lame, the blind and lepers were recipients.[51] And in these eleemosynary grants lay the root from

[45] Stenton: *Facsimiles of Early Charters from Northamptonshire Collections*, p. 6.
[46] Pollock and Maitland: op. cit. (Vol. I). p. 256.
[47] Op. cit., p. 326.
[48] Stenton: *The First Century of English Feudalism, 1066-1166*, p. 162.
[49] Op. cit., pp. 155, 157.
[50] Pollock and Maitland: op. cit., p. 241.
[51] Stenton: *Facsimiles of Early Charters from Northamptonshire Collections*, p. 154.

which, in the days when tenure is botanised, will come two spiritual tenures of divine service and frankalmoign.

Tenure in free and common socage. Thus, the stamp of feudal tenure was pressed over castle and kitchen, church and leper colony. But what of the husbandmen? Small military men, the radknights, have already been identified tilling the land. The obligation to rise to the summons of the fyrd still cast a common shadow over all free men.[52] But there was a class of freemen which had no peculiar military bearing about it. These men are neither *milites* nor *drengs* nor *radknights*. They are freemen, often peasants, of whom the *socmen* of East Anglia are type and representative. Among the pages of the Domesday Survey and in later cartularies and other documents numerous traces are found of free tenants, many appearing to hold land immediately of the king, whose tenure finds no place in any one of the developing tenurial conventions. The Danelaw was particularly prolific. Socmen were numerous there. By their side were men of similar standing, the *liberi homines;* and of like status were the *alodiarii* and *franklings*.[53] Differences of liberty and loyalty distinguish one from the other. But each and all hold land in free tenure, in exchange for services which resemble in many cases those of petty sergeanty when they are not agricultural work or money payments. Paradoxically it is from this heterogeneous class that time and the subtleties of lawyers will fashion under the epithet "free and common socage" a puissant tenure to assimulate all others. Socage tenure had no social eminence in the early days, but it was never subject to wardship and marriage and the other burdens of chivalry,[54] and therein lay its hidden advantage.

Socmen are sometimes distinguished from *liberi homines* by historians who place them on the weather side of the freedom line.[55] Socmen for them are outside the privileges of free tenants because they had no autonomy in matters of land alienation.[56] If freedom is to be defined as freedom of alienation (a state of tenure which in no way binds a tenant to the soil although he is bound to his lord as vassal) it is permissible to draw the freedom line between socmen and *liberi homines*. But there is a mystery in the socman's position, a vital, hidden, elemental something which later in time

[52] Stenton : *Types of Manorial Structure in the Northern Danelaw*, p. 30.
[53] Vinogradoff : op. cit., p. 418.
[54] Stenton, D. M.: *The Earliest Northamptonshire Assize Rolls A.D. 1202-1203*, p. xxxiii
[55] Vinogradoff : op. cit., p. 432.   [56] Jolliffe : op. cit.. p. 145.

reveals the advantage of socage tenure and makes of it a synonym for all free tenure standing over against villainage or bond tenure. But this freedom has little to do with alienation. A socage tenant because he is free has proprietary rights in his tenement,[57] rights which the king's court will acknowledge and protect,[58] and the limits of his service are precisely and immutably determined. All this, however, must await development. The idea that bondage ensues wherever service is uncertain makes nonsense in a day when tenure by knight's service is held in a similar uncertainty.[59]

The Domesday *villanus* is too broad a term by which all who are unfree are separated from the ranks of the privileged.[60] And yet among the villans are those *nativi* whom the formulators of the Leis Willelme have in mind when they provide that "no lord may eject his cultivators from their land as long as they can do their due service" and "nativi who leave the estate where they were born are to be arrested and sent back". Perhaps the freedom line can at so early a date be located between the landless villan and the villan or socman possessed of a tenement. There can be no certainty. In these first days, the geography of abstract tenure has no deep sunk valley of Jordan.

ASSESSMENT TO THE GELD

Hides as units of assessment. Maitland[61] contends that in the eyes of the Domesday commissioners the essential difference between villans, on the one hand, and socmen or freemen on the other, turns upon the incidence of the Danegeld. The freemen and socmen are assessed to the geld in their own right. The levy upon the villan is indirect. It is the lord of the villan to whom the tax demand is addressed and not the peasant himself. This view is understandable in one for whom the great Survey has no other significance than a nation-wide geld inquest.[62] Each and every question is freighted with the same burden : to determine for the king the true liability of land to the geld, to record the gelding-houses *(maneria)*, to note the assessments and to appraise the potentialities.

Right to levy Danegeld was among the first reins of kingship that William tried. The response was shy and the king in-

---

[57] Op. cit.. pp. 144, 145.
[58] Pollock and Maitland : op. cit., p. 362.
[59] Stenton : *The First Century of English Feudalism, 1066-1166,* p. 153.
[60] Jolliffe : op. cit.. p. 85.
[61] Loc. cit., p. 125.   [62] Op. cit., p. 4 et seq.

creased the burden, not twice but thrice. On the third occasion, in 1083, he levied an "exceeding muckle geld" of six shillings upon every hide. Multiplying the tax rate did not quicken the response. Either men were defrauding the sovereign or he had been misinformed concerning the assessment of the land. The great Survey, so it is argued, was an impassioned attempt to discover the roots of the matter and for this reason it follows hard upon the disappointing returns of 1083-1084.

There can be little doubt that the fiscal motive was a very real one with the Conqueror. Domesday Book regarded as a geld register throws a great light upon the contribution and assessment of land to the crushing Danegeld in early Norman times.

Fiscal confusion was bound up with the dual nature of the hide. To the Domesday question "How many hides are there?" the answer came from many counties in a manner which leaves no doubt that the juratores understood the question as one relating to geld assessment. The Huntingdon response used the formula *hidas ad geldum*; Cheshire and Shropshire referred to *hidae geldantes;* and in the south-western counties the phrase *geldabat pro . . . hidis* was coined.[63] Clearly the same thing is meant in each case; the number of hides is a record of geld liability. All would have been well had the number of hides given agreed with the number of ploughteams or ploughlands, either at the date of the Survey or at one or another of the times in respect of which information was sought. Geld assessment would then have borne obvious, direct and immediate relationship either to the actual or original area of land under the plough, or to the potential extent of cultivation. The hide for tax purposes would have been concrete and tangible, and the tax assessment a perfect reflection of the area of ploughed or ploughable land. Such was not the case. Admittedly Domesday records, here and there, instances of congruity between the number of hides and the number of ploughteams or teamlands.[64] The frequency of agreement, however, is insufficient to identify a constant or normal equation or to dispel the thought that the hide in the days of the Norman kings, when used for geld purposes, is nothing more than a financier's counter.

Hidation and dehidation. Nowhere is the artificiality clearer than in the principle of repartition of hides among the lands of the realm from the central office of the Exchequer. The great, centrally poised scheme was first discovered by Round.[65] Working upon the

[63] Maitland: op. cit., p. 405.
[64] Vinogradoff: op. cit., pp. 512, 544.
[65] Round: op. cit., p. 44 et seq.

G

Inquisitio Comitatus Cantabrigiensis, he noticed how the hidation, the assessment in terms of hides, of the hundreds tended as a general rule to be an exact quota of a hundred hides, and that the vills within each hundred were assessed according to a multiple of a five-hide unit. There are anomalies even among the Cambridgeshire evidence, but for the most part the principles hold good and traces of their presence in the hidated areas of England are discernible in other documentary evidence. Two perfect examples from Round's analyses[66] are seen in the hidation of the hundreds of Longstow and Erningford.

HUNDRED OF LONGSTOW

	Hides		Ploughlands	
Eversden	$8\frac{1}{3}$		$13\frac{3}{8}$	
Kingston	$8\frac{1}{3}$	25	8	38
Toft and Hardwick	$8\frac{1}{3}$		$16\frac{1}{8}$	
Gransden	5	25	9	$32\frac{1}{2}$
Bourne	20		$(23\frac{1}{2})$	
Gamlingay	20			
Hatley	$4\frac{1}{4}$	25		
(Unnamed)	$\frac{3}{4}$	5		
Croxton	7			
Eltisley	3	10		
Caxton	10	25		
Caldecot	$1\frac{3}{4}$	5		
Long Stow	$3\frac{1}{4}$			
		100		

HUNDRED OF ERNINGFORD

	Hides T.R.E.	Hides T.R.W.	Ploughlands
Morden (1)	10	8	20
Tadlow	5	4	$10\frac{1}{2}$
Morden (2)	5	4	$10\frac{3}{4}$
Clopton	5	4	7
Hatley	5	4	7
Croydon	10	8	$11\frac{1}{2}$
Wendy	5	4	$6\frac{3}{4}$
Shingay	5	4	6
Litlington	5	4	11
Abington	5	4	$3\frac{3}{4}$
Bassingburne	10	8	22
Whaddon	10	8	$14\frac{3}{4}$
Meldreth	10	8	$20\frac{1}{2}$
Melbourne	10	8	$19\frac{1}{2}$
	100	80	171

[66] Op. cit., pp. 48, 50.

These two examples are sufficient to illustrate the arbitrary nature of the assessment principle. It is seen in the lack of flexibility of assessment among vills of different area. A vill of 20 ploughlands is charged to the geld at 10 hides, while one of 11½ ploughlands has a similar assessment. The principle of dehidation is also apparent. For some reason or another the assessment of the hundred of Erningford suffered a wholesale reduction between T.R.E. and T.R.W. The perfect quota of a hundred hides at the later date is scaled down to eighty.

A true diagnosis of the Conqueror's trouble may probably be found just here. On the assumption that each hundred bore an assessment of hundred hides, it would be possible to calculate a hidation figure for the whole realm by merely multiplying the number of hundreds by the perfect assessment. The global result would be an admirable budgeting instrument. Indeed, it has been argued[67] that such a figure was 1200 hundreds of one hundred hides, and that the sums stated in the Anglo-Saxon Chronicle as the national yields of Danegeld are all multiples of £1,200. The Conqueror may well have been advised by his financiers to base his fiscal estimates on a total assessment of this order. But its rigidity left no place for dehidation, a practice that was widespread. The principles of dehidation, like the principles of original assessment, were not careful of land areas or values and if no exact assessment terriers were kept none could tell the true state of affairs with the nation as a whole. Too many stewards for too long had taken their pens and written fourscore where the original charges stood at a hundred. A national survey of existing hidation was a statesman's only path.

However calamitous dehidation may have been from a national standpoint, in the eyes of the landowner it was a boon greatly prized. The royal lands present many instances of unqualified and absolute immunity from geld.[68] Entire emancipation of land was not the general rule. Church property is found so privileged in 1085, doubtless an inheritance from some ancient comprehensive grant of immunities creating bookland. The common case is partial reduction of original or normal assessment, a phenomenon which historians have designated *beneficial hidation*. Immunity from geld and beneficial hidation meant that either the total hidage of the hundred, within which the emancipated or relieved land lay, would be curtailed or a greater hidage would be placed on the less fortunate lands of the hundred. Some evidence is forth-

[67] Ballard : op. cit., p. 254.
[68] Maitland : op. cit., p. 448.

coming that the demesnes of Wessex manors, the *inland*, always shifted the geld burden on to the tenant's land, the *warland*.[69]

Immunity or concession was often a condition accompanying royal grants of land. In any event only a royal writ or charter could substantiate the benefit, as instanced by the following Domesday entry:[70] "Harold held it of King Edward; before Harold had it, it defended itself (i.e., was gelded at the rate of) for 27 hides, afterwards for 16 hides because Harold so pleased. The men of the hundred never heard or saw any writ from the King which put it at that figure." Sometimes the motive lying behind the modified assessment is given. One interesting case tells how King Edward sanctioned 30 hides by toll, to be reckoned as 20 hides "because of the Vikings." This and similar records are strongly suggestive of a notion somewhere at the back of the recorder's mind that the fiscal hide should bear some relationship to the hide by toll.

What exactly the hide by toll was is not easy to say. Maitland[71] characteristically presupposes a normal assessment of one fiscal hide = one teamland. Equipped with this equation he shows how whole counties fared. Some are under-rated, others over-rated, some stand at par. He is unable to show why entire counties should be more lightly assessed than others. Now and again reason seems to prevail. Yorkshire[72] appears to change from a highly over-rated county to one lowly assessed because of the devastation and waste left in the wake of the northern harryings of post-Conquest days. Kent is always a land of Goshen. Admittedly it forsakes the English hide for its own peculiar sulung, but the number of teamlands far exceeds the sum of the sulungs and each sulung bears Danegeld as if it were a hide.

The carucate. Kent is not the only county where the hide was unknown. The Danelaw prefers the *carucate*. Its wapentakes and hundreds are for geld purposes neat bundles of six-carucate units.[73] The carucate may have had a greater affinity with the soil than the hide had. There is not so wide a difference between the actual land measure and the *geld-carucate* as existed between the physical hide and its fiscal wraith. For this reason, perhaps, the carucate is adopted as the unit of assessment when in later days determined efforts are made to relate the assessment of land to its ability to carry the tax burden.

[69] Ballard: op. cit., p. 247.
[70] Maitland: op. cit., p. 449.
[71] Op. cit., p. 447.
[72] Op. cit., pp. 448, 460.
[73] Round: op. cit., p. 73 et seq.

Hidage remains unaltered. The Domesday Inquest itself may have been a great foreshadowing of this polity. William may have intended sweeping re-assessments as a consequence of his enquiry. The material was to hand. Hidage could reflect reality, or assessment made to turn upon the number of plough-teams or the potential number of ploughlands or the value of the manor. But the fact remains that for over a century whenever Danegeld is levied the assessments to the tax are substantially the same as the Domesday commissioners found and recorded them.[74]

SAKE AND SOKE

Sake and soke obscure in meaning. Among the comparatively clear and understandable records of tenure and geldability the Domesday scribes intermingled references to *sake and soke*. Obscurity shrouds the meaning of the phrase. Its Saxon origin is certain enough. What lay behind the strange alliteration both for the Domesday surveyors and the Old English kings in whose writs it first appears has been the subject of much debate. The problem is made the more recondite by the use of the single word "soke" where the full phrase may have been expected. Weighty opinion fosters a tradition that sake and soke is but a periphrasis of the single word; the same thing is meant whichever is used. More recent writers question this confidence.[75] All views, however, tend to support the notion that sake and soke is in some manner concerned with rights of private jurisdiction. To adopt this interpretation clears the ground, but at once the opened pathway divides about many forks. Rights of jurisdiction mean a number of different things. Sake and soke cannot with certainty be assigned to any one meaning. In its fullest sense jurisdiction amounts to authority to preside over a court, pronounce and execute sentence and appropriate the profits from forfeitures and fines. So conceived, it is both an enabling power making for control and order at the instance of the lord in whom it vests and a valuable source of revenue. A lower usage omits the juridical function but retains the profits; lords have no power of presidency or summons but take the fines and forfeitures. Jurisdiction within both meanings differs in degree according to the nature of the pleas; some pleas are those of high justice, others pertain to low justice. Sake and soke can denote either plenary or limited jurisdiction but it never embraces

[74] Maitland : op. cit., p 473.
[75] Ballard : op. cit., p. 117.

the pleas of high justice;[76] grave mischief and the causes that spring therefrom are always a king's immediate concern.

Private jurisdiction under the Normans. By the end of the Norman period the king's court was becoming avaricious of all justice. Under the Angevin kings it embarked upon a policy of attrition which eventually wore down the feudal rights of private jurisdiction. The Norman period, however, was near enough to Saxon times for some honour still to be paid to the ancient words sake and soke and the other alliterations[77] which were often associated with them in definitions of private jurisdiction in petty justice. Exactly how far this jurisdiction ran is difficult to say. In all probability it was limited to disputes about land between freemen, the troubles that constantly outcropped from the practice of communal agriculture and to matters concerning toll and warrants given when cattle or goods were sold; and to the right to adjudge thieves taken in possession of stolen property on the land of the lord (*infangenetheof*).[78]

Sometimes the phrase "all customary payments" conjoined with a reservation of the king's forfeitures appears to do the work of the ancient words.[79] The king's forfeitures were the penalties of high justice, the outcome of Crown pleas — if such a term may be used of so early a time. Some reservations retained for the Crown more pleas than others. There was no universal standard. Where the reserved Crown pleas were few, it followed that either custom had gathered a wider range of pleas into the realm of low justice or the franchise of Crown pleas had been assigned to private hands with no intention that the pleas should pass from the sphere of high justice.

Acquisition of rights of sake and soke. A fundamental difference between low and high justice appears in this. Rights of jurisdiction over Crown pleas could never arise by custom in favour of private lords. Private jurisdiction over Crown pleas there could be but he who would claim title thereto must show evidence of a specific royal grant express or implied.[80] It is not so with rights of sake and soke for the jurisdiction implied by the words is always within the capacity of custom. Custom, however, did not give rights of sake and soke into the hands of Saxon lords by

[76] Vinogradoff: op. cit., p. 116.
[77] Toll and team; inne tid and ut of tide; binnan burh and butan burh; on straete and of straete.
[78] Stenton: *Anglo-Saxon England* (2nd Ed.), p. 491.
[79] Vinogradoff: op. cit., p. 112.   [80] Stenton: op. cit., p. 493.

virtue of their lordship and because they were lords of lands having tenants. Until Norman times private jurisdiction never sprang *ipso facto* from tenure. Social status was probably the criterion that attracted sake and soke before 1066.

Rights of administering high justice[81] not infrequently came into the hands of private lords when extensive royal manors of one or more entire hundreds were added to their fiefs, or granted to them as new fees carved out of royal demesne.[82] The new lord of the land of the hundred became the lord of the hundred court and presided where the king's sheriff had stood. Grants of hundredal jurisdiction were either made for life or lives or were inheritances passing down the intricate canons of descent. Royal gifts of jurisdiction over a hundred court in some instances stopped short of plenary authority and the grantee was given only the power to take the profits of hundredal justice. Analogous grants, here and there, and with greater frequency as time passed, were made in favour not of a private lord but of a body of doomsmen who in consideration paid a lump sum to farm the hundred.[83]

Soke and sokeland. Admitting the loose usage of "sake and soke" to mean nothing more than a right to take the profits of justice, scholars have attempted to find precise meanings for each word. "Soke" gives the sense of a power of summons, of the right to demand that the doomsmen seek the court; while "sake" denotes rights of cause, authority to adjudicate upon pleas[84] Obligation to seek the lord's court is probably responsible for the wider and detached usage of the word soke. It is used elliptically where the full phrase is spared, to connote rights of justice.[85] Title to profits of justice did not carry with it the presidency of the hundred court, because in a strict sense the soke of the hundred still remained with the king's sheriff. And there were other meanings. Peasants were required by the burden of foid soke to seek the lord's sheepfold with their own flocks that the manurial benefits of folding might enhance the lord's husbandry;[86] obligations to seek the fyrd were fyrd soke and to seek the navy ship soke, and so on. Nowhere is the wider use of the word more apparent than in the Danelaw counties.[87] A lord's authority to demand services many and varied from

[81] Maitland : op. cit., p. 92.
[82] Cam : *Liberties and Communities in Medieval England*, p. 71 et seq.
[83] Vinogradoff : op. cit., p.114.   [84] Maitland : op. cit., pp. 84, 85.
[85] Stenton : op. cit., p. 488.
[86] Jolliffe : op. cit., p. 70.
[87] Stenton : *Types of Manorial Structure in the Northern Danelaw*, p. 21 et seq.

socmen and from *liberi homines* who are not his tenants derives from a power of soke. A gossamer of obligation binds men, over whom a lord has powers of soke, not of tenure, to the economy of that lord's manor.[88] Soke is the integrating principle giving a semblance of unity to the loose manorial structures of the Danelaw. It binds the sokeland to the central landed interest; a lord's sokeland is of his manor but not in it. The sokeland renders soke, in the form of services and payments, to the manor and the men of the sokeland do suit of court at the central manor court.

Men of a sokeland were not necessarily socmen. They might be freeman, *liberi homines*, over whom the lord of the manor to which the sokeland was appurtenant had rights of soke.[89] No difference can be found distinguishing socmen from *liberi homines* in this matter, both could be within the soke of the same lord. There might be a difference where socmen and freemen inhabited extramanorial lands which were not sokeland. All socmen did not live within a sokeland. A man might be a socman solely because he was moot-worthy only at the court of the lord who had a right of soke over him, and in this he differed from the freeman who did suit of court to the county and the hundred moot. Again, a socman was not of necessity the commended man of the lord of his soke. Commendation and rights of sake and soke were not mutually attractive.

Sake and soke linked with tenure. If among the confused evidence of a confused age, it is possible to place a finger on one certain fact it is this: an act of commendation in Saxon England did not imply a right of private justice over a man[90] in favour of his commended lord. The act of commendation created the lord-vassal relationship, but it was local custom that endowed the lord with rights of sake and soke or other powers of petty justice. A lord so endowed could not prevent his socman seeking another lord by commendation; albeit the lord's power of sake and soke over him remained unimpaired. Lordship of the soke could divide from the lordship of the vassalage.

When the land came under the Norman yoke, the feudalists saw tenure in the vassalage and a seignory in the lordship. What was only a lord-vassal relationship became a privity of lord and tenant; and the tenants because they were tenants became subjects

[88] Stenton : op. cit., p. 12.
[89] Maitland : op. cit., p. 105.
[90] Stenton : *Anglo-Saxon England*, p. 484.

of the lord's rights of sake and soke. Such a fate appears to have overcome the socmen and freemen rendering soke in the Danelaw and other eastern regions.[91] Although it cannot be said with finality that all socmen and freemen were the commended vassals of their lords of soke, the heavy incidents of soke would look in Norman eyes uncommonly like the burdens of vassalage and hence of tenure and the right of soke over the tenants would become an incidence of feudal lordship. The theory may be an unjust critique of the Norman surveyors. It sees them mistaking soke for vassalage and vassalage for feudal tenure. None can dogmatise. The only certainty is the advent under the Norman settlement of the high feudal principle which gave to a lord of lands, by virtue of his seignory, rights of private jurisdiction, seignorial justice, over his tenants.[92] Exactly how the principle was related to the Saxon tale can only be left to conjecture. Whatever may have been the true history, seignorial justice, claiming lineage with the sake and soke of Old England and pointing forward to the traditional manorial and other feudal courts, was a salient feature in the unfolding land story of the Norman period.

MANOR AND VILL

No evidence for a typical manor. To what extent, if at all, the manor as an institution runs back into Old English society is an open question. In name it is truly Norman. The *manerium* of the Domesday Survey came with the scribes and the thought of the Conqueror.[93] The writing of the scribes is loose and the thought confused. Historians have laboured among the pages of Domesday to find a consistent idea, some simple mantle clothing the thought of the commissioners. Stenton[94] pleads for the recognition of a typical manor within the Danelaw; but this will not do for other parts of Norman England. One by one theories have stood up to be laid low. The attractive notion that the manor was a gelding place, a point to which the geld of bond tenants flowed for collection is happily maintained until villeins are discovered making payment to the sheriff.[95] Frequently the manor centred in a hall of residence; but at times there was no hall within a manor.[96] Demesne

[91] Maitland : op. cit., p. 63.
[92] Jolliffe : op. cit., p. 148.
[93] Maitland : op. cit., p. 108.
[94] Stenton : *Types of Manorial Structure in the Northern Danelaw*, p. 59.
[95] Vinogradoff : *The Growth of the Manor*, p. 227.
[96] Maitland : op. cit., p. 110.

land likewise was not an uncommon feature, but manors are known that had no demesne.[97] There is no irrefutable evidence supporting the simple, basic notion of the manor as the estate of one lord and his tenants; for freemen, who have no tenants have manors.[98] A recent view avoids any attempt at standardisation and regards the Norman manor as a place of local prominence. A property that is prominent in one countryside will differ materially from a property that stands out in another. Both are manors because of their setting; in other respects they differ.[99] No one definition holds. But the Norman manor cannot be escaped. It is a radical conception of Norman thought. The new statesmen are groping after a formula through which the political, economic, judical and social ideas of the age would express themselves.

The manor not the vill. One fact is certain: the manor was not the vill. The distinction is not unimportant. The decay of manorial structure and life has left the manor-house dominating the village and in the popular mind the vill and manor have coalesced. Vill is the Norman word for the Saxon tun, or township, and to distinguish the vill from the manor will give clearer conception of the essential qualities of both.

The vill. The vill is concerned with husbandry. It is indifferent of tenure and social status. Among the fields, the pastures and the woodland, free and bond, socman, villein, serf and slave find a common identity. All are men of the soil. Each is dependent upon the other, and their communal enterprise upon a reciprocal balance of arable land, meadows, pastures, woodland and water; a unified economy giving selfhood to the vill. Vills with scattered holdings and even wideflung hamlets were not alien to the normal principle, for common grazings and rights in the woodlands bound the discrete parts together.

Land measurement. Allusions to the features of contemporary husbandry are more frequent among Norman diplomata than among the Saxon documents. But the days are too early for the full manorial accounting which gives so generous a picture of husbandry practice.

Among the noteworthy features of the Norman evidence is a wealth of reference to land measurements. The hide is the basic

[97] Vinogradoff: *English Society in the Eleventh Century*, p. 333.
[98] Op. cit., p. 334.
[99] D. M. Stenton: *English Society in the Early Middle Ages (1066-1307)*, p. 129.

unit. It divides once into half-hides; twice into yardlands and virgates; and again as oxgangs or one-eighths. In the Danelaw the hide gives place to the carucate which sub-divides into one-eighth fractions. The Kentish sulung likewise is partitioned about four yokes. Areas are often given to the nearest acre as the ultimate common unit. Acres sometimes are real acres but the occasions are rare. For the most part acres and all other land measures must be regarded as fiscal expressions. As such they serve well the partitioning of land. Proportions between allotments are more important than the niceties of actual measurement.[100] The hide, the virgate and other land divisions are only exceptionally conceived as measures of arable-land severed from the many rights appendant over pasture, meadow and woodland. Arable-land is not measured by itself. The organic unity of the vill is maintained, and land parcels, although expressed as areas of arable land, stand in fact for proportionate parts of the vill as a whole.

Villeins did not hold the same proportion in each township. In some vills the typical holding was half a hide, in others a virgate or a yardland or a smaller division. But within each vill a crude equality was found. As a general principle the bordarii and cottarii held much smaller shares in the village lands than the villeins and other members of the peasantry.

The manor. The manor lay as an overprint across the vills and hamlets. Here and there perfect correspondence of boundaries suggests the illusion of the two being one, an illusion heightened by the tenurial, economic and jurisdictional bond between the manor and the vill.

Lord's demesne. The tenurial link was most obvious where the lands of the vill included lord's demesne land. Demesne, like so many other contemporary terms, has more than one meaning. Generally it denotes land in the immediate occupation of the lord of the manor and distinguishes it from the lands of the manor occupied by tenants, bond and free. Exceptionally demesne is comprehensive of land in the lord's immediate occupation and the land of his bond tenants.[101] The demesne might make common cause with the other lands of the vill as part of the agrarian unity, or it might stand apart in enclosed severalty. In any event, the services of the tenants meet its husbandry needs. In consideration

[100] Vinogradoff: op. cit.. pp. 282-283.
[101] Stenton: op. cit., p. 9: cf. p. 79 ante.

for the tenure of their land the men of the vill perform agricultural work upon the lord's demesne. The nature of the service tends
to distinguish freemen from bondmen. He who is free does
boon work only, work performed at set times of the year; while
the bondman groans under the burden of *week-work*, continual
service determined according to the daily needs of the demesne
husbandry. Certainty of labour service as the hall-mark of free
tenure is probably a lawyer's theory, and should be accepted with
considerable reservation, especially for Norman times.[102]

On many manors the proportion of demesne land to tenant's
land is not clear from the face of the records. Sizes are given in
hides or ploughteams. Oftentimes the demesne enjoys beneficial
hidation or complete immunity from the geld, and the geldhides
of the original assessment have shifted from the demesne to the
tenant's land. Ploughteam numbers are also misleading. The Domesday record for Middlesex[103] shows how actual land areas are related
to fiscal units, hides, virgates and so on. It is possible, therefore, to
check the number of ploughteams, which are also given, against
the areas so recorded. On many occasions the land of the villains
carries ploughteams beyond its capacity and an extensive demesne
is under-equipped.[104] The inference that the villains maintain
ploughs and the ploughteams for the sole purpose of cultivating the
lord's demesne seems reasonable. The incongruity clearly exposes
the danger inherent in accepting ploughteam numbers as indices of
area proportions between demesne and tenant's land.

Manor economically dependent upon the vill. The Middlesex
evidence is also eloquent testimony to the economic dependence of
the manor upon the vill. The industry of the working tenants won
from their holdings the greater part of the food needful for sustenance and enough to spare, for sale or barter in exchange for
a balance of diet and other necessities. The residue of energy was
given as service to the lord. In a full monetary economy this
would have been expended on the tenant's land to stimulate the
year's return and a money rent paid for the land. The result was
the same: labour services of manorial tenants are an expression of
rent. Service, however, was not in every case agricultural service.
Renders in kind displayed a lavish variety and reflected the complex needs of contemporary society. Tenants of salt-pans rendered

[102] Poole: *Obligations of Society in the Twelfth and Thirteenth Centuries.*
     p. 15.
[103] Vinogradoff: op. cit., p. 168.
[104] Op. cit., p. 174.

salt to the manor,[105] tenants of quarries minerals, craftsmen[106] the artefacts of their industry; a multiplicity of giving and taking.

Agricultural labour service. Detail of agricultural labour service in Norman times did not worry the Domesday scribes and surveyors overmuch. Little minute evidence is available until the twelfth century. Some authorities endeavour to match the peasants of the Recititudines[107] with the peasants of Domesday Book and other Norman evidence. The outcome is not altogether happy. The foundation charter of Revesby Abbey (c.1142) is the earliest extant document recording agricultural services rendered by tenants to a lay lord.[108] Agricultural services in favour of an ecclesiastical body are recorded in the *Liber Niger* (c.1130) of Peterborough. Ballard[109] translates an extract from its pages as :

"Liber Niger, Chronicon Petroborgense, p. 158.

In Pilesgete are 3 hides to the King's geld.

In the demesne of the Court is one plough of 8 oxen, and 1 boar and 2 calves, and 1 ram and 2 foals, and 9 score sheep, and 20 pigs.

And 8 villans hold 1 hide and 1 virgate. And they have 2 teams whence they plough for the lord's need, 8 acres of winter ploughing, and 8 acres of spring ploughing (*tremeis*), and work three days in the week.

And there is one bordar and 2 oxherds (*bovarii*), holding land by service, and one shepherd.

And 44 sokemen.

And all these with the villans aforesaid render 44s. per annum.

And all these sokemen have 8 teams and thence plough three times in the year; and each of them mows in August half an acre of the Lord's corn, and twice in August performs a boon-work, and each harrows one day in spring.

And one mill which renders 4s."

The vill dependent upon the manor. Lest the picture be onesided, the dependence of the vill upon the manor must not be overlooked. Title to land emanated from the lordly grant. Many necessities which the arable holdings of the tenants could not produce were supplied by rights over pastureland and woodland. In this way were obtained swine-mast for pigs; timber for

---

[105] Ballard : op. cit., p. 182.   [106] Maitland : op. cit., p. 45.
[107] cf. p. 68 ante.
[108] Stenton : *Facsimiles of Early Charters from Northamptonshire Collections*, p. 4.
[109] Ballard : op. cit., p. 158.

fencing, house repairs and fuel; honey for mead and sweetening; and a host of homely things indispensable in the economy of every day. Privileges of a private order between particular tenants of the manor, which in future times the lawyers will classify among the servitudes, were also sanctioned by manorial authority. All were woven later into the fabric of manorial custom. It must not be supposed that each thread was newly drawn. The Normans were tolerant of Saxons institutions[110] and the roots of much agrarian custom lay deep in the practice and precept of lordships long ancient.

Manorial courts. The growth of custom is one with the growth of law. Manorial customs were *lex loci* and it is difficult to imagine their culture without the husbanding of courts. The right of the Norman lord of lands to hold a court for his tenants has already been observed. How far the business of early manorial courts was burdened with the petty agricultural affairs of the vill is nowhere precisely recorded. Profits of jurisdiction were doubtless included in the valuations[111] of manors. The available figures, from eleventh and twelfth century sources, are rounded totals, too inelegant to distinguish the income of the court from other receipts, and identify the amount of fines and other amercements. It can only be postulated from the growth of custom and the nature of the later manorial courts that the early vill administration and the manorial organisation were true complements expressed through the growth of the manorial court.

Farming the manor. Valuation of the income of a manor often fell below the render or annual sum payable when the manor was granted *ad firman* for a period. *Farming* manors in this way is analogous to granting them on lease.[111a] To speak of leasing the manor is dangerous. A lease is a legal technicality and the punctilios which fashion it in modern law are unknown in Norman times. However exorbitant the render or prolonged the farming policy, the minds and pockets of the men of the vill were not affected. Farming the manor was exclusively a lord's affair.

Assarting. So was assarting. Land is assarted from the wild by taking new areas into the orbit of cultivation. The lord might grant permission to a tenant to clear and enclose a plot from the

[110] Stenton : *Anglo-Saxon England*, p. 674.
[111] Ballard : op. cit., p. 221 et seq.
[111a] Barlow : op. cit., p. 275.

waste, but generally the tenantry were disadvantaged by assarting. The lord himself moved against the wastes and enclosed them within his own demesne and he converted common grazings into private closes and cornered open ploughland in a ring fence. The processes in the eleventh century are obscure.[112]

Of greater consequence and concern to Norman vills was the pressure of the king's forest law against the liberties of freemen. Some vills of the forest suffered annihilation at the hands of the Norman kings, avaricious and jealous for the sake of their deer. But William and his sons were too shrewd and politic to undermine economic stability in pursuit of pleasure. Only poor, worthless villages were abolished.[113] The intolerant forest law ran not among the corn-favoured loams and open uplands but through virgin wood and over scrub and moorland where assarting would win little profit.

Manors within manors and manors within vills. Assarting could wear another countenance. Off-shoots from a parent vill planted in dense woodland or scrub created assartland. The stolons never ran beyond the span of the parental manor. In consequence a manor might have two or more vills within its purlieu. Each new vill would be linked with the manor by the close, double bond of proprietorship and seignory.[114] In this, the new lands differ from sokes,[115] where the bond with the manor is but an attenuated seignory and has nothing of land proprietorship about it. Some manors assimilated their sokes and became swollen forms of the original creations. Others were created as vast fiefs. However the great manors came into being many had small manors within them. Manors lay within manors. Also there were whole manors within a single vill. The open-fields and commons were not infrequently partitioned by intricate divisions between two or more manorial jurisdictions, the demesne of each manor lying *hide meal and acre meal* among the open-fields. At the opposite extreme, both in size and complexity of structure were *maneriola* or smallholdings, the home of single families without dependant tenantry.[116]

Honours and baronies. Extensive fiefs had many manors welded to-

---

[112] Vinogradoff: *The Growth of the Manor*, p. 171.
[113] Stenton: op. cit., p. 281.
[114] Stenton: *Types of Manorial Structure in the Northern Danelaw*, p. 61.
[115] In the Danelaw off-lying vills attached to central settlements were known as "berewicks." (Stenton: op. cit., p. 61).
[116] Vinogradoff: *English Society in the Eleventh Century*, p. 332.

gether into honours and baronies. Tenants-in-capite were often lords of honours and mesne lords held baronies of them. Honour courts developed,[117] but the greater seignorial unit was not a magnified manor on that account. Manorial courts remained autonomous within the honour and there was no question of a higher justice in the jurisdiction of the honour court. It has been questioned whether so-called courts of baronies were ever realities in the eyes of contemporary legal opinion. Honours and baronies were never more than embellishments of the feudal structure. Any estimate of Anglo-Norman landholding must accept the manor, in its bewildering variety and mutability, as the elemental thing, the brick by which the Conqueror built his feudal edifice.

[117] Stenton: *Anglo-Saxon England*, p. 674.

CHAPTER IV

SELECT BIBLIOGRAPHY

Ballard, Adolphus: *The Domesday Inquest* (1906).
Barlow, Frank: *The Feudal Kingdom of England, 1042-1216* (1955).
Cam, H. M.: *Liberties and Communities in Medieval England. Collected studies in local administration and topography* (1944).
Davenport, Frances G.: *The Economic Development of a Norfolk Manor, 1080-1565* (1906).
Freeman, E. A.: *History of the Norman Conquest of England, its causes and its results.* Vols. I and II (3rd Ed., 1877).
Galbraith, V. H.: *The Making of Domesday Book* (English Historical Review, 1942, Vol. LVII).
Galbraith, V. H.: *Studies in the Public Records* (1948).
Jolliffe, J. E. A.: *The Constitutional History of Medieval England from the English Settlement to 1485* (3rd Ed., 1954).
Madox, Thomas: *The History and Antiquities of the Exchequer* (2nd Ed., 1769).
Maitland, Sir Frederic: *Domesday Book and Beyond. Three Essays in the Early History of England* (1907).
Pollock, Sir Frederick, and Maitland, Sir Frederic: *The History of English Law before the Time of Edward I.* Vols. I and II. (2nd Ed., rep. 1952).
Poole, A. L.: *From Domesday Book to Magna Carta, 1087-1216* (2nd Ed., 1955).
Poole, A. L.: *Obligations of Society in the 12th and 13th Centuries* (1946).
Round, J. H.: *Feudal England. Historical Studies on the XIth and XIIth Centuries* (1895).
Sayles, G. O.: *The Medieval Foundations of England* (2nd Ed. 1950).
Stenton, Lady: *The Earliest Northamptonshire Assize Rolls, A.D. 1202 and 1203* (1926).
Stenton, Lady: *English Society in the Early Middle Ages* (1066-1307). The Pelican History of England, Vol. 3 (1951).
Stenton, Sir Frank: *Anglo-Saxon England* (2nd Ed., 1947).
Stenton, Sir Frank: *Types of Manorial Structure in the Northern Danelaw* (Oxford Studies in Social and Legal History, Vol. II, 1910).
Stenton, Sir Frank: *The First Century of English Feudalism, 1066-1166* (1932).

H

Stenton, Sir Frank : *Documents illustrative of the Social and Economic History of the Danelaw from Various Collections* (1920).
Stenton, Sir Frank (ed) : *Facsimiles of Early Charters from Northamptonshire Collections* (1930).
Stubbs, William : *The Constitutional History of England in its Origin and Development* (Vol. I, 6th Ed., 1897; Vol. II, 3rd Ed., 1887; Vol. III, 4th Ed., 1887).
Vinogradoff, Sir Paul : *The Growth of the Manor* (3rd Ed., 1920).
Vinogradoff, Sir Paul : *English Society in the 11th Century. Essays in English Medieval History* (1908).
Vinogradoff, Sir Paul : *Villainage in England* (1892).

CHAPTER FIVE

THE MIDDLE AGES: THE CONSOLIDATION OF TENURES

ABUNDANT WRITTEN EVIDENCE

Change and stability. Professor Levett is clear in her verdict upon The Middle Ages: "There is no heresy about the Middle Ages quite so pernicious as the theory that they were unchanging."[1] And yet it is difficult to avoid the conviction that the centuries between the drama of the Norman impact and the pageant of Tudor England were more stable than these crisis years. The true light probably shines upon a paradox: the growth of a deep-rooted stability which in itself is radical change.

The history of landownership gives a glimpse of the paradox. Feudal landright was a local thing, taking its colours from the changing customs of honours and manors. Custom changed with succeeding generations the consensus of the lord and his tenantry, whether bond or free, determined it according to current knowledge and circumstance. Landholding was, in consequence, plastic, moulded according to the political, social and economic exigencies of the fief. The transfer of power in the Middle Ages from the local feudal courts to the king as sovereign, his courts and his Parliament, established both common law and statute law; a twin-pillared worthy house within whose abiding shade the clay of plastic ideas could harden. Rights in land became determinate. Landownership passed from an empirical order of things to a realm of permanent definition, and at a time of unprecedented money-flow. The interaction stimulated the land market. Marketing of land began to move apace and the benefits and burdens of tenure were written up in money terms more widely than before. It is these two changes which economists have in mind when they denounce theories of medieval immutability. But the changes are made possible by the steady growth and consolidation of common law and statute law.

Common law and court rolls. In the beginning the common law of England is the common sense of England, as the king's justices in eyre and central court understand it. And yet it is not judge-made law; it is revealed law. Learned judges merely declare what was and is and evermore shall be. A

[1] Levett: *Studies in Manorial History*, p. 42.

principle once enunciated remains constant, changeless; but it needs to be recorded. The growth and perfecting of the common law was assisted by careful preparation of court rolls. The use of court rolls in the king's courts inspired similar care in the seignorial courts. Many court rolls from the Curia Regis and later supreme courts, the assize courts and the multitude of feudal courts, have been preserved and it is these among much else that form an invaluable corpus of written evidence telling something of the story of land-ownership in the thirteenth, fourteenth and later centuries.

Statute law. The evidence of the court rolls of the royal courts is impregnated with and expanded by case judgments standing upon statute law. The statutes and ordinances of Parliament are in themselves a rich deposit of information. The historian is indebted to the growth and doings of Parliament, for he has in consequence a library of Parliamentary memoranda in which more than one direct reference is made to land affairs.[2]

Pipe rolls and ministers' accounts. During the period of transition between baronial power and the establishment of Parliamentary authority, the king gathered about him a personal bureaucracy. Officers of the royal household and other select courtiers became bureaucrats and statesmen towering in quasi-majesty over the affairs of the realm and the narrower interests of the royal demesne. However much the barons and other great landowners, who were not numbered among the chosen, may have resented the new growth, they were not blind to its administrative advantages, and the pattern was followed on a smaller scale throughout the great fiefs. The rule and arrogance of baronial officials, especially the auditors,[3] became a common complaint among the lesser tenantries. The bureaucratic fervour produced the pipe rolls and other official documents of the royal Exchequer. It also initiated the ministers' accounts of private estates and possibly stimulated the preparation of extants, surveys, rentals, custumals, cartularies and inquests which make the medieval centuries of England so rich a mine for the economic, social and legal historian and provide an unprecedented range of documentary matter dealing with details of landownership.

Commentaries, Year Books and other writings. The sources of evidence illustrative of contemporary landownership are richer still.

---

[2] Maitland: *Selected Essays* ed. Hazeltine et al., pp. 32, 34.
[3] Denholm-Young: *Seignorial Administration in England,* pp. 140-143.

Chronicles and commentaries were written. It was the age of Glanvil and Bracton, the first law codifiers of England. Their monuments of learning inspired lesser men who came shortly after them — Fleta, Britton and Gilbert de Thornton — and Littleton's great work on tenures in the fifteenth century. Alongside these known commentators laboured a host of anonymous legal writers who have left the invaluable law reports known as the Year Books, dating from the fourteenth century onwards. Contemporary text-books, however, were by no means all lawbooks. At this time also appeared the earliest treatises upon estate management; four writers,[4] more idealistic than practical, advised landowners and their stewards upon land administration which promised to become a profound wisdom. An instance of the heightened interest in land administration is the formulary book of the Abbey of St Albans, a collection of standard forms designed for the better and more uniform management of estates. To that great ecclesiastical landowner is also attributed one of a number of chronicles telling the story of lord and tenant upon ecclesiastical liberties. Besides what may be so classified, there are miscellaneous writings bearing in various ways upon land affairs. Notable among them is the Dialogue of the Exchequer, the Constitutio Domus Regis, the Calendars of Letters Patent and Close and The Ladies Roll.[5]

Whatever the Middle Ages may have been in other respects, for the land it was an age of ceaseless administrative activity and documentation. Rivers of ink flowed over acres of parchment to create a geography which, even to-day, leaves much to be explored.

ESTATES IN LAND

"Estate" the measure of the duration of interest. The fiefs of the Conqueror's England are not cradled in a system of tenures made neat and perfect by the precision of legal thought. Whatever show the Conqueror may have made of his boasted intention to respect the landed interests of the English, there seems little room for doubt that he gave the forfeited lands to his military chiefs as reward or "fee" for service and what remained in English hands rested upon his sanction. The original enfeoffment has all the marks of a

[4] Denholm-Young: op. cit., p. 120.
[5] Poole: *Obligations of Society in the Thirteenth and Fourteenth Centuries*, p. 100.

military diplomacy[6] executed by an autocratic prince in the plastic circumstance of a conquered land and people. The terms upon which land is held reflect the will of the Conqueror and the relationship in society between himself and the grantee, small or great. The fee is an interest held at will or at most for life.

Settlement raised the question of inheritance. A generation of invaders gave place to a generation at peace, and sons naturally expected to secure the soil their fathers had won and held. The royal grantors gave no guarantee of inheritance at first but circumstance seems to have forced an early development. By the year 1100 Henry I acknowledges the right of the heir to the father's land.[7] When Bracton is codifying the law a century and a half later, "fee" has become synonymous with inheritance[8] to the exclusion of the life interest, and legists are casting about for a word great enough to embrace, as an expression of duration, all interests in land, inheritable and otherwise. In the early days of the Year Books they were successful and the "estate in land" first found utterance in legal thought: the "estate" is the measure of the duration of interest.[9]

The entailed fee. Attempts were made in the thirteenth century to introduce an estate between the fee and the life interest. The upshot were fees dependent upon a limited range of heirs. To such belonged the *maritagia* and the entailed interests modelled upon them.[10] Estates would be given to the donee and the heirs of his body, instead of to the far wider range of heirs which the common law recognised in the expression *fee simple*. The lawyers endeavoured to frustrate the attempts by treating the limited gifts as conditional gifts of the fee simple not taking effect until an heir is in being: at the moment an heir is born the entire fee, the fee simple, passes to the grantee. Such an interpretation manifestly did not accord with the intents of the grantor, and the statute De Donis Conditionalibus, 1285, was passed to uphold the entail.

Alienation by subinfeudation and substitution. Creation of an entail was but one of many forms of alienation. A fee simple owner could transfer his entire estate so that the grantee stood in his shoes; or the transfer could operate to expand the feudal chain by introducing the grantee as a tenant of the grantor who

[6] Jolliffe: *The Constitutional History of Medieval England* (2nd Ed.), p. 181.
[7] Plucknett: *A Concise History of the Common Law* (5th Ed.), p. 524.
[8] Op. cit., p. 523.
[9] Pollock and Maitland: *The History of English Law before the Time of Edward I* (Vol. II), p. 11.   [10] Plucknett: op. cit., p. 548.

became a mesne lord. The former process is alienation by substitution and the latter alienation by subinfeudation. In practice only fee simple estates were alienated by substitution.

Subinfeudation allows a tenant to sub-grant his estate and reserve service of the same or a different nature from the service he renders his immediate lord. A tenant by knight's service can subinfeudate his estate in sergeanty or socage. By mid-thirteenth century subinfeudation had created a vast, intricate web of estates. A simple example instanced by Poole[11] shows no less than four mesne lords holding fees in one parcel of land and to these must be added the king as supreme lord and the tenant in demesne — six people in all. Growing confusion led to the statute Quia Emptores, 1290. This statute is one of the foundations of English land law and abolishes alienation of the fee simple by subinfeudation. All transfers of fee simple estates, henceforth, place the transferee in the shoes of the transferor. Substitution became the only mode of alienation available to the owner who wished to transfer his fee simple estate. In consequence as estates in fee simple determined through failure of heirs the feudal chain contracted link by link until there remained only the extremities — the king and the tenant in demesne.

Feudal incidents.   Subinfeudation was distasteful to the great fiefs. By introducing mesne interests between superior lords and their tenants it deprived the former of the benefit of many feudal incidents. The features of feudal incidents, in common with the land law in general, were being chiselled to a fineness by the legal sculptors. At the same time the swing towards a money economy tended to commercialise them, especially the incidents of military tenure. The monetary value of relief, aids, wardship, primer seisin, escheat and forfeiture endeared military tenure to the heart of kings and great lords long after the essential character of the tenure had changed beyond recognition. Abuse of the royal right to feudal incidents moved the barons to force the king's hand at Runnymede. The incidents of military tenure were an anvil on which politics, law and principles of land management were forged. To safeguard them the medieval legislature drafted the mortmain laws. And to avoid them in the fifteenth century men granted estates to uses under the protection of the courts of Chancery.

What are these incidents? Relief is payment made to an overlord by an heir succeeding to the inheritance. When a knight's

[11] Poole: op. cit, p. 5.

fee was eventually determined in the twelfth century the amount of relief appears to have been fixed, at all events in theory, at one hundred shillings per fee and proportionate amounts for fractions of a fee; baronies suffered arbitrarily at the hand of the king, although there is some evidence for £100 a barony as a maximum relief.[12] Aids are levies made upon tenants by an overlord when the shifting winds of fortune are blowing adversely. Aids are levied on the knighting of the lord's eldest son, the marrying of his daughter and to raise a ransom when the lord is a prisoner of war. Royal aids were levied upon the tenants of the "honour" of England, and when the days of strict feudalism passed they became a form of imperial taxation in the hands of the king.[13] Wardship and marriage are perhaps the greatest irritants of the conventional tenures in chivalry. When a tenant in chivalry dies and leaves his heir a minor, the lord has wardship over the land until the coming of age of the heir. The lord is impeachable for waste,[14] but subject to the limitations of that doctrine, he can exploit the estate and the right of wardship can be a most valuable asset. Rights of marriage empower an overlord to arrange the marriage of a ward, male or female, and of the widow of a deceased tenant. The right, like wardship, became an object of commercial traffic and to lawyers of later days a chattel real. The hand of an heiress in marriage often meant a great fortune and social distinction, and one who sought her would pay handsomely for the lord's sanction of marriage. Early in the thirteenth century Geoffrey de Mandeville was content to incur a debt of 20,000 marks for the hand and lands of Isabel, Countess of Gloucester.[15] Widows were often compelled to buy their liberty at great price. The practice was repugnant to influential opinion, and Magna Carta brought some protection. Even so, in the late thirteenth century, the heiress of Clare paid 3,000 marks to secure freedom of marriage and the wardship of her son.[16] Primer seisin is a kingly right. The supreme feudal lord has right of seisin of all estates while the seisin of the heir is in dispute or an enfeoffment awaits the formalities of delivery. Escheat and forfeiture restore the land of a tenant to the hand of the immediate overlord; land escheats to the immediate overlord when the line of heirs fail and the fee simple determines; an estate is forfeited when the tenant commits felony.

[12] Poole : op. cit., p. 96.
[13] Jolliffe : op. cit., pp. 308-312.
[14] *Statute of Marlborough*, 1267.   [15] Poole : op. cit., p. 97.
[16] Denholm-Young : op. cit., p. 43.

Law and practice not in harmony. Although Blackstone in later centuries refers to the incidents of military tenure as the seven fruits of chivalry, the records of the early Middle Ages do not reveal one of them, not even wardship and marriage, as exclusively the mark of tenure in chivalry. Blackstone is but an echo of the early law writers. They are burdened to formulate principles of tenure; to draw boundary lines of service and incidents, each differing from the other, and by means of the diversity to point the distinguishing features of knight's service, sergeanty, frankalmoign, socage and villeinage. Actual life did not fit the ideal abstractions of the lawyers.[17] Medieval society, depicted in the stark boldness of the legists' formulae, is an approximation, a picture of simple washes. Life and the ways of living on the estates are variegated; secondary and tertiary colours, half-tones and quarter-tones, soften the hard edges of the lawyers' impressions. As rare examples of this general rule, socage tenants, the strict agriculturalists of Bracton's text,[18] render in the early years military service to their lords.[19] Wardship and marriage are also demanded of them.[20] And the spiritual service, the classical hallmark of frankalmoign, is a service not unknown to sergeantry tenure.[21]

Expedients in estate management may well have accounted for the practical ways of land affairs running loose from legal formulae. Life ranges wider than law. The law to-day places the incidence of income tax squarely across the landlord's shoulders, but it is the tenants who in modern practice receive and meet the demand notes; again, common law imposes no responsibility for repair of buildings upon landlords but where tenancies are created by parol the landlord's contribution towards repairs is often an accepted principle of tenure. So it is in medieval days. Scutage payments, in the eyes of the lawyers, betoken tenure by knight's service only, but in practice on some estates the burden is carried by villeins,[22] the bond tenants, men who at common law have neither inheritance nor estate in land; as an expedient of land management lords of estates holding by knight's service are raising scutage by shifting the burden to their lesser tenantry. A similar transfer of incidence takes place where tenants-in-capite, responsible for maintenance of county bridges, compound the obligation for a money payment defrayed as pontage and charged upon

17 Poole: op. cit., p. 3.
18 Pollock and Maitland: op. cit. (Vol. I), p. 294.
19 Poole: op. cit., p. 7.
20 Pollock and Maitland: op. cit., p. 321.
21 Poole: op. cit., p. 7.   22 Op. cit., p. 47.

villein land.[23] Perhaps the emphasis placed by medieval lawyers upon the public livery of seisin as an essential feature of valid conveyancing of land at a time when charters were being widely used[24] as instruments of land transfer, also shows the eddies of life flowing freely beyond the runnels of law.

The fate of the manors.   Research in medieval social and economic affairs is blurring at many points the neat geometry of landownership which the legal historians of a generation ago accepted. The Middle Ages in matters of estate management and landownership do not fit the ideal, simple, logical world of the legists. Nor, indeed, can confidence be placed upon the impressions of earlier economic historians who see land owned and managed, almost universally, as a chequer of orthodox well-balanced manors. The evidence they had was weighted evidence for the records of great ecclesiastical houses had been taken as guides. Recent studies of lay evidence redress the balance and destroy the illusion.

The uniform mosaic of Seebohm's thought has been overlaid by crazy paving. Opinions may differ about Kosminsky's theory linking manorial structure to size[25] but, leaving cause aside, the brute fact remains that manors vary greatly in size and structure throughout medieval England. Small manors bond in with the great, and the precisely circumscribed with the discrete. The pattern is kaleidoscopic. There is more than a hint that it moves through disintegration to integration and back again. The Normans are seen gathering small freeholds "to make manors"[26] and in the thirteenth and fourteenth centuries the great feudatories are falling apart. Certainly this is so on the Bigod manors of Forncett: the two manors of Anglo-Norman times have become fourteen by 1565.[27]

Fission of compact estates was but one among other movements destructive of a simple ownership pattern. Colonisation must also be reckoned with. Assarting, the making of *terra perprestura*, was a continuous activity against waste, woodland and common. The clean lines of an open-field vill marking arable land from common pastures became thickened; barnacles of closes, separate and conglomerate, free and bond, grew upon them. Sometimes, as at New Yatt in Oxfordshire,[28] newly broken land meets

[23] Neilson : *Customary Rents,* p. 137.
[24] Plucknett : op. cit., pp. 611, 612.
[25] cf. Postan : *The Manor in the Hundred Rolls,* Econ. H. Rev., 2nd Series, Vol. III, No. 1, 1950, p. 122.   [26] p. 83 ante.
[27] Davenport : *The Economic Development of a Norfolk Manor,* p 8.
[28] Ballard : *The Manors of Witney, Brightwell and Downton,* p. 186.

newly broken land, and between two open-field vills a settlement of enclosures is born. Everywhere in Kent settlements were pecking at the vast Andredweald. Pasture grounds, the *denns* of Kent, were claimed within the great woodland mass by vills lying many miles away; the denns in time broke loose from their parent settlements and developed *terra sulingata* on their own account.[29] Petty freeholds outcropped everywhere and the word "manor" ran with a vulgar intimacy among them. Whatever technical connotation the word may have had for the Anglo-Norman is lost in Plantagenet England. Demesne land served by a free and servile tenantry is certainly manorial but it does not depict the only kind of manorial structure.

Administrations other than manorial. Other administrations, specially among marsh, fen and forest, further complicate the picture. Vills in the fenland and elsewhere enjoyed rights of intercommoning and turf-cutting. The waste was held *pro indiviso* according to local custom (*consuetudo marisci*) and administered in the fens by special courts (*curia de Barra*).[30] Common obligations were the counterpart of common benefits, and distributed between vills maintenance obligations in respect of sea-walls, embankments and dykes. Men attended to the benefits of custom more conscientiously than to the burdens and, in the fourteenth century, the king was moved to appoint commissioners of sewers. The commissioners held inquests and generally stiffened the maintenance obligations and enforced their observance. Such a commission in the able hands of Henry de Bathonia perfected, as early as the reign of Henry II, the custom of Romney Marsh, a code of conduct applied in later years by commissions in other areas, notably the fens. The forests also had institutions peculiar to themselves. Forestmoots, justices of the forest, wardens and lesser officials administered the forest law. The royal law of the forest ran or stopped at the king's word, expressed by charter.[31] To be neighbours of the forest was not enviable, although there is evidence enough that the rights of customers were preserved whenever the wastes were afforested,[32] and even assarting was sanctioned by the justices of the forest in some places.[33]

[29] Neilson: *The Cartulary and Terrier of the Priory of Bilsington, Kent,* pp. 8-13. [30] Neilson: *A Terrier of Fleet, Lincolnshire,* p. xvi.
[31] cf. Neilson: op. cit., p. xxiii.
[32] Neilson: *The Cartulary and Terrier of the Priory of Bilsington, Kent,* p. 35.
[33] Stenton, D. M.: *The Earliest Northamptonshire Assize Rolls, A.D. 1202 and 1303,* p. xxxii.

The growth of officialdom. The passing of the great honours and the fissipation of the larger manors coincided most suggestively with the growth of officialdom. The supreme honour of the realm came to be administered by a central Exchequer and a domestic bureaucracy.[34] Lesser estates soon followed the royal form.[35] Feudal lords of the thirteenth century neglected the feudal constitutions and instead of seeking advice from the body of their tenantry they leant towards estate officials.[36] Private bureaucracy lead to seignorial councils. The constitution of the councils varied, but Professor Levett[37] is able to identify four common elements: selected men of influence, permanent officials, legal experts and the king's justices. The waning of seignorial courts was a consequence of the new policy. And the decline of the great territorial fiefs and lesser manors may have been largely due to the shift of the reins of power from the homage to factitious, conciliar administration. The strength of the old order was its freedom of spirit. The new vogue was legalistic and, therefore, brittle.

The new legalism left an impressive record of itself. Although fashions change, it is possible to distinguish between officers of the households and officers of the landed estates. The arch-administrator of the lay estate is the steward, corresponding to the sheriff of the royal demesne; in one instance at least the royal title is appropriated.[38] The cellarer acts in a similar capacity on ecclesiastical estates. The pattern is not uniform. Duties falling to a steward on one estate may be the responsibility of a receiver on another. The liberty of St. Alban's Abbey[39] has a law administrator, the seneschal, and a special official, the *refectorarius*, over the courts of the liberty. Manors are grouped into bailiwicks, under bailiffs or constables, regardless of the boundaries of honours and the old feudal structure.[40] The administrator of a bailiwick, although a bailiff, is often a more mighty personage than the manorial bailiff. The manorial official is responsible for the day to day affairs of one or two manors and in particular for maintaining association with the working tenantry through the person of the reeve. The highlights of medieval officialdom are the auditors, in whose ears the detailed accountancy of a year's management is

[34] Jolliffe: op. cit., pp. 182-190.
[35] Denholm-Young: op. cit., p. 1.
[36] Cam: *Liberties and Communities in Medieval England*, pp. 213, 214.
[37] Levett: op. cit., p. 26.
[38] Denholm-Young: op. cit., p. 47.
[39] Levett: op. cit., pp. 105-112.
[40] Denholm-Young: op. cit., p. 99.

rehearsed, checked against manorial extents and committed to account rolls.

Account rolls. The form and content of account rolls are not only revelations of sources of income and policies of expenditure, they are eloquent commentaries on contemporary estate management. Items vary with locality, custom and management, but in structure the accounts display a remarkable standardisation. The earliest account rolls known, the accounts of the Bishop of Winchester's manors, may be prototypes.[41] Much work remains to be done on this mass of medieval material. Studies so far pursued show clearly how thirteenth and fourteenth century manorial administration is concerned with monetary matters and extra-manorial marketing; a fact which spells ruin to any theory of manorial self-sufficiency.[42] The detail in which expenditure and receipts are minuted would dismay easy-going, stub-pencilled farmers of to-day. The intricacies of the items convey an impression of a great complexity in medieval estate management. Two worlds are at grips: the old world of tradition, custom, lordship and villeinage and the restless world of contract and nascent capitalism. The estate manager has to know how to honour the former and woo the latter. Rents of assize have to be kept separate from other money payments and from the income from hired lands, the farms of medieval manors. The value of labour service must be balanced against money payments from "sale of works". Sale of works has to be carefully distinguished from commutation proper if flexibility of management is to remain unimpaired. Heriots, merchet, reliefs, tallage and other customary incidents might mean gain in money and prestige, yet at a time when men can flee the manor and suffer little in consequence, when wages are rising and when sound tenants will take demesne leases, a rigid adherence to the old order is likely to damage the efficiency of the new. Vacillation was disastrous. The successful land administrator was he who with steady hand and set purpose established precedent and practice.[43]

Accountancy method did not aspire to anything more than a statement of receipt and expenditure of money. Where labour service was not commuted to money, the full range of internal economy remains hidden. A wealth of labour could be expended

[41] Levett: op. cit., p. 46.
[42] Levett: *The Black Death on the Estates of the See of Winchester*, p. 30.
[43] Op. cit., p. 134.

on demesne land, hall and buildings but not appear in the accounts.

Repairs and waste. The important matter of repair expenditure was obscured in this way on those manors where the customary tenants repaired the lord's hall and buildings[44] or carried responsibility for arterial drainage channels, sea-walls and roads. Freeholders often discharged similar obligations, especially in respect of roads, dykes and sea-walls. Villeins were held liable for the structural condition of their own meagre homesteads, but on some manors allowances were made from money rents in cases where the tenant was admitted to a dilapidated holding.[45]

Repair liability of freeholds was bound up with the doctrine of waste. Limited ownerships inevitably raise the question of safeguards. There can be only one person in possession of land and where such a person is limited in his ownership, he must be restrained lest his actions impair the proprietary interests of others. The doctrine of waste is the answer the Middle Ages gave. It is a common law doctrine. But the common law only applied it to the special tenures of courtesy and dower and to estates held in wardship by knight's service. Termors, life tenants and guardians in possession of a minor's estate in free socage were made impeachable for waste by the Statute of Marlborough, 1267. Fee simple owners and the possessors of entails whether of extensive manors or small holdings were not liable for waste; to have made them so would have been repugnant to the nature of their estates.

BY FORK AND BY FLAIL

Criteria of villeinage uncertain. There is great temptation to divide feudal society into two all-embracing classes, a military aristocracy and a toiling peasantry,[46] and to see in the former the ancestors of medieval estate-owners and in the latter the forebears of a servile tenancy. But it will not do. Between the knightly class and the peasantry lay a promiscuous professional stratum and parallel to the three ran the hierarchical society of the church. Furthermore, the nobles were not all landowners. Among them were important people holding no estate in land but enjoying the

[44] Bennett: *Life on the English Manor, 1150-1400*, pp. 107, 108.
[45] Op. cit., p. 230.
[46] Hilton: *Peasant Movements in England before 1381*, Econ. H. Rev., 2nd Series, Vol. II, No. 2, 1949, p. 118.

use of land at the will of the king.[47] And beneath them, with the peasantry, were true estate-owners, sturdy men boasting estates in socage. The number of estate-owners among the peasantry was relatively low and raises the question of the interest in land of the majority; answer turns upon the vexed problem of villeinage. The mass of the peasants in medieval times is in bondage. The peasants are servile persons holding base tenements "by fork and by flail".[48]

Villeinage stands over against free tenure; so much is certain. But despite the new age of documents, case law and treatise the exact whereabouts of the freedom line is no more certain than it had been centuries before. The criteria of medieval villeinage are indefinite. The lawyers are struggling towards two simple tests: one, the uncertainty of labour service; and two, the obligation to pay merchet. These are the twin sides of the lawyer's cleaving axe by which he tries to sunder the bond from the free.[49] Yet once again legal theory seems to fail in the face of facts. *Utrum sit villanus?* is the nagging question, running by fireside, field and fold to the bar of justice; and the lawyer's touchstones fail to clear the minds of judge and jury in every case. Uncertainty of labour service was frequently an accepted criterion of villein status, but it did not follow that commutation of labour service to money rent, or the acceptance through leniency or laxity of more certain and lighter burdens were acts of manumission. Pedigree could be a material factor and in support of the writ *de nativo habendo* an overlord would drag kindred of the defendant into the witness box to prove a taint of villeinage in the blood of their kinsman.[50]

All attempts to establish universal principles floundered amid the cross-currents of manorial custom. The badge of bondage in one manor differed from that in another.[51] Custom is fundamental to the problem. To realize this will safeguard against accepting the too clear-cut view of the lawyers and bring some cogency to bear upon the often conflicting statements of different writers. Where one points to merchet[52] as the mark of bondage another will instance freebench;[53] a third the indignity to be tallaged high and

---

[47] Pollock and Maitland: op. cit., p. 357.
[48] Vinogradoff: *Villainage in England*, p. 170.
[49] Poole: op. cit., p. 13.
[50] Cam: op. cit., pp. 131-135.
[51] Clapham: *A Concise Economic History of Britain*, p. 97.
[52] Bennett: op. cit., p. 240.
[53] Op. cit., p. 251.

low;[54] a fourth carting service;[55] and a fifth the obligation to repair the mill dam.[56] On some manors the freedom line appears to have been approached by stages and various gradings of tenure divide the peasantry, as "free, molmen, werkmen and Mondaymen."[57] Vinogradoff aggravates the confusion by seeing the mantle of free status fall upon each villein whenever he takes his place as a doomsman in the manorial court.[58] Free status is not the same as free tenure. Villeinage can be a virus in the soil contaminating the freeman who becomes tenant upon it and, contrariwise, free tenements occupied by villeins become *soiled*.[59]

Classification of burdens of bondage. So obscure was the dividing line between bondage and freedom and so intractable the evidence that some cases of doubt seem never to have been settled. Once, however, the courts have passed judgment of *nativity* upon a peasant, or his status has been unquestionably accepted by him, then, as a general rule, a greater weight of manorial obligation fell upon him than upon the free tenant. The sum of the incidents of bondage varies, like the marks of bondage, from manor to manor. It was the total that outweighed the incidents of free tenure. Item for item there may be little or no difference. A free tenant may have the same ploughing service to discharge, or be liable for merchet and in these matters his lot differs not at all from his bond neighbour. All attempts to analyse and group economic and tenurial data must be more or less misleading, but allowing for unavoidable error, the burdens of bond tenants can be summed up under four heads: labour services and rent, other manorial dues, royal obligations discharged through manorial organisation, and church dues including tithe.

Labour services and rent. Although money rent is suggestive of free status, bond tenants were frequently liable for rents of assize and other money rents in addition to labour services. Labour service had many forms. A basic obligation arose from the villein tenement proper but some villeins undertook works in consideration of special privileges; an example is the ploughing duty known as "averearth" to secure extra pasturage rights.[60] The basic oblig-

[54] Hilton : op. cit., p. 120.
[55] Neilson : op. cit., p. 26.
[56] Ruston and Witney : *Hooton Pagnell*, p. 300.
[57] Neilson : *A Terrier of Fleet, Lincolnshire*, p. lxv.
[58] Vinogradoff : op. cit., p. 389.
[59] Davenport : op. cit., p. 70.
[60] Vinogradoff : op. cit., p. 280.

ation generally involved week-work and boon-work.[61] Ploughing,
mowing and reaping with their attendant obligations of harrowing,
stacking and threshing were common services. Carrying service also
is widely recorded. Other services are less in evidence. In Fenland
and low-lying coastal regions, drainage and repair to sea-walls are
typical. Repairs to manor-house, demesne homestead, the lord's mill
and the mill-dam, and the upkeep of roads are other examples.
Authorities differ over the question of uniformity. Some maintain
the villein labour services were the same, holding by holding,
within the vill.[62] Others speak of a marked irregularity.[63] Difference
could arise from one writer searching the custumal (the law of the
manor) and another observing the facts of rentals and account
rolls. Time undoubtedly brought change. When uniformity of
tenement area gave way in the fourteenth century, uniformity of
obligation followed suit. Labour service might not fall upon
individual holdings nor their tenants but upon the tenantry as a
body. In this event, the obligation was often expressed in terms of
ploughteams and not holdings; thus at Guiting in Gloucestershire
in 1185 "each team must . . . plough two acres of pasture."[64]
When demesnes were leased in the fourteenth century it is noticeable, on at least one honour, that villein labour services changed
from agricultural work to tasks in the wider activity of estate
management.[65]

Other dues in bondage. The median of the Middle Ages was the
darkest hour for servile tenants. The thirteenth century had settled
the law: all villein property, land and goods, is held *nomine
alieno* — it is the lord's. About this doctrine was woven an ever-
increasing restrictive practice. A villein had no right to dispose of
his goods or land save as the lord should let him. Force of
circumstance mitigated the rule, villeins had to sell their corn to
live, but the harsh doctrine was logically pursued in many other
directions.

From it derive the manorial incidents of tallage, heriot,
fine or relief, merchet, chevage, suit of oven, mill and fold and
impositions peculiar to particular manors. Tallage reflects the
political power of the lord of a manor.[66] It is a local levy imposed
by the lord upon his villeinage as occasion requires. Eventually
custom bound his hand. But to be tallaged high and low *ad*

[61] cf. p. 138 post.   [62] Vinogradoff : op. cit., p. 169.
[63] Davenport : op. cit., pp. 62, 63.
[64] Poole : op. cit., p. 16.
[65] Davenport : op. cit., p. 54.
[66] Vinogradoff : op. cit., p. 163.

I

voluntatem domini lingered long in some places. The right to take a heriot arises upon the decease of a tenant in bondage. The overlord claims the best beast or the most valuable chattel or a number of chattels and sometimes the entire chattel wealth of the villein, according to custom. When an heir is admitted to a tenement a relief or fine is taken by the lord. Fines are also levied on the occasion of sales or exchanges of land.[67] Tallage, heriots and fines were the greatest economic burden but they were not the most resented. The nadir of a bond tenant's subjection is the payment of merchet; a sum rendered by the tenant for permission to give his daughter in marriage. Chevage follows a tenant beyond the confines of the manor. When residing away from his tenement, whether he has fled or left the manor with permission, a tenant is liable for the payment, a yearly reminder of his lord's rights over him. In so far as all things in bondage are the lord's it was not inconsequent for a lord to require his bond tenants to grind their corn at his mill, to bake their bread at his oven and to fold their sheep upon his land.[68] To these burdens of suit must be added suit of court, with its threat of fines and amercements.

Manorialisation of royal dues and church dues. Royal dues and church dues, the ancient church scot and the tithe, became manorialized on some manors.[69] The lord of the manor levied the burdens, which fell primarily upon himself as tenant of the fief, so that the incidence shifted to the tenements of his seignory. Thus it came about that villeins paid scutage and other royal dues. Apart from manorialized church dues, villeins in common with other occupiers of productive land rendered tithe annually to the rector of the parish. Tithe was begrudged.[70] The church was aware how unwillingly the tenths were rendered and met the open, stiff-necked attitude of the peasants by an overt demand for a *mortuary*: a sum payable at death to make good tithe divagation practised by the deceased during life.[71] The mortuary when taken was usually the second best beast or chattel after the heriot.

The sum of these burdens was great. To the older historians the weight pressing upon the peasant and in especial the ignominy of merchet, chevage and heriot spelt the essence of personal servility. Modern views are moving towards an economic interpretation of

[67] Levett: op. cit., p. 44.
[68] cf. p. 95 ante.   [69] Neilson: *Customary Rents*, p. 6.
[70] Bennett: *Life on the English Manor*, 1150-1400, p. 84.
[71] Coulton: *The Medieval Village*, p. 290.

the situation.[72] The thickened seignorial whip of the thirteenth century was not a resurgence of feudal domination, a movement to elevate the autocracy of the lord over the person of the servile villein, but rather a symptom of change, a sign of an emerging, new economic order. Lords are concerned to impose merchet, chevage, fines and restrictive codes in the interests of their rent, and for no other reason. Freedom gained by a bond tenant meant loss of labour service, tallage, heriot and other wealth and a weakening of the production potential of the demesne.

Clearer legal thinking upon villeinage. The underscoring of seignorial power in the late thirteenth and early fourteenth centuries coincides with the development of clearer legal thinking about the nature of base tenure. From the villein's point of view, the lawyer's concepts grow darker. At one time, in the early days of the thirteenth century, it looked as if the protective robes, the assize of novel disseisin and the assize of mort d'ancestor, which Henry II had fashioned to secure land titles against custom and caprice, would be within the reach of villeinage where freemen were holding villein land or villeins free land.[73] The thirteenth century cases which promise this protective recognition were, in Maitland's view,[74] probably belated rather than premature. They reflect the uncertainty of the earlier legal opinion and are not heralds of a coming day when the king's courts of equity would fashion protective actions for villein subjects. They are unbaked soft spots in a doctrine hardening against the villein.

Villeins held land at the will of the lord and had protection for their land in the lord's court and in none other. Nevertheless the language of the pleadings in the manorial courts is remarkably similar to the speech of free men in the king's court.[75] The lord's court speaks of seisin and disseisin but with this difference: it is seisin within the custom of the manor.[76] Interests in villeinage are coloured and fashioned by manorial custom. Custom in legal theory does not conflict with the lord's will, it is the express image of it. For practical purposes, before the weakening of the manorial courts, custom was a lively oracle, the

[72] cf. Hilton: op. cit., p. 120.
[73] Vinogradoff: op. cit., pp. 73, 78.
[74] Pollock and Maitland: op. cit., p. 359.
[75] The same principle is observable in the greater and lesser franchise courts where the common law did not run. (Cam: *Liberties and Communities in Medieval England*, p. 212).
[76] Pollock and Maitland: op. cit., p. 361.

consensus of the lord and his tenantry sitting as a court.[77] Later the personal opinion of the lord became more ascendant,[78] especially when voiced through the baronial council whose opinions tended to create a seignorial equity over against custom.[79] On some manors two distinct tenures evolved, true villeinage and land held openly *ad voluntatem dominï*.[80] This decline towards arbitrariness led, in the fourteenth century, to the development of a species of written title and registration.[81] Tenants and tenements in villeinage were recorded on the court-rolls of manors and copies of the registrations became evidence of title in the hands of the tenants. Henceforth the villein held "by copy of the court roll". He was a copyholder.

The duration of villein interests after death. Empirically base tenure differs little from the free tenures. Always it is more precarious but its workday features bare a resemblance. The two tenures differ as black from white in their soul-structure. Heritability is illustrative of this. Custom governs the passage of bond tenements at death. The pattern varies. Frequently the youngest son is admitted into possession. The custom of freebench, by which possession passes to the deceased's widow, was common. Equal division among all the sons of a father is another form. In one fashion or another custom deals with the problem. And yet it is avidly maintained by common law that villeins have no heirs but their lords, and hence no inheritance. Common law is rude: pigs have no heirs, pigs have litters, so do serfs. It is the brood, the *sequela*, of the villein that the common law knows.[82] There is however at least one ancient reference to a villein's heirs,[83] but whether it represents an exception to the general rule, or is a mark of ignorance or merely an accident of some scribe, none can say. When a tenement passed to all sons equally there naturally followed a sub-division of the striplands or small enclosed parcels. After division the holding was still regarded as an entity for the purposes of manorial incidents and obligations. There is reason to believe a subsequent reduction in the number of sons or their

[77] Vinogradoff: op. cit., p. 361.
[78] cf. Neilson: *A Terrier of Fleet, Lincolnshire,* p. viii.
[79] Plucknett: op. cit., p. 186.
[80] Vinogradoff: op. cit., p. 173.
[81] Pollock and Maitland: op. cit., p. 375.
[82] Pollock and Maitland: op. cit., p. 381.
[83] Vinogradoff: op. cit., p. 173.

descendants did not occasion a re-shuffle. Sub-division of striplands meant lamination[84] and gave topographical appearance similar to the horizontal markings of the ancient Celtic fields which, as suggested earlier,[85] could also be due to partition among descendants.

Custom not only created a quasi-inheritance of land but on some manors, notably those of the Liberty of St Albans, it recognised a villein's right to grant land by testamentary disposition.[86] Wills of villeins came to be enrolled on the court rolls of St Albans, especially after the Black Death. Curiously enough, the practice did not continue. The fifteenth century had run but a quarter of its span when villeins are found surrendering their holdings on death and naming the successor whom it is hoped the lord will admit into possession. This is retrogression. Surrender and admittance are the twin acts which always attended transfer of bond tenements.

Theory and later practice made bond tenure precarious. Forfeiture was an ever-present threat. A tenant who did not perform the tasks of servitude or meet the rent or repair[87] his homestead was liable in theory to forfeit his holding. Prior to the late fifteenth century enclosure movement, eviction was bad economy and practice did not, as a rule, follow theory. Enclosure brought practice into line and breach of custom was seized upon and forfeiture enforced whenever possible.

THE VILL ECONOMY

Villein tenure does not imply open-field husbandry. Reference was made earlier to the balance of vill economy, but no attempt was made to describe it. The classical writers, a generation ago, especially the lawyers, knit their estimates of villein tenure to descriptions of the open-field system of communal agriculture, generally accepting Seebohm's original outlines as standard. The impression given was twofold: that a villein holding always lay in the open-fields, with ancient rights of common, estovers and botes over the woodland and waste; and, because of the universality of villeinage, the open-field system of husbandry itself came near to being ubiquitous. This impression is misleading. Modern regional

---

[84] Coulton : op. cit., pp. 40-41.   [85] p. 40 ante.
[86] Levett : op. cit., pp. 208-223.
[87] The right of bote opened the manorial woodland to the tenant for the purpose of gleaning timber, so much as was necessary for repairing house, implements and carts, for fuelling and other functions.

studies of manorial surveys and other records track down the open-fields proper to the great Midland plain and even there, among the forests, moors and woodlands, orthodoxy by no means holds undisputed sway,[88] but everywhere villein tenure is found. A typical villein tenement, therefore, no longer lies in the open-fields. It lies nowhere. There is no such thing! The open-field system nonetheless has some claim to special recognition. It appears as the great master-pattern in which all other agrarian systems may recognise one or more of their own features. For example: the elongated vills of the coastal fenlands display the scattered strips of open-fields within their many *inliks* and *fen ends*;[89] and the compact tenements of the Kentish *doles* are liable for the villein services of ploughing, harrowing, mowing and carting,[90] suggestive of a manorial organization harnessing the working villeins to the lord's fields and other parts of his domain.

Open-field vills. What then are the motifs of open-field vills? Open-field husbandry was self-admittedly communal.[91] The main-spring of communal activity was long thought to be the practice of co-aration. The great expanses of arable land were ploughed by joint ploughteams. Each villein and small freeholder, according to his ability, would make a contribution of plough oxen or plough parts to the village plough which, lumbering and incommodious, moved over the fields regardless of property boundaries of lord and tenant.

A plough=a team. Today the picture of massive ploughs and group ownership of the implements in the open-fields is fading. Here and there among contemporary writings and documents hints are given of each tenant being responsible for his own ploughing,[92] and the good husbandry of his own tenement,[93] a state of affairs which could never have arisen if co-aration were practised. Moreover, it is by no means certain that villeins ganged up their animals to make a phalanx of eight or ten oxen harnessed to a single whipple-tree to plough the lord's demesne. Admittedly there is abundant evidence referring to plough teams of eight oxen but a plough team need not necessarily be associated with only one

---

[88] Clapham : op. cit., p. 86.
[89] Neilson : op. cit., pp. lx. lxiii.
[90] Neilson : *The Cartulary and Terrier of the Priory of Bilsington, Kent,* p. 62.
[91] Vinogradoff : op. cit., p. 232.
[92] Bennett : op. cit., p. 45.
[93] Stenton, D. M. : op. cit., p. xxxi.

plough. The word, team, may have an altogether different connotation. In a custumal of Battle Abbey the following ordinance occurs:[94]

> "Each free tenant, who has a whole plough or some part of a plough, ought to come with his plough or with his part, if he has not a whole plough, to one ploughing boon-work at the sowing in Lent, and each one that has a plough ought to plough an acre at each boon-work, and he who has less than a whole plough shall plough according to what animals he shall have joined to the plough."

The word plough here obviously refers to a team of oxen of known size; it does not denote the instrument. He who has a full team is required to plough an acre and he with only a proportion of a team a corresponding proportion of an acre. That a plough means a team and not an implement is supported by references to villeins having half-ploughs in circumstances where they could not join with others to make a full plough team, and yet it is obvious they have holdings to cultivate. Such an instance occurs in the Domesday record of Rolvenden hundred[95] where a denn lying in Bircholt has two villeins with half a plough. These two, presumably, have no immediate neighbours from whom to borrow extra plough beasts and an implement. Yet they must plough. If "half a plough" means half a plough team of eight oxen, or two pairs of oxen each pulling a plough, the reference has meaning: the villeins have a two-oxen plough each.

The hide a criterion of the plough team. There is a hint here that the hide, instead of being as some have thought, the amount of land a plough can cultivate in a year, is rather the criterion of a plough team. A team is the number of plough animals necessary to cultivate a hide. A serious oversight is implicit in the older notion. To assume that the difference between a hide and a virgate is that the former is a full ploughing task for the year and the latter but a quarter of the task, implies that ploughing a hide can take four times as long as ploughing a virgate. Practice knows better. Ploughing seasons are limited in time. Is it not

[94] Orwin and Orwin: *The Open Fields* (2nd Ed.), p. 41.
[95] cf. Neilson: op. cit., p. 10,

more logical to assume that the hide needed four ploughs of two oxen and the virgate one plough of two oxen to master the ploughing each season, and that a plough team was the necessary number of ploughs for a hide? This supposition provides also a reasonable interpretation for the meaning of the villeins' holdings in the open-fields: a virgate would be a holding needing one two-oxen plough (a quarter team) to cultivate it; a half-hide two such ploughs; an oxgang or bovate a single-ox or one-horse plough or, where the land was heavy, a two-oxen plough procured by two holders of bovates entering into the partnership known as *marrows*.[96]

Villein takes own plough to demesne. An interpretation on these lines would also avoid the unlikely situation to which, in some instances, the theory points which assumes that villeins ganged their animals to eight-oxen ploughs to cultivate the lord's demesne. Where a virgate has to contribute one acre a week ploughing,[97] if the tenant can only plough as and when his neighbours, likewise burdened, brought their beasts to join with his, it would mean that when he was ploughing his neighbours would be idle and when they were ploughing he would be idle. On the assumption that an eight-oxen plough ploughs an acre a day, each virgater, with two oxen, would in fact give four days a week of his time to the lord's ploughing; an unlikely, although not impossible, arrangement. No doubt oxen were ganged together when soil and circumstance required it, but the discharge of each man's obligation to his lord appears to have been generally an individual effort. This is further borne out by the fact that when a villein defaulted his labour service fell upon the other members of the community. If massive communal ploughs were doing the ploughing service, a private default would not be felt; a hand would be missing, but nothing more alarming. On the face of some custumals the individual nature of ploughing service is quite clear: at Park in Hertfordshire in 1284 the labour services of a holder of a virgate were "three days' ploughing in the year with one plough and harrow."[98]

Scattered strips. Among the many mysteries of the open-fields and systems displaying like features,[99] the scattering of the holdings into strips peppered over the fields is perhaps the greatest enigma. Many explanations have been advanced. No doubt there is

[96] Bennett : op. cit., p. 45.   [97] Vinogradoff : op. cit., p. 279.
[98] Levett : *Studies in Manorial History*, p. 194
[99] cf. p. 126 ante.

much truth in Vinogradoff's[100] strong advocacy that a simple desire for equality was the only reason. Recently the Orwins[101] have maintained that the cause was nothing more than the inevitable consequence of many ploughteams going into action in one field. Whether each team ploughed for many stripholders or for one stripholder, the order of original alignment would be repeated day by day as the array of ploughs moved round the field. Another explanation finds the secret not in the brown earth but the blue heavens. A superstition, running back with the roots of nations, warned men lest they walked withershins or counter-sunwise; all movement must be sunwise to avoid the evil fairies! It is thought that the alignment of strips in the open-fields in some places, notably on the Continent, followed furlong by furlong the path of the sun's daily traverse.[102]

Whatever communal sanction may have originated the distribution, by the late Middle Ages it no longer has strength enough to check movements of re-allotment and consolidation.

The mensuration of the open-fields. The mosaic of the strips is not without a general principle. Ideally, each strip is an acre: a furlong, or furrow of forty rods in length and four rods in width, so that each quarter acre, or rood, is forty square rods. Actually, the strip varies greatly with soil, contour and custom. Parcels of strips are sited together as furlongs, shotts or flatts. Where strips are fore-shortened they are termed butts, and a furlong running out into a point or apex is a gore acre. Each strip, by the action of ploughing, is thrown into a ridge and valley formation running lengthwise.

Grass-baulks. Difference of opinion has arisen over the grass baulk. Some historians, following earlier opinions, divide the strips by grass baulks. The Orwins have challenged the traditional view; for them the double furrow made by ploughland meeting plough-land, and specially placed landmarks are the boundaries of strips.[103] Such an explanation would account for the loss of strips and acres from time to time.[104] A recent study of the plough and furrow technique of the open-fields accepts both opinions, pointing out that practice was not uniform and the presence or absence of grass baulks depended upon the nature of the soil.[105] Baulks are recog-

[100] Vinogradoff : op. cit., p. 236.
[101] Orwin and Orwin : op. cit.,, p. 40.
[102] Homans : *English Villagers of the Thirteenth Century*, p. 94 et seq.
[103] Orwin and Orwin : op. cit., pp. 43-48.
[104] Bennett : op. cit., p. 47.

nised by Orwin; they are grass edges to roadways and trackways, and mark parish boundaries in the open-fields. Together with sikes, unploughable areas of grass among the strips, the baulks provide grass for tethered animals; on Forncett manors there is much record of similar odd grazings being let off at money rents to tenants.[106]

Community and common rights. The communal element in open-field vill economy is not to be looked for among the plough teams but in the common rights, in the court customary, in the sense of joint responsibility for the manorial burdens and in a shared dependence upon the services of the reeve and other officials and the craftsmen and functionaries who serve the community.

Common grazing rights were the foundation of stock policy. Without commons no villein or small freeholder, unless he had an enclosed paddock, could keep plough beasts for the plough, or sheep for the fold. Arable husbandry was dependent upon the common grazings. Impair the commons and the arable cultivation immediately suffers. Common grazings, as a general rule, were available over either a half or a third of the arable land, according to whether the two-field or three-field system was practised. Actual location changed year by year for the common rights were limited to fallow ground and stubbles. After harvest the stubble became common grazings until needed for ploughing again. In each vill, where possible, land was shut up for meadow, allotted in doles or strips among the arable tenantry, and after hay-harvest opened as common grazings. Permanent common of pasture was afforded over the pasture land and wastes of the vill. The pasture land and waste were the hinterland of the vill and into them the lord of the manor would make assarts to augment his demesne.

Against such inroads, the villein tenants had only the manorial court and custom to protect them, a vulnerable armour. Statute law, in the Statute of Merton, 1236,[107] protected the freeholders. Lords were permitted to enclose the waste provided they did not impair the freeholders' common of grazing. It was the ancient common rights associated with freehold strip-holdings in the open-fields that gave rise by Littleton's day[108] to the legal notion of common of pasture appendant. Other common rights could not be claimed as appendant to the arable; they could only arise by a grant from the lord, express or implied, and were known as rights

---

[106] Davenport : op. cit., p. 32.
[107] Plucknett : *Legislation of Edward I*, pp. 84-6.
[108] Vinogradoff : op. cit., p. 266.

appurtenant. Intercommoning among fenland vills has been noted elsewhere;[109] these practices and all common rights in overlapping wastes between vills were known as *common de vicinage*.

The officers and functionaries of the vill. Cattle and sheep on the arable, pastures and wastes, and pigs in the woodlands were not tended by their owners. The vill community was served by shepherd and swineherd and many other functionaries selected from among its members. The requirements and customs of vills differed, but the reeve appears, by the early Middle Ages at least, as an almost ubiquitous personage. Generally a villein, sometimes elected to serve year by year, but more often annually, the reeve is the major-domo of the villein community. He is responsible to the manor for the proper discharge of all agricultural service. Under the reeve on some manors are found the messor and hayward performing specialized functions, among which the organisation of boon-work in hay-harvest is frequently included. The beadle is the policeman who knocks at doors calling the tenantry to remember their boon-days. A pindar is employed to impound straying and trespassing cattle. Many of these functionaries, especially the reeve, in later days appear to have held designated holdings in the vill, of which reevelands[110] are examples. Besides these functionaries the vills are served by craftsmen, blacksmiths, wheelwrights and so forth, villeins who for their services held villeinland subject to rent payments and other burdens of bondage but not the customary work on the lord's demesne. They are small men standing half-way between tenants in villeinage and wage-earners.[111]

So then, the web of common rights, not co-aration, welds the open field community together. Because the arable fields have to be broken, and turned over to common grazing at a day appointed, there must be a calendar of harvesting, sowing and ploughing binding every stripholder, and an open forum, or court, governing husbandry policy. The common meadow also demands communal attention, and the common pastures and wastes have to be stinted and controlled. While all this is surely true and so well exemplified by the open-field system, it does not mark that system off as something unique among other agrarian systems. The greatest factor giving all vills selfhood is the enjoyment and administration of common rights.

[109] p. 115 ante.
[110] Neilson: *Customary Rents*, p. 104.
[111] Op. cit., p. 66.

CHAPTER SIX

THE MIDDLE AGES: MONEY RENT AND LEASEHOLDS

COMMUTATION OF SERVICES

Change of accent in dual economy. Money rents were no innovation in the Middle Ages. Tribute, rent and taxes had been paid in money alongside renders in kind and labour service in the days of Old England. The picture of medieval rent audits bright in the lustre of newly minted coin, strange alike to a wondering peasantry and wily officialdom, is illusory. Both medieval tradition and the earlier modern schools are to blame for the misconception. The redactor of the Dialogus de Scaccario refers to "the tradition handed down to us by our fathers" according to which in the early state of the kingdom after the Conquest, the kings used to receive from their manors not sums of gold or silver but only provisions, from which were supplied the daily necessities of the king's household. Cursory acquaintance with the mass of exchequer documents, manorial and regal, outcropping abruptly in the thirteenth century has been another false guide. The wealth of documents contrasts with the paucity of the records of the earlier centuries and has been taken as evidence that the monetary interests and financial practices of the thirteenth century were as novel as the documents that record them. The inference is too hasty.[1]

Recent historical opinion favours a steady, expanding use of money that forced services and payments in kind to yield to monetary commutation until, in the last decades of the fifteenth century, the accent which previously had fallen upon the barter aspect of a dual economy now fell upon the monetary. The change of emphasis was inevitable. Money once introduced into an economy tends to leaven the whole sooner or later. An incident recorded in the Dialogus[2] is illustrative; "when King Henry was engaged abroad or in remote parts of the country in suppressing rebellion, it became necessary that he should have coined money for his expenditure. And at the same time there poured into the King's court crowds of complaining husbandmen . . . as a sign that agriculture was decaying. Accordingly the King . . . acting upon the advice of his magnates, sent through

[1] Levett: *Studies in Manorial History*, p. 42.
[2] Lipson: *The Economic History of England* (Vol. I), p. 601.

the kingdom men whom he knew to be wise and fitted for the work, in order that they might visit and inspect each manor with their own eyes and then estimate in money the value of the payments in kind." The writer does not attempt to give a reason for all this. It is clear that the renders of tribute in kind from the royal demesne manors were over-burdensome and conversion to money was advocated as a just alleviation. Perhaps the growth of commodity markets was bringing coin to the hand of the peasantry with greater frequency than before but instead of money being taken for tribute, levies in kind were being made upon what may be regarded as essential, working capital — seed and breeding ewes — to the detriment and damage of husbandry. Money in the markets set up a demand for commutation on the land. Generally the leaven did not act so quickly and directly. Tradition frustrated its working. And paucity of money supply, so characteristic of medieval England,[3] was another retarding agent.

Scutages and fines. True commutation of tenurial services to money came sooner to some tenures than to others. Invariably the change came by stages. As early as the reign of William I barons were hiring knights to make good the *servitium debitum* of the fiefs.[4] It was the first stage. The hiring rates provided a measuring rod for scutage, the shield-money which military tenants were soon to pay in lieu of performing military service, or providing retinues of heavy armed retainers. Scutage therefore in the early days reflects the cost of maintenance. When the knight's fee became fixed, a scutage of two marks on the fee was a common levy, representing a knight's remuneration rate of eightpence per day for the full feudal obligation of forty days military service.[5] Scutage from military fees of less than noble rank, the lands of *serviens*, was a sum corresponding to the rank and lower cost of maintenance. On the other hand, it is questionable whether scutage ever discharged a tenant-in-chief, who was also a great baron, from his personal military obligations. Two marks are no equivalent of the service which an exalted tenant-in-capite can give; the king alone can evaluate his service. Heavy fines or *dona* imposed upon the great military fiefs, ecclesiastical and lay, in the teeth of loud-voiced protests, are probably the redemption price of the mighty men.[6]

[3] Op. cit., p. 532.   [4] Round : *Feudal England*, p. 271.   [5] Op. cit., p. 270.
[6] Pollock and Maitland : *The History of English Law before the Time of Edward I* (Vol. I), p. 269.

The top rungs of the feudal ladder were thus burdened with scutage and fines in lieu of military service. Scutage was dealt with by passing the burden of it down the ladder. The lesser knights, the mesne tenants by knight's service and non-military sub-tenants and, in some cases, even the bondmen of the vill carried the burden. Aids were handled difffferently. A similar policy, shifting the incidence of aids to the lands of lesser tenantry, was invalid unless sanctioned by the writ raising the levy.[7] Fines were, however, raised from estates in sergeanty not as impositions passed down from superiors but as commutations of sergeanty service. The arbitrariness of these fines fits well the essentially personal character of sergeanty. But scutage is not unknown to sergeanty tenure.[8]

Scutages and fines passed through the hands of the county sheriffs to the royal Exchequer and eventually all rental significance was lost. Together with aids they moved into the province of taxation. Fines, aids and scutages became categories of imperial taxation and were levied alternately with a seeming disregard of historical origins. The fine and aid of military tenure inspired, in the twelfth and thirteenth centuries, a fine on the plough, and later a tax on money rent.[9]

The commutation of the service of the noble tenures to money payment was probably, at all events in its later stages, more a political manoeuvre than an economic expedient. Certainly political consideration weighed equally with the economic. William I had aspired to increase his enfeoffed army as an insurance against English insurrection and had encouraged and fostered subinfeudation by knight's service. But the Angevin kings, suspicious of baronial power, welcomed and sponsored the payment of money in lieu of heavily armed knights maintained and equipped by the mighty and potentially rebellious.[10] Royal armies were now the ranks of mercenaries. Money wages kept the fighting machine together. The king's view dovetailed with the new interests of his military tenants. Commerce, attendant upon the expanding woollen industry, was leading the minds of lords of lands to calculate the worth of their acres in terms of cash-counters instead of fighting tenantry. Change was slow, especially along the marches of the kingdom.

Money equivalents made a mockery of noble military tenure. Division of the knight's fee was quickened and men of small

[7] Jolliffe: *The Constitutional History of Medieval England* (2nd Ed.), p. 308.
[8] Poole: *Obligations of Society in the Thirteenth and Fourteenth Centuries*, pp. 59, 60.   [9] Jolliffe: op. cit., p. 309.   [10] Round: op. cit., p. 273.

social stature who would never aspire to knighthood and possession of an entire fee came to hold land in chivalry. Knight's
service tenure moved downwards through society.

Commutation of socage service. Socage moved upwards. The
great and ancient estates were embarrassed more by the fruits of
chivalry than by the money equivalents of knight's service,
the exorbitant *dona* or fines. Socage tenure avoided wardship
and marriage and other detested feudal incidents. But socage
was socially disparaging with its mean and ignoble service. Money
rents changed its nature. What does it matter whether the money
paid is the sign and symbol of ancient fighting service or agricultural labour ? It is money. The shillings of socage rent are the
peers of the shillings of scutage. So the great and the noble
sought socage estates at money rents; although the day was
far distant when military tenure would give way entirely to
free and common socage.

Money rent always a feature of free socage. Ignoble labour
service was a repellent feature of free socage tenure, but it was
not the hall-mark of the tenure. While theorists were struggling
to establish uncertainty of service as the essential difference
between free socage and villeinage, practice looked to the payment
of money rent as a rude, ready-to-hand test of free socage;[11] land
held *ad censum* was free, land held *ad opus* was bond. Money
rent, in some cases, was the only form of socage service. Normally
money payment and labour service were a joint obligation. But
it is the monetary element that is significant and tells for freedom;
emphasis is upon the money rent rather than the labour service.
This principle applied also to the intermediate tenures between
free and bond. The ascendancy of the molmen of the Fens over
their servile neighbours is marked by higher monetary rents and
less weighty labour service.[12]

The money rents of free socage came from many origins.
Curiously enough scutage was contributory in some cases. The
division of a knight's fee into minute fractions created tiny
parcels too small for the fruits of chivalry to be worth plucking,
and the small scutages resembled the ancient money rents of
socage plots. Noble origins were obscured[13] and knight's service
tenure lapsed into socage. Another probable origin of socage
money rents lay far back in Anglo-Saxon times. Many free

[11] Vinogradoff : *Villainage in England*, p. 171.
[12] Neilson : *A Terrier of Fleet, Lincolnshire*, p. lxxi.   [13] Poole : op. cit., p. 36.

socage tenements in the Middle Ages paid the mysterious rents of assize. Professor Levett[14] suggests that the rents of assize were the consequence of the Anglo-Saxon gafol passing through an intermediate stage as *gabulum assisum*. So far as this interpretation is true, free socage rents originate in part from the commutation of ancient land dues to gafol payments. Beside this archaic element and contrasting with it is a contemporary contribution to the fixed rents of medieval socage: lords colonised woodland and waste and reclaimed land from the sea by granting tenements at fixed money rents in free socage to colonisers and pioneers. A fourth origin is the commutation of socage labour service to money equivalent. The commutation of free agricultural labour service differs from the commutation of villein services. Labour service is commuted for a fixed sum, often merged in the *redditus assisus* and, unlike the commutation of bond service, does not become *redditus mutabiles*; and there does not appear to have been a sale of superfluous works prior to commutation proper, as is the case with villein commutation. On some manors redundant free socage obligations lapsed altogether.[15]

Commutation of bond services. The commutation of bond services to money rents was a complex process. Customary tenure has a character and purpose of existence essentially its own. It is the tenure of the vill, the one social institution above all others, with the exception of the church, that remained intact under the impact of the Conquest. Hence the tenure in its medieval dress carries traces of fashions long forgotten; archaic food renders and purveyance obligations. Contemporary renders, rents in kind and labour services in exchange for special privileges are also a mark and sign of the same character and purpose. Labour services and status payments lie at the heart of the tenure. Commutation to money rents has to account for the assimilation or treatment in some other way, of three diverse elements. Two distinct principles can be traced through the prolonged, localized processes: a change to money payments, at comparatively early dates, of the many renders in kind given for special privileges, and a tendency for these payments to coalesce with the ancient payments, tallage and other annual payments under the accommodating rubric, *rents of assize;*[16] and the conversion of labour

[14] Levett: op. cit., p. 50.
[15] Davenport: *The Economic Development of a Norfolk Manor 1080-1565,* p. 63.
[16] Neilson: *Customary Rents,* p. 46. Bennett: *Life on the English Manor 1150-1400,* p. 138.

services into money equivalents by annual *sales* of the services to the villein tenants, as a first step to commutation.

Sale of works. Sale to the bond tenants of the lord's right to demand labour services is known as *sale of works* and was an established feature of medieval estate management. It gives the impression of commutation. This is misleading. Sale of works was not commutation. The transaction was yearly and in no wise effected a permanent change. The number and type of the works sold varied from year to year. On some manors success or failure in management must have depended upon the acumen of the steward, or other advisor of the lord, when judging where the point of division lay between works to be performed and works to be sold. Prices and other features of these sales were not uniform. They varied from manor to manor according to local custom.

Professor Levett's researches through the manorial records of the Bishop of Winchester's estates show four clearly identifiable principles in operation by the fourteenth century. A distinction is made between the sale of works proper and what appear to be arrangements more akin to permanent commutation, although included in the documents among the sales of works.[17] Quasi-commutations of this kind doubtless account for the petty payments, quaint of name and bewildering in number, so characteristic of medieval manorial arrangements.[18] To such belong the *hedernewech* of the Ely extents, a money payment in lieu of the customary week-work of guarding the stores and granaries; and the *woodsilver* of the Romsey lands, payment given in the place of wood-carrying service from the woodlands to the lord's hall in winter. Woodsilver is a good example of how the nomenclature of change can obscure identity, for tenants in some parts render woodsilver to the lord for the privilege of taking timber from the woodlands for housebote or similar purpose.[19]

The Winchester evidence shows also the Lord Bishop bargaining, not with individual tenants, but with the entire tenantry of a vill. For the sum of £16. 13s 4d the bond tenants, as a body, are freed from manual and carrying services subject to the ancient obligation to provide from among themselves a reeve, a beadle, a shepherd and other servants to work the

[17] Levett: *The Black Death on the Estates of the See of Winchester*, p. 32.
[18] Neilson: op. cit., p. 50 et seq.
[19] Op. cit., p. 53.

demesne land.[20] The third and fourth principles are the sale of ploughing, harrowing, threshing, reaping and other specific services; and the sale of manual or general services. Specific services are sold at unit prices, the unit depending upon the nature of the work. Thus, ploughing service is sold at a given sum per acre (e.g. 6d—9d) while threshing is sold at so much a quarter. The mere announcement of prices does not imply willingness to sell. Each year has to await the declaration of the lord's policy.

Work and money payments are entered as alternatives in rentals and extents. Two examples from the extent of the manor of Orchard, 1347-48 show the form of record:[21]

Holding	Rent	Services
1 messuage 10 acres in bondagio	3s. 10d.	June 24 to Aug. 1. Mowing or 10d.
1 messuage 10 acres in bondagio	3s. 2d.	Aug. 1 to Sept. 29. Reaping or 3s. 4d.

General works are the unspecified and indeterminate services rendered to the lord as so many days' work in the week, and the work demanded as boons. A work, for the purposes of sale schemes, is not a day's work. Definitions vary. A work may mean the services of one man for half a day, or for half a day in winter and a whole day in summer. The length of a day itself is not constant. A work may require only the services of the tenant or his substitute, or it may mean the attendance at the demesne of the entire family with the exception of the housewife. On some manors more precise formulae are used. At Stoke "a work in mowing-time meant mowing three swathes of grass each twelve feet wide, in some meadows, while in the park, which was estimated at 31½ acres, the three swathes were only to be 4 feet in width."[22] Allocation of the works between the sold and the performed depended upon the manorial policy which circumstance and prudence governed. Most manors had a large reserve and a lord's bailiff had a very wide margin of manoeuvre. On certain of the Winchester manors on one occasion a number of works were sold late, as though a sale policy had been determined upon and carried out before the labour services were in fact required, and a number of works were in consequence held in reserve as a margin of manoeuvre

[20] Levett: op. cit., p. 33.
[22] Op. cit., p. 41.
[21] Op. cit., p. 23.

against the time when the final labour demands would be known. The following works schedule for Nailesbourne, 1348-1349,[23] is a typical specimen of a sales policy:

NAILESBOURNE, 1348-49

Total number of general works owing	4755

In acquittance to 1 reeve and 1 beadle	98	
,, ,, ,, 1 ploughman	122	
,, ,, 9 workers for festivals	45	
Total number of works acquitted	——	265
Reaping and harvesting &c. by 62 customers ..	248	
Mowing, and haymaking, 12 acres	96	
Mattocking demesne for winter sowing	15	
Sowing	4	
Harrowing	104	
Making 'grips' or trenches	17	
Mattocking demesne for Lent sowing	15	
Sowing	4	
Making 'grips'	2	
Hoeing corn	64	
For 1 rook-herd	10	
Repairing bridge	2	
Total number of works performed	——	581
,, ,, ,, ,, sold	——	3863
,, ,, ,, ,, sold (after account was made up.)		61
		4770

Sale of works and policies of estate management   The sale of labour services to tenants in bondage is generally regarded as one aspect of the medieval labour problem. It paid the overlord to have his demesne land cultivated by hired labour and not by the *customers* of the vill, hence he would take money in lieu of service from the tenants and pay hired labour with it. The facts, as manorial evidence gives them in detail, do not bear out this conception at every point. There is no doubt that the simple economic fact, the substitution of hired labour for villein service, was one among many stimuli prompting sale and commutation, especially when rising food prices made the customary boons uneconomic; those boons at which the lord was required to provide meat and drink for the tenants and "the work did not pay for the breakfast." But this substitution was not a simple *quid pro quo* policy of hired labour replacing servile labour.

[23] Op. cit., p. 89.

Prices for the sale of works do not correspond with wage rates. The sale price of the one does not reflect the other. All the labour services of a virgate, for example, may be sold at 2s. and include ploughing operations which in terms of contemporary wages rates would cost from 2s. to 6s. each.[24] Even more conclusive is evidence from the Winchester estates. Professor Levett shows that the manors having a superabundance of works sold were the very ones where the amount of hired labour was lowest.[25] Works sold do not invariably mean the employment of hired wage-earners.

In the detailed accounts of receipts[26] covering the period 1204-1376, the sale of works shows a remarkable constancy after 1346, except for the years of the Black Death. Where sales increase, the increase is accompanied by improvements in the income from leases and assize rents. Professor Levett[27] gives the following figures for Nailesbourne reproduced in the Table opposite.

[24] Levett : op. cit., p. 43.
[25] Op. cit., p. 104.
[26] Op. cit., p. 177.
[27] Op. cit., p. 174.

NAILESBOURNE

	1284-5			1346-7			1347-8			1348-9			1349-50			1350-1			1351-2			1352-3			1376-7		
Minister ..	—			John Cade			John Waterman			Roger de Torre			Roger de Torre			Roger atte Torre, John Waterman						John Waterman			Adam atte Mersch		
	£	s.	d.	£	s.	d.	£	s.	d.	£	s.	d.	£	s.	d.	£	s.	d.	£	s.	d.	£	s.	d.	£	s.	d.
Arrears	—			12	16	7	26	9	5¾	2	17	10¼	18	0	0¾	26	10	8¼	—			2	9	7½	None		
Assized rents ..	21	2	6½	26	19	2¼	26	19	5¼	26	19	5¼	26	19	5¼	26	19	5¼	—			26	19	5¼	27	11	6¼
Increments ..	—					3																					
—Acquittances ..	1	12	0	1	1	0	1	1	0	1	1	0	1	1	0	1	1	0	—			1	1	0	1	1	0
—Defects ..		7	1½		7	1½		7	1½		7	1½		7	1½		7	1½	—				7	1½		7	1½
—Defects *per pestilentiam* ..	—			—			—			c.4	14	9½	3	12	8¾		13	0¼	1	10	3¾	1	1	11¾	None		
Leases	—			1	11	4	1	11	4	1	11	4	1	9	8	1	11	4	1	11	4	1	11	4	1	1	4
Custom	—			3	4	6½	3	1	8	2	19	0	2	19	11½	2	18	4	—			2	17	4½	3	8	9½
Annual recognition	2 plough shares 6½ lbs. wax				1	3			9			9			3			4	—					8		3	4
Issues of the manor	9	4	1	2	1	0	2	3	6½	2	10	8½	4	4	4	4	0	9	—			4	18	0	7	9	4
Sale of pasture ..	—			5	11	0	5	2	9		14	1	c.1	0	8	1	11	0	—				19	8		3	0
,, ,, corn ..	28	11	0½	36	0	7¼	21	16	5½	10	4	11	9	5	0	12	7	6	—			9	18	8½	14	4	2½
,, ,, stock ..	—			1	13	3	1	6	0	1	16	0	3	10	8	6	13	0	—			4	6	6	5	0	0
,, ,, works	(1	18	0)	9	12	11¾	9	12	6¾	9	12	8¼	4	3	9½	6	0	7¾	—			5	14	5¼	9	16	5½
Fines & marriages	3	18	10	7	9	8	4	2	8	16	18	8	10	3	8	14	10	6	—			2	16	8	2	6	4
Perquisites of the court ..	6	1	10	3	7	0	2	16	2	1	18	7	2	17	8	4	9	11	—			23	0	1	2	13	7
Heriots in pence	—				1	0		4	6	1	5	6		2	6		8	0	—				1	0		1	0
Miscellaneous ..	—				6	8½		3	5¼		17	9¾	1	1	5	—			—			3	0	3½		18	6
Total receipts	63	0	4½	109	8	2¾	104	2	8	74	4	5	80	14	8	106	0	3½	—			86	3	8¼	74	9	3¼
Expenses ..	12	7	2½	13	6	10½	8	19	9¾	7	18	7¾	4	18	1¾	17	7	0½	—			10	6	6¾	11	1	5½
Paid over ..	50	13	2	69	11	10½	92	5	0	48	5	8½	49	5	10	67	11	0	—			54	10	8	59	17	9¾
Owing	—			26	9	5¼	2	17	10¼	18	0	0¾	26	10	8¼	21	2	3	—			21	6	5½	2	10	0

Although there is insufficient evidence to establish a proof, the figures are suggestive of two alternative movements. The increase in works sold and the improvement in income from leases may indicate the expansion or introduction of demesne leaseholds. If this were so, the area under immediate cultivation by the lord would be curtailed, there would be a slackening of demand for customary labour services and a corresponding augmentation of works for sale and these changes would be accompanied by an enhanced rent roll from leases. Alternatively, improved assize rents and rising sales of works may have been due to a policy of colonisation. New intakes would be let at assize rents and the holdings become subject to the customary burdens of the vill. The total obligations of the vill would increase and this increment would be entirely redundant. The demesne land would not want the labour, and the reserve of works for sale would be inflated.

It might be reckless to argue from these isolated examples of the Winchester estates to general conclusions for the whole country, although Professor Levett maintains that the bulk of the material is weighty enough to give a substantial degree of probability to any general conclusions it may point to.[28] The evidence points to a considerable monetary element in manorial rents prior to commutation of labour services; and to sums of customary services quite disproportionate to the requirements of the demesne. Even in the dark days of the great pestilence, 1349-50, the number of works actually performed remains normal at Nailesbourne.[29] The marked decrease in the number of works sold is not due to a greater number of works performed, but to the abnormal death-rate among tenants to whom works were usually sold. The reserve of works is ample enough to meet the unprecedented toll of death and allow the sales of works to average fifty per cent of normal. Clearly on these manors in the fourteenth century, the lord is reaping from works sold a money return which has no practical connection with the manorial origin of the works.[30]

This income casts a reflection upon the deep waters of commutation. Conversion of labour service to money payment is an adjustment of manorial labour policy; especially so when wages are low and the sale of works more than compensates for wage payments, and when the cost of food at boons

---

[28] Levett : op. cit., p. 142.   [29] Op. cit., p. 89.
[30] Hilton : *Peasant Movements in England before 1381*, Econ.H. Rev., 2nd Series, Vol. II, No. 2, 1949, pp. 119, 120.

makes customary service unprofitable. But adjustment of labour policy is not a complete explanation of sales of works and commutation. The income from the sale of superfluous works looks uncommonly like the true rent of the economists' schools: it is money consideration paid to the owner for the benefit of possession. This is more obvious when it is remembered that money payments in lieu of service were eventually demanded by the tenants themselves. The lords were the prime movers; they had to be. The villein's first reaction was hostile. But time swung opinion to the opposite pole. Money payments opened the road to emancipation and the voice of bond tenants is heard praising the change and crying after the new order. Commutation became a tenants' cause. The lords reacted and in the late fourteenth century tried to reverse the process. Their efforts were in vain; tide of circumstance was flowing against them and forcing commutation. Early historians regarded the Black Death, 1349-50, as a turning point, if not the origin of the commutation movement, a gateway of death into life through which the villein gained bargaining power over distracted overlords. Whether true or not, the emphasis on the tenants' role in the drama is a warning against thinking of sales of works and commutation as being nothing more than adjustments to manorial labour policies.

Modern opinion rejects the cataclysmic role of the Black Death.[31] Movement towards commutation now appears as a constant and steady process, little affected by the social upheaval of the great pestilence. By the thirteenth century, money rent has a greater total value than the equivalent value of labour service.[31a] Commutation displays but few signs of dramatic acceleration until the last decades of the fourteenth century. And why, it may be asked, does commutation quickly advance then?

Leaseholds a new principle of estate management. Perhaps too little attention has been paid to the decline of population, the rise of wages and the new principles of estate management which resulted from the social and economic movements of this time.

Throughout the fourteenth century and the first half of the fifteenth century there was a precipitous rise in money wages, mainly due to a decline in population.[32] Sale of works was no answer to the new wage rates for it had never been policy to adjust sale

---

[31] Levett: op. cit.
[31a] Kosminsky: *Studies in the Agrarian History of England in the Thirteenth Century*, p. 191.
[32] Postan: *Some Economic Evidence of Declining Population in the later Middle Ages*, Econ.H. Rev., 2nd Series, Vol. II, No. 3, 1950, p. 229.

prices to wage levels. Income from the sale of works was rigid, traditional, rental in nature and unrelated to the price of labour. Moreover, employment of villein labour was daily proving more unsatisfactory. A spate of money flow, especially near the towns, had made villeins prosperous and avaricious of emancipation. Landowners had to change their principles of estate management. Everything pointed towards a more independent peasantry. Peasant families working their own small plots were little affected by the problem of high wages. Manorial lords and others, therefore, met the demands of the hour by encouraging the growth of leaseholds. Manorial demesnes were let in parcels or as entire units on stock-and-land leases and customary holdings in the vill granted to the tenantry at fee farm rents. By these changes lords avoided paying high wages and villeins became leasehold tenants holding at money rents, under *ad hoc* contracts or the custom of the manor recorded on the court roll. Labour services on the manorial demesne became anachronistic and were either sold, mere book entries in the manorial records, or fell into desuetude.

DEVELOPMENT OF LAND MARKET AND LEASEHOLDS

Lord and vassal transactions do not create a land market. From the days of Anglo-Norman England and earlier there was a land market, if the transfer of proprietary interests from one to another is a market. Feudal lords granting estates to be held of them by tenants are trafficking in land. In exchange for military support or less colourful service an estate in land is granted, and where estates are created and pass in this way there is a market in land.

Yet this thought does not come easily. A certain hesitancy overhangs it. The creation of a feudal estate is something above a mere bartering of service or money in exchange for land. It is a political and social event. So much more than the mere possession and enjoyment of land is involved. Personal privities arise and relationships vital to the constitution of the realm are created. Estates in land are too sacrosanct, they hang too close to the heart of national life and social order for their creation and alienation to be nothing more than a movement in a land market. Is it going too far to suggest that while estates in land were fused with a vital, personal affinity between lord and vassal, to speak of a land market is profane?[32a] It is only when history allows an estate owner to realize his proprietary interest as something standing apart, detached from his vassal personality, that estates become marketable. This thought must not lead to the assumption that subinfeudation retarded the growth of a land market and alienation by substitution assisted it. The lord and vassal affinities, so close in the days of early feudalism, became attenuated and weakened as services were commuted to money payments. Money payments were the acid that wore away the feudal bond and opened the way to the development of a land market. And money on which commutation of service depends is itself the great fertiliser of all market growth.

How far feudal tenants were at liberty to transfer estates without the sanction of overlords is not at all clear in the early years of feudalism. What emerges in thirteenth century jurisprudence supports the view taken above. The feudal obligation of tenant to lord, especially tenants-in-chief to the king, conditioned and clogged alienation of land. The personal bond had to be honoured. Transactions and traffic in land were always subject to its requirements, unless the feudal lord to whom service and homage were due licensed a grant. The principle is clearly enunciated in Magna Carta 1217: "No free man shall henceforth give or sell so much of his land as that out of the residue he may not sufficiently do to the lord of the fee the service which pertains to that fee."[33] This prohibition seems to have been imposed with exceptional rigour upon the king's tenants-in-chief. And Henry III in 1256 categorically ordained that no barony or fee held of him in chief should pass to another without his licence. Although Bracton merely mentions the Great Charter of 1217 and its severe restrictions in favour of the king, other writers coming after him hint that the king differs from other lords and his licence is a necessary condition of all valid transfers of fiefs held in chief.[34]

The power of the personal, feudal loyalty acting as a clog upon land transactions is prominently displayed by the universally accepted dogma that sergeanties were in all respects inalienable without licence because of the peculiarly personal nature of sergeanty service.[35] Despite the dogma, sergeanties were alienated and so frequently that the transactions created a chaos of minute holdings. By the mid-thirteenth century the state of

---

[32a] Holmes: *The Estates of the Higher Nobility in XIVth Century England*, pp. 7, 8.
[33] Pollock and Maitland: op. cit., p. 332.
[34] Op. cit., p. 336.
[35] Op. cit., p. 334.

affairs was so serious that royal commissions were set up to seek out alienations of sergeanties, so that the tenure might be converted to knight's service or socage and a money rent reserved.

The structure of the medieval land market has never been closely studied. The royal commissions enquiring into socage, and what is known of the development of a money market in the thirteenth century are grounds for thinking that by then traffic in estates was becoming active. The statute Quia Emptores at the end of the century supports this opinion. The transfer of estates meant subinfeudation. Although in the process of subinfeudation the grantor does not pass his entire estate, what is reserved is often a nominal interest, acknowledged by the gift of a rose at Midsummer or some other yearly token proffered by the grantee. Subinfeudation therefore did not prevent the substance of an estate passing from grantor to grantee. Apparently the spate of the land market so increased that the tenurial complexities attendant upon subinfeudation caused concern and Parliament was called upon to face the fact and attempt to solve the riddle. The significance of Quia Emptores appears on the face of the statute: henceforth vendor and purchaser transactions in land will not create a feudal privity, they are economic and strictly within the land market.

Reference to sales of estates for money sums is infrequent. An example among the entries of the Northamptonshire Assize Roll of 1202 refers with great clarity to the purchase of land: "the jurors do not know whether the land was bought with the pennies of Maud or the pennies of her husband."[36] A liberal run of statistics similar to Delisle's figures for three monasteries in Normandy is necessary before any reliable word can be written about the land market. Delisle showed how between 1217 and 1384 the monks bought small freeholds by paying lump-sums and granting possession back to the vendors in consideration of receiving money rents in perpetuity which, on the average, gave investments at ten per cent and pointed to a ten years' purchase figure as the measure of capital value.[37]

A market in chattels real. The restraining influence of the feudal privities on the land market possibly lies behind the fact that most references to capital transactions are not concerned with the sale of fees or estates in land but with a market in chattels real.

[36] Stenton : *The Earliest Northamptonshire Assize Rolls, A.D. 1202 and 1303*, p. 57.
[37] Coulton : *The Medieval Village*, p. 285.

There is considerable traffic in leaseholds. The purpose of the transaction is not the creation of a limited term for its own sake. Leaseholds are used as gages to support money advances. For example, in 1190 Simon of Pattishall took upon himself a debt which one Robert, son of Hugh, owed the King and in consideration of this, Robert granted his land to Simon for a yearly rent of a pound of pepper to himself and ten shillings to the chief lords.[38] The lease gave a tangible possessory interest but no status or feudal standing, and in the early Middle Ages was essentially a financial instrument.

Leaseholds are to the lawyer chattels real and not real property. Of like nature are the wardships and marriages pertaining to military tenure. Sales of wardships and marriages and the exorbitant money sums which passed to secure the guardianship of heirs and control of marriage have been mentioned.[39] Possessors of the right were not seised of the ward's estate as of fee. The fee vested in the ward as heir. The guardian's interest was a right of enjoyment, an interest in land which stood apart from his own person and social status and therefore lent itself without difficulty or embarrassment to monetary investment. Maitland[40] draws attention to the probability of both types of chattels real being the essential form of free capital investment in the early Middle Ages.

Gages. It was logical for leaseholds to be given as gages to secure debts. The law in the thirteenth century, where it touches or concerns gages, is by no means clear, but among its certainties is the distinction between the *vifgage* and the *mortgage*. Manors were leased to creditors, *gagees*, in exchange for money loans. The manorial income could be set against the debt and the sum outstanding reduced year by year: such was the living gage, the vifgage. Or the debt might remain outstanding for the term of the lease: such was the dead gage, the mortgage. In mortgage transactions the manorial income was of the nature of usury and though the arrangement was upheld at law it was not entirely a desirable transaction. With the passage of time the leasehold gave place to the conditional fee as security for loans;[41] a further sign that the fee became more marketable as its feudal significance waned.

[38] Stenton, D. M.: op. cit., p. xvii.
[39] cf. p. 112 ante.
[40] Pollock and Maitland: op. cit. (Vol. II), p. 116.
[41] Op. cit., p. 120.

Seisin. The leasehold was free from feudal incidents and on that account alone was a cleaner instrument for the purposes of the financier. Its streamlining, however, was a weakness. Feudal dues and other incidents were a token of seisin, and seisin was the rock, the only rock upon which at common law a valid title to a fee could stand. He who is seised is truly owner against the world at large. An interest in land upon another foundation is by comparison an edifice built on sand.

No alienation of a fee was complete until seisin had passed from the old to the new owner. Livery of seisin was the true act of conveyance. A charter may rehearse what was done or presume to be itself the instrument of disposition. In both events the writing was valuable as evidence, but whatever form the words took they were impotent to effect feoffment. Livery of seisin had to be public and notorious. Frequently a simple ritual on the land was the order of procedure.[42] At other times the seisin was conveyed in court or other public place by the transfer of a symbol—a rod or sod or branch taken from the land. As the symbol passed from the hand of the transferor to the transferee physical possession of the land and ownership of the fee moved too and the conveyance was perfected thus. Seisin was the self-consciousness of feudal landownership : when it ceased ownership ceased.

The use. The later Middle Ages avoided the notoriety of land transactions which livery of seisin created. Recourse was had to the device of the *use.* The use was a flame kindled from a stray spark. A conflagration between Papal and lay opinion had flared up to a white heat at the end of the thirteenth century. People had given gifts "to the use of" the Franciscans and the meaning of this condition was the cause of strife.[43] Long after the origin of the use had been forgotten in the diminishing glass of memory, the device of granting land to the use of another remained. Its legal standing in England was a matter of grave doubt. Late in the fourteenth century common law finally set its face against the use, and then it was that the Chancellor, for the sake of the King's conscience, stepped in to defend the intentions of a donor who had given land to one to hold to the use of another. The Chancellor's action exposed a great fissure that was opening, and dividing common law from equity. Equity upheld the use; common law did not.

For   landownership   the   great   divide   had   far-reaching

[42] Pollock and Maitland : op. cit., p. 83.
[43] Op. cit., p. 238.

consequences. Gifts made to one person to hold to the use of another would at common law convey the estate to the immediate donee in the normal way. Common law was not concerned with the obligation in the gift, but equity's conscience was tender and honoured the terms of the use. Thus future interests in land abhorrent to common law, and other forms of gifts which at common law were invalid were accepted by equity under the cloak of uses. Furthermore, the great dichotomy gravely affected the value of feudal incidents. The burden of feudal incidents never encumbered the equitable estate. He who was seised of the fee at law was liable for the incidents, and not the one for whose benefit the estate was given to uses. These developments facilitated the disposal of land. The story of the role of the use in the growth of the land market has yet to be written. It is not without significance that the perfecting of the use in the fifteenth century coincides with the rising tide of a money economy and the advent of merchants and moniers among the lordships of landed estates.

The use undermined the feudal structure. An adroit gift to uses could deprive an overlord of much precious fruit. An estate owner *in articulo mortis* could give his estate to another to hold to the use of an heir yet in his minority. The gift would deprive the overlord of the benefits of wardship. By vesting an estate in a number of persons to hold to the use of a beneficiary, liability for relief could be postponed indefinitely.

Mortmain. Another process which deprived a feudal lord of the fruits of chivalry was the grant of land in mortmain. The dead hand of mortmain was at first the hand of communal religious bodies. Religious communities never died, never married, were always full-grown and seldom alienated their land. A monastery was a profitless tenant in the eye of a seigneur. A tenant's death was a savour of life to the feudal lord, and a tenant who never died touched the seignory with the chill hand of death. Not until the thirteenth century was any conscious expression given to the ill consequence of the fashionable gift of land to religious bodies. Provisions of Westminster led, in 1279, to the first mortmain statute, De Viris Religiosis.[44] The new law forbade gifts to religious bodies but did not preclude the king and other lords from a purposeful evasion of its protection. Hence, in practice, land passed legally into mortmain providing the licence

[44] Pollock and Maitland : op. cit. (Vol. I), p. 334.

of the king and the immediate overlord concerned accompanied and upheld the transaction.

A freer market among socage tenures. The mortmain laws, the doctrine of uses, the sensitiveness of common law towards seisin and the crisis of 1290 were all effects of the tension between the tenants and lords of military fiefs. The tenants were manoeuvring towards freedom of management and disposal. And the overlord, jealous of the fruits of chivalry, countered the moves point for point. As a consequence a land market did not develop easily at high social levels. Socage tenure, on the other hand, was freer. At this level signs of a vigorous land market are evident. The market in socage land was also probably due to the fact that socage was the tenure of the free peasantry. The noble classes would not be moved to sell estates for money : apart from financing a crusade or other military undertaking, there was little cause to convert land to money. The land was the hall-mark of aristocracy. The noble would only exchange land for land. But the peasant of the thirteenth century with free money in his pouch faced a prospect of many horizons, and among the fields of the vill the economic historian has discovered evidence of an early, widespread land market.

Disruption of the open-field regularity. The land market among the peasantry widened with the accelerated flow of money. The flow was swiftest in the immediate vicinity of markets and fairs, and the socage lands of the boroughs give the earliest evidence of a land market. Uniform tenements, scattered in fragments about the open-fields change in shape and size. Regularity gives place to irregularity. Plot has exchanged with plot. Strips once shy of each other have come together and lie engrossed in blocks. Movement is everywhere : "the market has mobilised the land."[45]

What was true of burghal fields soon became a common experience. As early as the thirteenth century the change has come to the St. Albans' manors. "On most of the St. Albans' manors it is clear that the break-up of the virgate as the normal holding, the growth of the custom of sub-letting, the beginning of a process of exchange in order to secure compact holdings and separate closes, the planting of hedges, and the sharing out of their timber and firewood, was in full swing by 1300 and can be traced back to 1250 or 1240".[46] The break-up of the regularity is everywhere in

[45] Maitland : *Township and Borough,* p. 66.
[46] Levett : *Studies in Manorial History,* p. 185.

evidence by the late fourteenth and early fifteenth centuries. Professor Tawney[47] makes much of this evidence, and argues the case for a virile land market and enclosure movement among the peasants which activated the plots in the fields of the vill throughout the fifteenth century.

Engrossing was often preceded by sub-division.[48] This fragmentation is more marked among the free tenements than among the virgates of the villeins,[49] probably because free socage land was less hampered by manorial custom. Manorial custom could fetter the sale of villein tenements and make the transaction dependent upon the sanction of the lord. This might be so even where a villein had a fee simple tenement among the manorial freelands.[50]

Early historians writing of economic processes unduly emphasized the existence of a nature economy. The comparatively rapid change to a money economy in later medieval times makes it difficult for them to account for the differences of wealth between villeins. In their eyes a villein was wholly dependent upon his villein tenement for subsistence, and villein tenements were equal to each other in size and barely sufficient to meet daily needs. The idea of a gradually developing land market among the peasants does not fit easily this straightened view of the economic and social order.

Modern knowledge needs no persuasion. The monetary aspect of villeinage makes a land market quite feasible. A normal virgater of a 30-acre virgate could have a useful balance of corn to market[51] after allowing for home consumption, seed and manorial levy. From early times villeins were hoarding corn to buy their freedom[52] and the more diligent could likewise accumulate money to invest in extra land. Rents did not alter where they were fixed by custom and the improved marketing of corn and wool would immediately increase the saving power of the peasant who held his land at a fixed rent. Above all, the human factor, the innate differences of persons, must have played a decisive part in the disruption of the stereotyped orthodoxy. One man would outwit and outwork his neighbour and profit thereby, whatever theory of equality governed their fortunes. The quick drop in population after the Black Death and the

[47] Tawney: *The Agrarian Problem in the 16th Century*, p. 72 et seq.
[48] Coulton: op. cit., p. 41. Levett: op. cit., p. 185.
[49] Neilson: *A Terrier of Fleet, Lincolnshire*, p. lxxii.
[50] Hilton: op. cit, p. 132.
[51] Bennett: op. cit., p. 89.
[52] Coulton: op. cit., p. 66.

steadier decline in the fifteenth century must have aided a redistribution of the land.[53]

Three types of leasehold.   The general disintegration of the old regularity was further accelerated by the creation of leaseholds. Medieval husbandry leases were of three types: the stock-and-land lease, the customary lease and the contractual lease at an economic rent. Economic historians and even legal historians have introduced the word "leasehold" into the medieval setting without any attempt to define it precisely. A loose, general convention has been unanimously, perhaps unwittingly, accepted: the leasehold is an interest in land created by *ad hoc* agreement, for a definite period. As such it stands aloof from tenancies at will or of indefinite duration, and apart from freeholds for life and inheritance.

Husbandry leaseholds were among the innovatory measures in the fundamental principles of estate management provoked by the labour problems of the fourteenth and fifteenth centuries.[54] An early form of lease was the "stock and land lease.[55] Husbandry in the early Middle Ages could not boast wealthy, stock-laden villeins and yeomen capable of equipping and financing enclosed demesne lands. Lords who were turning their minds towards a policy of letting the demesne had to face the prospect of providing both land and stock for their tenants. The stock-and-land lease was inevitable. Lords of manors departed from the old bailiff husbandry and let the entire demesne land, together with stock and seed, to willing and acceptable tenants. At first the role of the demesne in the manorial economy was little affected. Rents reserved by stock-and-land leases were produce rents and so as of old, the demesne land provided for the family larder. Stock-and-land leases at produce rents lingered long on monastic lands and this form of leasehold became associated with ecclesiastical corporations of the fifteenth and early sixteenth centuries. Savine[56] suggests that the hardening of social opinion against the monasteries in the late fifteenth century was, in some respects, responsible for the tardy change to money rents.

Customary leasehold is a paradoxical term. Customary leaseholds were a new species, a spontaneous generation and yet customary, grafted into what had been long established. Like the stock-and-

---

[53] Postan : op. cit., pp. 242, 243.
[54] cf. p. 144 ante.
[55] Lipson : op. cit., p. 119.
[56] Savine : *English Monasteries on the eve of the Dissolution*, pp. 154-165.

land lease, the customary lease was born of conflict, of the travail of landowners struggling to contain the demands of a new economic order within the confines of the old. Because customary leaseholds were entered upon the court rolls[57] of the manors they became tainted with the pigments of manorialism. They were not truly contractual. Custom and the manorial court intervened. And yet, these leaseholds unlike the custom of the manor are temporal creatures of time and hence of change. As old leases fell in and new ones were made, the terms of tenure changed. It is this elasticity which distinguishes customary leaseholds from true customary tenures. The decline in land values as a result of the population shrinkage of the fifteenth century makes bold the distinction. Premiums and rentals of husbandry leases dropped precipitously while the rents of customary tenures remained relatively constant. In fairness to customary tenures it should be noted that the slow demand for tenements reduced in the long run the entry fines and accelerated commutation.[58]

For practical purposes the customary lease was a useful instrument. Overlords, who for one reason or another did not let their demesnes as entire units, split the land into parcels among the customers of the vill. On the Forncett manors there was a definite change of policy: the demesne was at first let as an entire husbandry unit, and subsequently parcelled out in small leaseholds among the customary tenants.[59] Customary leaseholds were not confined to demesne land. Customary tenements themselves were let on lease and leasing became a widespread practice among assarts from woodland and waste. Leases, moreover, were not always the creations of the manorial overlord. His tenants leased land among themselves. On some manors this was frowned upon when it spread to the villeins. Manorial restriction upon the leasing of land was one of three major causes of rebellion in the early fourteenth century on the manor of Darnhall in Cheshire, when the tenants rose against their overlord, the Abbot of Vale Royal.[60]

There was a magic in the small customary leasehold: it turned the husbandman of the open-fields into a *farmer*. The *farms* of the medieval village were the leased plots for which the tenants

[57] cf. Davenport: op. cit., p. 53 n.
[58] Postan, op. cit., pp. 237, 238.
[59] Davenport: op. cit., p. 57.
[60] Hilton: op. cit., p. 129.

paid an inclusive money rent. "Farm" is an old word from Anglo-Norman England. Burghs were *farmed*, when they rendered an inclusive sum in lieu of tribute and other royal dues. Counties were farmed. Manors were farmed. And now the bits and pieces of the latter day manors are farmed; and rural England is populated by farmers. At first the overlords administered the new policy with care and hesitation, and farms were of short duration. Especially is this noticeable in some districts after the Black Death, 1349-50. Villeins and others were granted leases of land on the understanding that if and when anyone should come who was willing to take the land at the old customs the lease would determine. In Berkshire much land was let on nine-year leases as a consequence of the Plague and after the terms had expired the tenure reverted to customary tenure.[61]

In other shires the grip of the leaseholds never relaxed. A remarkable instance is again provided by the manors of Forncett: immediately after the Plague leases were granted for three years, but, as hope of recovering tenants on the old customs faded, the terms were gradually extended until the leaseholds became indeterminate, held in perpetuity.[62] Leasehold tenants holding land in perpetuity were said to hold it at fee farm. Fee farm is a mongrel growth. The attitude of the law towards it is difficult to trace. For the most part lands at fee farm seem to have been treated much the same as copyholds, entered upon the court rolls and conveyed from one tenant to another by surrender and admittance.[63]

The earliest documents show how the problems of present day agricultural leaseholds are in fact as old as the tenure itself. Tenant-right and dilapidations, the everyday anxieties of twentieth-century landlords, tenants and agents were common concerns on the manors of the thirteenth century. On the St Albans' manors a lease drawn in 1265 put a joint liability for hedges upon both lessor and lessee.[64] In 1307 a fine, recorded on the court roll of Hiperium, was imposed for breach of agreement to repair.[65] And at Wakefield in 1274 a reference to tenant-right is unmistakable: "Agnes, the wife of Philip atte Lidgate, claiming the right of the crop of a bovate of land of which she had been dispossessed was granted, not only the current year's crop from

[61] Levett: *The Black Death on the Estates of the See of Winchester*, p. 145.
[62] Davenport: op. cit., p. 77.
[63] Op. cit., p. 57.
[64] Levett: *Studies in Manorial History*, p. 187.
[65] Ruston and Witney: *Hooton Pagnell*, p. 336.

the cultivated land, of which she had been deprived, but also the next year's crop whether it was sown with wheat or barley, on account of her manure."[66]

The stock-and-land lease underwent a radical metamorphosis. From it emerged the contractual, economic agricultural lease, the ground of the traditional landlord and tenant system destined to become a bulwark of England's landed greatness. Little need be said of the process here. Historically it almost escapes the scope of this work. The commercialism of the late fifteenth century initiated it and Tudor enterprise and trade completed the process. The economic leasehold was the tenure of the great sheep ranches of the Tudor enclosures. Unlike the stock-and-land relationship, the tenants were capitalists, stocking and equipping the lands of their landlord. Like its parent stock, free contract was the essence of the tenure and distinguished it from feudal and customary tenures.

[66] Op. cit., p. 335.

CHAPTERS V AND VI

SELECT BIBLIOGRAPHY

Ballard, Adolphus: *The Manors of Witney, Brightwell and Downton* (Oxford Studies in Social and Legal History, 1916).
Bennett, H. S.: *Life on the English Manor, 1150-1400* (1948).
Cam, H. M.: *Liberties and Communities in Medieval England. Collected studies in local administration and topography* (1944).
Clapham, Sir John: *A Concise Economic History of Britain from the Earliest Times to 1750* (1949).
Coulton, G. C.: *The Medieval Village* (1925).
Davenport, Frances G.: *The Economic Development of a Norfolk Manor 1080-1565* (1906).
Denholm-Young, Noël: *Seignorial Administration in England* (1937).
Hilton, R. H.: *Peasant Movements in England before 1381* (Economic History Review, 2nd Series, Vol. II, 1949).
Holmes, G. A.: *The Estates of the Higher Nobility in XIV Century England* (1957).
Homans, G. C.: *English Villagers of the 13th Century* (1942).
Jolliffe, J. E. A.: *The Constitutional History of Medieval England from the English Settlement to 1485* (3rd Ed., 1954).
Kerridge, Eric: *Ridge and Furrow and Agrarian History* (Economic History Review, 2nd Series, Vol. IV, 1951).
Kosminsky, E. A.: *Studies in the Agrarian History of England in the Thirteenth Century* (1956).
Levett, A. E.: *Studies in Manorial History* (1938).
Levett, A. E.: *The Black Death on the Estates of the See of Winchester* (Oxford Studies in Social and Legal History, 1916).
Lipson, E.: *The Economic History of England*, Vol. I (8th Ed., 1945).
Maitland, Sir Frederic: *Selected Essays* ed. Hazeltine et al. (1936).
Maitland, Sir Frederic: *Township and Borough* (1898).
Myers, A. R.: *England in the Late Middle Ages* (Pelican History of England, Vol. IV, 1956).
Neilson, N.: *Customary Rents* (Oxford Studies in Social and Legal History, 1910).
Neilson, N.: *A Terrier of Fleet, Lincolnshire, from a manuscript in the British Museum* (1920).
Neilson, N.: *The Cartulary and Terrier of the Priory of Bilsington, Kent* (1928).
Orwin, C. S. and Orwin, C. S.: *The Open Fields* (2nd Ed., 1954).

Plucknett, T. F. T.: *Legislation of Edward I* (1949).

Plucknett, T. F. T.: *A Concise History of the Common Law* (5th Ed., 1956).

Plucknett, T. F. T.: *Statutes and their Interpretation in the 14th Century* (1922).

Plucknett, T. F. T.: *The Medieval Bailiff* (1954).

Pollock, Sir Frederick, and Maitland, Sir Frederic: *The History of English Law before the Time of Edward I.* Vols. I and II (2nd Ed., rep. 1952).

Poole, A. L.: *From Domesday Book to Magna Carta, 1087-1216* (2nd Ed., 1955).

Poole, A. L.: *Obligations of Society in the Thirteenth and Fourteenth Centuries* (1946).

Postan, M.: *The Manor in the Hundred Rolls* (Economic History Review, 2nd Series, Vol. III, 1950).

Postan, M.: *Some Economic Evidence of Declining Population in the later Middle Ages* (Economic History Review, 2nd Series, Vol. II, 1950).

Powicke, Sir Maurice: *The Thirteenth Century 1216-1307* (1953).

Round, J. H.: *Feudal England. Historical Studies on the XIth and XIIth Centuries* (1895).

Ruston, A. G., and Witney, D.: *Hooton Pagnell* (1934).

Savine: *English Monasteries on the eve of the Dissolution* (Oxford Studies in Social and Legal History, Vol. I, 1909).

Sayles, G. O.: *The Medieval Foundations of England* (2nd Ed., 1950).

Stenton, Lady: *English Society in the Early Middle Ages* (*1066-1307*), Pelican History of England, Vol. 3 (1951).

Stenton, Lady: *The Earliest Northamptonshire Assize Rolls A.D. 1202 and 1203* (1926).

Tawney, R. H.: *The Agrarian Problem in the 16th Century* (1912).

Vinogradoff, Sir Paul: *Villainage in England* (1892).

CHAPTER SEVEN

LAND IN THE BOROUGHS

Origin and nature of the borough. The story of the English borough is truly English. The beginning lies remote in the Old English *burh*, a fortress or fenced place. This remoteness has provoked conflict of opinion among historians. Maitland[1] seizes upon the Anglo-Saxon burh to construct his garrison theory which places the origin of the boroughs in the fortified tuns and great houses of Old England. The theory receives some support from later historians, notably Ballard,[2] and in a special sense from Stephenson,[3] but it is not widely accepted. The market vies with the fortress as the originator of the borough, and scores some success. Another approach to the problem conceives the borough as a logical outcome of the tun, expanding into an urban centre and developing in consequence a social structure and administration peculiar and appropriate to itself. These are the main avenues by which authoritative opinion[4] moves towards the problem. No one theory can claim pre-eminence.

The nature and essential character of the borough community are obscure. No one has succeeded in formulating a tenable definition of the early medieval borough. The ancient documents and medieval writers scatter the word "borough" too promiscuously for any investigator to say: here is the typical borough. In the thirteenth century, the golden age of borough creation, the term is used of a great variety of communities. A newly developed building estate is a borough. Hoar ancient and extensive communities, of which London, York and Norwich are examples, are boroughs. And the term is used of every conceivable variation of urban growth between these two extremes. The agrarian element which remained in the boroughs undoubtedly helped to blur the outlines of burghal character. To see the ancient borough through modern eyes as a compact urban centre with habitations cut clean

---

[1] Maitland: *Domesday Book and Beyond*, p. 184 et seq.
[2] Ballard: *The Domesday Boroughs*, p. 35; *The English Borough in the Twelfth Century*, pp. 66-70.
[3] Stephenson: *Borough and Town: A Study of Urban Origins in England*, p. 207.
[4] Tait: *The Medieval English Borough*, pp. 1-5.

from rural life is a fundamental mistake. The history of towns must not be unduly hurried by filling them too full.[5] Danger lies also at the other extreme. Tait[6] has entered a caveat against the over-weighted rural view of Stephenson, who sees the Anglo-Saxon borough as a rural community, living, acting and ordering itself in conformity with other rural communities but with the difference that it clusters about a fortress or defended strong-point and is a special sphere of royal administration. The desire for a clear, unequivocable definition cannot be satisfied. In a general sense, the borough can be regarded as an oasis of liberties breaking into the arid country of strict feudalism. What is found differs from place to place. There is no essential quality common to all boroughs, no irreducible minimum of liberties.[7] In consequence a brief study of the medieval borough can best be presented as an outline of burghal characteristics, any one or more of which may identify a community as a borough com-munity and distinguish it from a rural manor and vill.

Burghal privileges territorialized. The privileges and responsib-ilities of borough life are doubly important to a study of landownership. Not only were they vital aspects of borough life but to a large extent they became territorialized. Ownership of burghal land and tenements carried with it the privileges of borough life, and tenants of burgages, in their capacity as tenants, were invested with burghal status. The privileges may be classified as privileges of court; privileges of tenure; privileges of trading; and privileges of self-taxing and self-government. Although listed in this way, it must not be forgotten that only the foremost boroughs displayed examples of all classes of privilege, and within each class were variants peculiar to one or a few boroughs only.

Privileges of court. The origin of the borough court and the part it played in the saga of courts from the folkmoots of Old England to the clearly identifiable system of the later Middle Ages are profound subjects. The answers to the questions they provoke are caught up in a tangled skein of evidence, and much time and scholarship have been expended in attempts to give them.

Fortunately, for the present purpose these provocative perplexi-ties can be left on one side. The fact of jurisdictional privileges, a

---

[5] Maitland : *Township and Borough*, p. 24.   [6] Tait : op. cit., p. 27.
[7] Pollock and Maitland : *The History of English Law before the Time of Edward I* (Vol. 1), p. 635.

highly valued feature of burghal life, is apparent on the face of the borough charters which from the eleventh century onwards grant the liberty in favour of the burgesses.[8] These grants are irrefutable evidence of a court peculiar to the borough and standing apart from the ordinary system of popular courts. The core of the privilege is the right to plead only within the walls of the borough.[9] Privileges of this order were naturally limited by the competence of the borough court. Beside them, charters frequently gave other liberties which reduced the influence of the royal courts and their procedures within the boroughs. The main privileges were of two types: power to attach the pleas of the crown,[10] and the right to the return of writs.[11] Both were introduced in the thirteenth century. The attachment of pleas enabled the burgesses before the arrival of the king's justices in the borough to arrest and take sureties from culprits summoned by the justices. The return of writs vested in the burgesses the right to execute the precepts of royal writs in lieu of the sheriff or other royal officer.

The degree to which the burden of suit to the borough court pressed upon the shoulders of burgesses is difficult to ascertain.[12] Probably in the distant past the obligation had a wider incidence than the evidence of post-Conquest charters reveals. The view taken by Bateson[13] imposes a general duty upon all burgesses to attend the great assemblies of the boroughs, held once, twice or thrice a year, but excuses them from the regular interim courts corresponding to the normal meetings of hundred courts, unless specially summoned. Liability to summons may have been a characteristic of all burgesses enjoying the privilege of a borough court, and in this sense it can be said they owed suit of court. Attendance at court did not carry with it in thirteenth century London and elsewhere the responsibility of deeming dooms; an aldermanic bench of judges had come to judgment and a panel of specially summoned assessors gave verdicts upon the judgment of the aldermen.[14]

The prerogative of the borough court was in many of the larger boroughs broken by incisions of foreign jurisdiction. Lords and lesser freemen had rights of sake and soke within the borough.

---

[8] Ballard: *British Borough Charters 1042-1216*, p. liii.
[9] Pollock and Maitland: op. cit., p. 643.
[10] Ballard and Tait: *British Borough Charters 1216-1307*, p. lx.
[11] Op. cit., p. lxi.
[12] Maitland: *Domesday Book and Beyond*, p. 211.
[13] Bateson: *Borough Customs* (Vol. II). p. cxlvi.
[14] Op. cit., p. cxlviii.

These autonomies varied in size and seriousness. Great places often had large isolated *sokens* within the boundaries of which the burgesses were the justiciables of the lord of the soken.[15] Rural landowners who had houses within a borough but appurtenant to a rural estate exercised rights of jurisdiction over the occupiers and took them apart from the general burghal jurisdiction. A common feature of borough jurisdiction was a right of sake and soke vesting in burgesses severally, in respect of their individual houses. References to this privilege in Domesday Book and elsewhere have occasioned much cogitation. The most reasonable theory conceives the privilege as the right to settle disputes out of court, when grievances or crimes within the jurisdiction of the borough court were committed in the house or other place over which the privileged burgess had sake and soke.[16]

Tenurial privilege. The advantages of tenure which burgesses enjoyed are, of course, the main theme of landownership in the boroughs. Mention is made of them here merely to list the privilege among the others. The privilege is more particularly considered later on.

Mercantile privileges. Mercantile privileges are the pride and boast of the medieval burgher. Trading monopolies had been features of the burhs and ports of Old England, but they were not secured by the gild merchant, the fraternal and commercial organisation so characteristic of Angevin and later boroughs. The trading privileges enjoyed by the burgesses of the Old English boroughs were the outcome of the early markets which had grown up in the peace of the burhs and ports. Wealth had gravitated to the nascent urban centres, and society within them became more commercialized and viable than the society of the rural tuns. The king's ban that created the wealth was not freely given; the royal exchequer benefited by tolls levied upon traders within the privileged places. Receipt of toll became a royal franchise. The royal hand could assign the benefit of the receipt of toll or remove the burden of payment.

Freedom from toll was to become in post-Conquest England the essential content of mercantile privilege in the boroughs, but there are hints of exemptions being allowed as early as the ninth century. Lack of evidence for the gild merchant in Anglo-Saxon

[15] Ballard: *The English Borough in the Twelfth Century*, p. 53.
[16] Ballard: *British Borough Charters* 1042-1216, p. liv.

days is probably a reliable indication that freedom from toll was
seldom vested in burgesses at large. Gild associations were known
to the Saxons, especially in later days. Gilds formed in the burhs,[17]
and in tenth century London a *frithgild* came into being to enforce
royal ordinances against cattle-thieves,[18] but nowhere was there
anything suggestive of a gild merchant. The gild merchant was
a practical expression of the enjoyment of legal immunity from
royal tolls. The right to a gild merchant was granted by charter
in favour of the burgesses of the borough in which the gild was
established. Exemption from toll was confirmed and strengthened
in a practical way by permitting all burgesses, who wished to
trade and take advantage of the immunity, to associate together
and organize themselves for the purpose. The wider the range of
privileges the greater the necessity for a gild merchant. It was
quite usual for the trading privilege to extend to other boroughs
besides the home borough, and the burgesses of some boroughs
enjoyed freedom from toll throughout the entire kingdom.

The corpus of gildsmen within a borough was not necessarily
identical with the borough community. A gildsman was not
always a burgess and a burgess was not always a gildsman.[19] A
view taken by Lipson[20] sees the gradual merger of the two fundamental institutions of gild and burghal commonalty; the
commonalty was subsumed by the former, and the trading elite
sat in the seats of government. A gild merchant was not an
invariable feature of boroughs. Many great cities, notably
Norwich and London, appear never to have possessed one. That
does not mean that the burgesses of those cities had no mercantile monopolies and trading privileges. The essential quality of the
borough trading privilege was freedom from toll and the right to
establish a gild merchant was only a particular expression of that
privilege.

Privileges of self-government. All burghal liberties were concessions to freedom at the expense of feudal suzerainty. They
called forth, in one way or another, policies protecting their
freedom against the feudal interests which ever threatened to
appropriate the emancipated territory. The greater the degree of
autonomy the greater was the need for vigilance and the firmer
were the measures taken. In highly privileged boroughs the

[17] Pollock and Maitland : op. cit., p. 639.
[18] Stephenson : op. cit., p. 64.
[19] Pollock and Maitland : op. cit., p. 667.
[20] Lipson : *The Economic History of England* (Vol. I), pp. 277, 278.

generous liberties led to the creation of local governing authorities. In early constitutions the borough court and gild merchant shared the administrative and organising responsibility, or the borough court reigned supreme. By the thirteenth century duality of government tended to give place to a unity under the mayor of the borough. The complicated history of constitutional development is not relevant to the land story. All that is required here is to note that a burgess with few exceptions was a member of a community which enjoyed local governmental autonomy.

Governmental authority was probably legislative and administrative in some boroughs. Little is known of the making of bye-laws. Maitland[21] sees evidence of governmental authority in the borough customs, but he hesitates to pronounce a word suggestive of legislative authority beyond a "necessary definition and development of ancient customs". Where a charter in 1188[22] gave to the burgesses of Bristol the right to improve their dwellings provided no damage was done to borough or township, some authority had to provide a code of principles or bye-laws giving expression to the privilege. The famous assize of Fitz-Alwyne, passed in London a year later, appears to be a code of bye-laws of similar intention; it has stringent prohibitions and rules regulating the erection of houses.[23]

Self-government was fostered when the burgesses were permitted to farm the borough. Instead of the sheriff or other royal officer intruding upon the privacy of the burgesses in the collection of the royal dues, elected bailiffs of the borough pay a farm to be quit of the sheriff and collect burghal dues from their fellow burgesses to defray the expense.

Privileges of self-taxation. Farming the borough does not imply a power of self-taxation. The right to raise money for building and maintaining walls and bridges, paving streets and other public utilities is not inherent in any of the normal liberties granted to burgesses; although Maitland thinks common law could not reject a claim by the burgesses of a borough to tallage themselves.[24] Specific power of self-taxation is the gift of kings. Sometimes in charters, but more frequently by royal letters patent,[25] a borough receives authority to levy murage to meet the cost of walling, or pontage for bridging, or pavage for paving. At first sight power

---

[21] Pollock and Maitland : op. cit., p. 662.
[22] Ballard : op. cit., p. 50.
[23] Pollock and Maitland : op. cit., p. 660.
[24] Op. cit., p. 663.
[25] Ballard and Tait : op. cit., p. xix.

of self-taxation seems a dubious blessing. But the privilege virtually means permission to spend money on improving the borough which otherwise would go to the king as tallage or other payment. But there is another side to the picture; borough improvement could be compulsory, especially the burden of bettering the walls and ramparts, and building the castle.[26] It is on record how the king was moved to admonish the authorities of certain boroughs because of neglect to pave and remove nuisances.[27]

The lord of the borough is not the feudal lord of its land. The establishment of boroughs by granting burghal privileges set up a system of proprietary interests that cut across the strict feudal proprietorships. Kingly sanctions of market, mint, court and so forth are expressions of royal prerogative, not acts of a feudal lord. Although the burgesses look to the king for their burghal privileges, and in that sense acknowledge him as lord of the borough, they are not invariably the immediate feudal tenants of the royal lord. Mesne feudal lordships remain within the borough. Burgesses owning suit of court and service to a rural lord are nonetheless burgesses. Their neighbours might be tenants of another lord, or king's men residing on royal demesne. This admixture of tenure led Maitland to coin the expression "tenurial heterogeneity"[28] and Ballard the term "composite borough."[29] Lack of homogeneity was a characteristic of the ancient boroughs, nurtured through the centuries of Old England in the lap of royal favour, and to the commissioners of Domesday it was an inscrutable riddle.

With few exceptions the ancient royal boroughs grew within the abandoned walls of deserted Roman cities. They provided a pattern and inspiration for the borough-creators of later days.[30] There were great differences between the ancient royal boroughs, the charter boroughs of later Saxon England created on *terra regis* by the King, and the crop of charter boroughs that blossomed in Norman and Angevin times. Differences were not only differences of origin. There were proprietary differences. Charter boroughs were, with few exceptions, proprietary interests of their creators, and wholly within their seignories. This was true whether the hand that sealed the

26 Tait : op. cit., p. 171.
27 Ballard and Tait : op. cit., p. lxxiii.
28 Maitland : op. cit.. p. 179.
29 Ballard : *The English Borough in the Twelfth Century*, p. 39.
30 Op. cit., p. 75.

charter was the royal hand or the hand of a lay or ecclesiastical lord. Boroughs are, therefore, capable of classification as ancient royal boroughs; royal boroughs standing wholly on *terra regis* or royal demesne; and seignorial boroughs. Of the boroughs in the last two classes, the lord of the borough revenues was also lord of the land on which the borough stood.

Mediatised boroughs. Borough revenues were valuable. In Old England they were often shared between the king and an earl, on a two to one basis; the earl was said to take the third penny. Saxon kings kept the boroughs in their own hands, a reason, Tait thinks,[31] for the dearth of borough charters in the years before the Conquest. But the Norman kings mediatised the royal boroughs. The boroughs were granted to high dignitaries as a mark of royal favour. Mediatisation meant a further complication of proprietary systems. Lords of boroughs, who were not in the strict sense territorial lords, stood between the king and the burgesses.

The benefits and risk of borough creation. By the thirteenth and fourteenth centuries the creation of boroughs had become common practice in land administration and estate management. Admittedly, a vill and its population benefited when king or lesser lord exalted the place to burghal rank. But it was not done for nothing. There was another side to the bargain. Lords were not wont to be moved by altruism. Profit and reward were behind their policies. Burgesses paid handsomely for borough charters and the privileges they bestowed. The rise and fall of kingly fortunes often corresponded with fluctuations in the rates of charter-mongering. A spate of charters granting the right to farm the borough in fee attended the financing of the crusades of Richard I.[31a]

What was given up in the creation of a borough must be set against what was gained from the action. A feudal lord would surrender rights of seignory but in return he would gain a valuable source of increasing revenue. Commerce and wealth grew within the liberties of the borough. Moreover, borough activity helped defence. When William the Lion built a castle at Ayr, he established a borough community at its gates so that the market would prove a supply base for the garrison.[32] Some charters expressly require burgesses to garrison the castle in time of war

[31] Tait : op. cit., p. 2.
[31a] Op. cit., p. 177.
[32] Ballard : op. cit., p. 23.

and in time of peace provide watching and riding services.[33] Borough creation could be the most expeditious and successful way of colonising and settling virgin land. Borough privileges with special taxation concessions were offered in one case as attractions to potential settlers.[34] Income from the land must have multiplied many times when a vill became a borough and developed a successful burghal life.

Making a borough involved risk. The enterprise was not always successful. A lord's feudal rights were at stake and might be impaired with little or no gain to himself. Townships once proud with burghal life are known to have lapsed to unprivileged communities. In one case at least the entire burghal community vanished and the burghal land became the land of a single agricultural holding.[35] A great decline is noticed among the lesser boroughs in the fourteenth century. Many became *villae mercatoriae*, mere market towns.[36] The greater boroughs were advanced at the expense of the lesser and the most favoured became the cities of medieval England.[37]

BOROUGH TENURE

Borough tenure the outcome of burghal freedom. Throughout the complexities of borough development an underlying movement is discernible. Borough life revolves round the garrison and the market in the beginning, and becomes increasingly commercial with the passage of time. Whether soldiering or selling predominated, the life of the borough worked loose from agrarian ways. This detachment led to the growth of a land tenure peculiar to the boroughs. The ordinary tun or vill was predial at heart because it was agricultural. And because it was predial, tenants were one with the soil; when they spoke of labour service their speech was of work among the fields and the woodlands. All men of the vill were not *adscriptus glebae*; socage tenants were free, but they were rarities. The detachment of the borough from agrarian ways lifted its life above the predial. Burgesses still had plots in the common arable fields beyond the gates, but the borough as a whole was free and within its walls there evolved a free tenure. The great contri-

[33] Ballard : op. cit., p. 24.
[34] Ballard : *British Borough Charters 1042-1216*, p. liii.
[35] Ballard and Tait : op. cit., p. lv.
[36] Tait : op. cit, p. 205.
[37] Pollock and Maitland : op. cit., p. 634.

bution which the freedom of borough life brings to the lands of England is borough tenure. This tenure has traits and behaviourisms peculiar to itself and stands apart, if not aloof, from the orders of feudal tenure.

Money rent a basic feature of borough tenure. Money rent was a most endearing and enduring feature of borough tenure, and its earliest glory. The tenure was unknown by name in Anglo-Saxon days. Some[38] would deny its very existence. But the burhs of Old England were familiar enough with a money rent called *landgable* and in this Tait[39] sees the Saxon precursor of the Norman borough tenure.

Money rent was a logical development with the commercial activity, military character and social structure of the early burhs. Maitland[40] peoples the royal and ancient boroughs of Old England with warriors who enact the drama of his garrison theory. They are the king's militia within the king's burh, the fortress which defends the county, but they come from the wide-flung lands of the county; the county supports the burh and the burh defends the county. The folkright imposes upon all lands the three-fold obligation of borough bettering, bridge building and fighting in the king's host.[40a] To discharge these duties the landowners of the shire send militia and retainers to live in the burh. The barracks of the burhs are part and parcel of the lands which contribute the militia, and the landownership pattern in the burhs is in consequence a microcosm of the lands and titles of the county. So runs Maitland's thought. Later historians have questioned the soundness of this theory. None however deny the contributory principle[41] although its essential military character has been challenged.[42] The principle itself is what is important in the development of borough tenure, and in particular monetary rent. Distance weakened communication between the barracks of the burh and the contributory lands. As burghal life organised itself under the patronage and dominance of the king the link became weaker still. By the eleventh century many of the erstwhile military houses were occupied by merchants and chapmen paying money rent to the parent lordships.[43] The purpose here is not to suggest that the contributory principle initiated money rents in the boroughs;

[38] Tait: op. cit., p. 4.   [39] Op. cit, pp. 96, 97.
[40] Maitland: op. cit., p. 180 et seq.
[40a] ante p. 55.   [41] Ballard: *The Domesday Boroughs*, p. 14.
[42] Tait: op. cit., p. 31.
[43] Maitland: op. cit., pp. 189-196.

it did not. Domesday gives evidence of renders in kind sent from tenements within the borough to outlying parent lands. The contributory principle is important because its inherent relationships made money rents logical and profitable and because it introduced heterogeneity of tenure within the borough. This promiscuity raised questions of lordship, especially in the minds of the feudal lawyers[44] who were doubly perplexed by tenements within the ancient burhs which were neither part of the original tun nor contributed places. Tradition seems to have established the principle that such properties stood upon the royal demesne, and there the occupants paid a money rent known as landgable or hawgable into the royal hand.[45]

Ballard[46] calls the ancient royal boroughs with their hetero-geneous tenure, composite boroughs, and distinguishes them from simple boroughs. Simple boroughs are those created by charter upon the royal demesne or the fiefs of mesne lords. In them were neither contributed places nor a confusion of lordships. The simple boroughs were glorified manorial structures. Borough tenure with its money rent did not grow intrinsically within their walls. It was a gift, along with other burghal privileges, conveyed by the royal or seignorial charter that created the borough. Indeed, minor boroughs might be nothing more than vills in which free borough tenure had been by charter substituted for villein tenure and free socage.[47] Borough tenure in the simple boroughs was patterned upon the tenure in the composite boroughs; it shone with a borrowed light.

Twofold nature of the money rent. Money rent in the boroughs had a double nature. In part it was the ancient landgable, in part a money payment reserved from burgages as a condition and consideration of sale or lease.[48] The division was probably of late development, although the description of the customs of Buckingham in Domesday Book points, with great clarity, to money payments of two different types.

"In this borough the Bishop of Constances has three burges-ses whom Ulward Fitz Edith held; they render 6s. 6d. and to the king 11d. Hugh has 1 burgess formerly the man of Burcard of Shenley: he renders 20d. and to the king 5d."[49]

[44] Pollock and Maitland : op. cit., p. 638.
[45] Maitland : *Township and Borough,* pp. 70. 71.
[46] Ballard : op. cit., p. 7.
[47] Ballard and Tait : op. cit., p. liv.
[48] Hemmeon : *Burgage Tenure in Medieval England,* p. 80 et seq.
[49] cf. Ballard's quote : *The Domesday Boroughs,* p. 72.

Ballard interprets this entry to mean that the payments to the Lord Bishop and Hugh, the earl, were true gable because they were rendered to the mesne landowners and not the king, as were the lesser payments. Nevertheless, the payments to the king of 11d. from 3 burgesses and 5d. from another are remarkably similar to the landgable payments discovered by Hemmeon[50] among the evidence of a hundred different boroughs. Landgable was ancient and boasts a lineage from the early days of borough growth under the Saxon kings. It was, in common with so much else of borough life, a precedent for the guidance and policies of future days. The new chartered boroughs of Norman and later times paid gable, a burgage rental payment constant and uniform throughout the borough area. If the origin of the gable had been the occasion of free Saxon burgesses seeking lords and offering payment in consideration of vassalage and protection, it is fairly certain the creators of thirteenth century and later boroughs knew nothing of it. For them it was sufficient that the kings of old had had gable from the tenements of the borough, and hence the kings of their day can demand similar payments from the burgesses of the new creations. Lesser lords follow the king in this. Mesne lords who create boroughs specify in the charters the burgage rents, which are in consequence uniform and fixed.

Uniformity of rentals was not evident in the old traditional boroughs, with the exception of the boroughs in the Danelaw. In no case was payment high.[51] In some boroughs it was not paid at all. Receipt of landgable was one of the regalities the king could give away and when he mediated a royal borough the new lord of the borough received the landgable. Frequently the king is found sharing the gable with the earl. The landgable was immune from the pressure of economic forces. There is no identifiable relationship between the amount of landgable and the value of the tenements as reflected in the rents and sale prices of the land market within the boroughs.[52] Rents, however, are not very reliable guides. In many cases they were mere nominal renders or payments reserved by the vendor after conveying the tenement for a premium or other capital sum.

Money-rent was the hall-mark of burgage tenure. As a general principle the conversion of a vill to a borough involved commutation of all manorial services to money payments,[53] and the

---

[50] Hemmeon : op. cit., pp. 67-70.   [51] Op. cit., p. 165.
[52] Op. cit., p. 80.
[53] Pollock and Maitland : op. cit., p. 645.

newly created burgess became one with the company of all free tenants of England.[54]

Services in addition to money rent. In some boroughs traces of the husbandry days lingered on. Tenants, though burgesses, were required to render agricultural service to the contributing manors to which their tenements were appurtenant. The evidence suggests that these reminders of a past rusticity were not heavy burdens, although at Tamworth the burgesses "worked as other villeins."[55] More frequent were renders in kind made by tenements in a borough to their parent manors. Some burgesses sent plough-shares as house rent;[56] others salmon or herrings or eels; corn was sent from mills and salt from salt pans.[57] Although Ballard can trace little evidence of the ancient obligation to "better the borough" among the charters of twelfth century boroughs,[58] there appear to be a number of references in Domesday to military obligations and services of other kinds rendered by burgesses. For example, at Warwick it was provided "that when the king went on an expedition by land 10 burgesses of Warwick went for all."[59] Customs of other boroughs provide for naval service, riding service and hunting assistance. It is difficult to tell, however, whether these services were rendered to the king as lord of the borough or as territorial lord of the borough tenements. In some cases the answer is fairly clear from the nature of the service; thus the custom of Hereford which required all "who dwelt within the wall" to reap and gather hay must refer to the service of tenure.

Time simplifies the tenurial pattern. The confusion of tenures which existed in the composite boroughs between lords many and tenants many and the borough lordship of the king clarifies with the passage of time. The original state of affairs was undoubtedly different from the picture revealed when the mists clear in the early fourteenth century. Tenure by then had gravitated either towards the king, and he appears as feudal lord, or towards the farmers of the borough who held the borough from him. Mesne tenures had almost vanished. Maitland in one place[60] ascribes the disappearance of mesne tenure to the prevalence of

[54] Tait : op. cit., p. 82.
[55] Ballard : op. cit., p. 57.
[56] Op. cit., p. 79.   [57] Op. cit.. p. 79.
[58] Ballard : *The English Borough in the Twelfth Century*, p. 16.
[59] Ballard : *The Domesday Boroughs*, p. 80.
[60] Maitland : op. cit., p. 74.

the landgable. Great lords of rural lands pay landgable to the bailiffs of the king's boroughs in respect of contributed tenements within the boroughs. The money rents which bound the contributed places to the rural manors had sunk into insignificance and had been forgotten, and the bailiffs accept the landgable as rent due to the king from a tenant in demesne. In another place[61] he suggests the disappearance is a consequence of the strengthening of the borough court and the burghal right to plead within the walls; seignorial justice, a concomitant of feudal tenure, is undermined and with it the tenurial relationship. The passing of mesne tenures is in line with what was taking place on a general and grand scale among all feudal tenures since Quia Emptores 1290.

Whether borough tenure was a species of socage tenure or another free tenure in its own right is not altogether clear. Maitland and Pollock[62] tend to see it as a tenure apart, but opinions differ. Some[63] are more certain than the legal historians; others[64] are against them altogether and regard burgage tenure as a variety of socage.

Feudal incidents and manorial privileges. The freedom of borough tenure creates too rarefied an atmosphere for feudal incidents to flourish and the decline of mesne tenures also has a withering effect upon them.[65] Freedom, however, is not so perfect as to render the borough tenure entirely clear of all incidents. Feudal aids, *per se*, are of little significance until they appear re-incarnate as royal taxes levied upon the larger and more important boroughs. Relief and heriot are known, mostly among the lesser and agricultural boroughs; they linger in the customs of seignorial charters, but the heriot is not the villein heriot but the ancient Saxon levy of arms.[66] Restraint on marriage, where it exists, does not follow the paternal ideal of the tenures in chivalry but is reflected in the obligation to pay the abhorred merchet of the villein classes. Wardship also is not chivalrous; guardianship vests, according to borough custom, in borough officials, or next of kin or by *ad hoc* devise.[67] Escheat has little chance of survival; not only are mesne tenures becoming

[61] Pollock and Maitland : op. cit., p. 646.
[62] Op. cit., p. 295.
[63] Hemmeon : op. cit.. p. 4.
[64] Ballard : *The English Borough in the Twelfth Century*, p. 3.
[65] Maitland : op. cit., p. 71.
[66] Tait : op. cit., p. 99.
[67] Bateson : op. cit., p. cxxviii.

obscure but the burgess has liberty of devise and can create an heir where none existed otherwise at law. As a general rule, lands of burgesses dying intestate without heirs pass to the immediate feudal lord,[68] a principle that works in the king's favour when the whereabouts of mesne tenures become difficult to locate.[69] Forfeiture for felony is general although modified by borough circumstances. The oath of fealty is sworn to a feudal lord by all burgesses and not only on personal grounds: the burgess-oath is to be loyal to the borough customs and the lord of the borough.[70] Homage is alien to burgage freedom.

Parallel with the survival of feudal incidents run remnants of what can only be regarded as manorial privileges. The transmutation of a villein or freeholding peasant to a burgess is not an absolute conversion. The golden light of harvest lingers long in the memory and the burgess holds in high esteem ancient rights from the open-fields and manorial wastes. Rights of common of pasture are frequent; other rights of cutting timber, fishing,[71] and hunting in the greenwood[72] belong to the burgess in his capacity as burgess and are not to be confused with the rights appendant and appurtenant to the holdings in the open-fields of the borough. The arable shell of the borough is not true borough land[73] and privileges of pasturage, fishing and the like are appurtenant to the burgage tenements by prescription or charter gift.

Burgages the building plots of medieval urban development. Borough tenure in the nomenclature of Old English references was "burgage." In later days when great men are creating boroughs upon their estates, the word burgage denotes a building plot or tenement.[74] The burgages of medieval boroughs illustrate one of the timeless principles of urban development. A landowner of the twentieth century setting out a housing estate on the outskirts of Burton-on-Trent would be of one mind with the founders of that borough in the Middle Ages, who carried out the intention of the original charter which prescribed the length and breadth of the burgages or building plots that first broke the rural alignments.[75]

The similitude between modern urban estate development

---

[68] Hemmeon: op. cit., p. 24.
[69] Pollock and Maitland: op. cit., p. 646.
[70] Hemmeon: op. cit., p. 46.
[71] Ballard: *British Borough Charters 1042-1216*, p. xlv.
[72] Op. cit., p. xlvii.   [73] Tait: op. cit., p. 89.
[74] Op. cit., p. 99.   [75] Ballard, op. cit., p. xlv.

and the foundation layouts of the new boroughs of the twelfth and thirteenth centuries is most remarkable. Small areas were cut up into what were virtually building plots and burgesses were encouraged to take up the plots. Some charters restrict the size of the plots by prescribing a maximum area[76] or fixing the frontage.[77] Nascent development values were apparent even among the landgable. Although landgable was fixed in amount and immune from economic pressures,[78] differences in site values are evinced by the rents as originally determined; at Hereford the rent of a tenement within the wall was 7½d and outside 3½d;[79] at Scarborough rents of plots where house development was parallel with the street were 6d, while narrow plots confining the frontage to the gable-end were 4d.[80] And Maitland imagines ribbon development creeping out of thirteenth century Cambridge towards Newnham.[81] Borough development differed from the estate development of modern towns, in that the latter knows nothing of the establishment of borough courts. When the thirteenth century Abbot of Eynsham created the borough of Eynsham he selected a site of some twenty acres, divided it into plots or burgages and set up a court for the handful of burgesses who came to settle upon the twenty acres.[82]

Building covenants. The building covenants of modern estates also have antecedents in the principles of borough establishment. At one place the borough charter imposes time limits within which the burgages had to be built upon;[83] and at another, similar obligations are the substance of conveyances granting building plots to developers.[84] Burghers were permitted to enlarge and alter their burgages in London provided no damage was occasioned to the borough interests.[85] Common law seems to have required burgesses to repair the roadway in front of their plots for the benefit of the community.[86] Certain tenements in the ancient boroughs carried exclusively the burden of repairing the borough walls and bridges. And the repair and maintenance of "castles,

---

[76] Tait: op. cit., p. 7.
[77] Ballard: op. cit., p. xlv.
[78] cf. p. 169 ante.
[79] Ballard: *The Domesday Boroughs*, p. 72.
[80] Ballard: *British Borough Charters 1042-1216*, p. xliv.
[81] Maitland: op. cit., p. 52.
[82] Ballard: *The English Borough in the Twelfth Century*, p. 32.
[83] Ballard: *British Borough Charters 1042-1216*, p. xlv.
[84] Op. cit., p. civ.
[85] Bateson: op. cit. (Vol. I), p. 279.
[86] Maitland: op. cit., p. 79.

walls, ditches, parks, bridges and causeways" fell in some boroughs as a burden on the burgesses in general.[87]

Apart from the common obligations of borough tenure and the local rates and requirements of bye-laws already noted,[88] the freemen of the borough had to meet the Danegeld or its equivalent in the form of royal aids and tallages.[89] The boroughs were woven into the hundred system for assessment to the geld; some were of hundredal rank in themselves but the smaller of them were assessed with the hidage of the hundreds in which they stood.

Freedom to alienate and devise. Freedom's greatest gift to the burgess, that which marked his tenure as one more privileged than the tenures of chivalry, was the right of alienation and devise. Burgages passed from hand to hand with great facility, and with a heightening rapidity as movement in land speculation quickened. The degree of freedom varied with the borough customs. A greater freedom of sale usually matched a greater freedom of devise. The most formidable restraint was the *retrait lignager*, which permitted a burgess's kin to re-purchase an inheritable tenement sold by him without their consent. The limitation virtually gave the kin a right of pre-emption and in some boroughs where the *retrait lignager* was operative, right of free sale was narrowed to lands of purchase only, as distinct from land of inheritance.[90] The two different categories were important also in connection with the burgess's powers of devise. Freedom of devise was no common privilege. Some boroughs knew nothing of it,[91] and others enjoyed only the limited power to devise lands acquired by purchase.[92] At Northampton rights of alienation were trammelled by the *retrait feodal*, which amounted to a right of pre-emption vesting in the lord of the land. At Nottingham there were two boroughs, one English, the other French. The principle of inheritance within the former gave the burgage to the youngest son and was distinguished from the custom of the French borough by referring to it as the custom of *borough English*; a title which subsequently embraced other tenures where the inheritance passed to the youngest son.[93]

All privileges summed up as borough customs were in fact

---

[87] Tait : op cit., p. 98. [88] pp. 170, 171 ante.
[89] Ballard : op. cit., p. lxxx.
[90] Hemmeon : op. cit., p. 111.
[91] Op. cit., p. 135. [92] Op. cit., p. 135.
[93] Pollock and Maitland : op. cit., p. 647.

tenurial privileges. The custom of the borough ran with the burgage or tenement and was not personal to the burgess.[94]

THE GROWTH OF CORPORATENESS

Factors making for corporateness. Medieval boroughs had personality and bodiliness. The borough was corporate. There was a selfhood greater than the mere association of the burgesses. In the beginning it was not so. Growth moved in step with the whole process of borough development. Mature corporateness did not blossom until late in the Middle Ages. The process is important for landownership because the incorporate borough came to be, in its own person, a controller of the pattern of ownership within the area of borough jurisdiction, by acquiring power to make and impose bye-laws and levy rates and other burdens. And moreover, the borough in its corporateness became a landowner among landowners.

The history of early corporations is shadowy and abstract. It is only possible here to note the factors in borough life and structure which initiated and prospered the development of corporateness. There is no unanimity of opinion but, allowing for the change of stress under the pens of different writers, the salient factors appear to be the granting of the *firma burgi*; the establishment of the gild merchant; the existence and functions of the borough court; granting of privileges to burgesses as a whole; and the holding of a common purse.

The firma burgi. The *firma burgi* was the farm of the borough. For the privilege of stepping into the shoes of the collector of income from the borough, lump sums were paid annually to the king or the sheriff of the county in which the borough stood. The principle was in all respects the same as that followed when manors, vills, mines and other income-producing properties were farmed.[95] The borough attracted premiums or *gersumae* over and above what must be regarded as the fair market quotation of the rent;[96] a fact which suggests the farmer could not avoid being an extortioner towards the individual burgesses who would use every expedient and offer willing sacrifices to have the matter in their own hands.

The sheriff as the king's representative often farmed the

[94] Tait : op. cit., p. 90.   [95] ante p. 154.
[96] Ballard : op. cit., p. lxxvi.

borough of the county himself. He and other private farmers were ousted from the financial affairs of a borough when the farm was granted to the burgesses themselves. To acquire the farm of the borough became a set purpose of every borough, and its acquisition a highly coveted liberty. The greatest freedom derived from a lease or farm of a borough direct from the king to the burgesses. The earliest recorded farm in the hands of burgesses is the Domesday Book description of Northampton, but this was not an immediate grant from the king; the sheriff of the county was the lord of the borough and farmed it to the burgesses, and whether the grant was in favour of the whole body of burgesses or only a few privileged people is not certain.[97] The first known direct grant was made to the burgesses of Lincoln in 1130.[98] Farms were granted for a term of years absolute or were grants revocable at the instance of the royal will.[99] Not until the reign of Richard I was it the practice of the king to grant the farm of a borough to the burgesses in fee.[100] Fee farm rents from the boroughs became a regular entry in the Royal Exchequer from that time onwards. Nevertheless fee farm rents were not exclusively a privilege of royal boroughs for mesne lords offered seignorial boroughs in similar manner.[101]

The story of land tenure within the boroughs moves with uncertainty as a consequence of the policy of granting the farm of the borough in fee to the burgesses. The words of gift in the charters are absolute, as exemplified by a charter of 1155 in favour of the citizens of Lincoln:

"Know ye that I have delivered my city of Lincoln to my citizens of the said city at that farm at which it was wont to be in the time of King Henry my grandfather with all the liberties and customs to the said city pertaining within the city and without."[102]

On the face of it the charter purports to give all that the king has to give of royal interest, privilege or prerogative in Lincoln and in the grand sweep of its generosity includes the landed demesne of the king. If this were so, the citizen grantees would become tenants-in-chief of the king and tenants in demesne of all waste places, markets, streets, walls, commons, woodlands and all else that pertained to wastes and commons, and into their custody

[97] Ballard : op. cit, p. lxxv.
[98] Tait : op. cit., p. 140.
[99] Op. cit., p. 162, et seq.   [100] Op. cit., p. 179.
[101] Ballard and Tait : op. cit., p. lxxxii.
[102] Ballard : op. cit., p. 221.

would fall the escheats of burgage tenements. So the charters make things appear. But practice points another way. Maitland is confident of this. He could see no interpolation of mesne tenure between the king and high tenants-in-chief in favour of the burghal community.[103] And so the situation appears to Ballard and Tait[104] although they strike a note of caution by referring to the support of the opposite doctrine by the Crown in 1330 when the matter was at issue in Norwich. The date in this case is advanced and it is not impossible to conceive at Norwich the working of circumstances towards a reversal of the original position; this certainly came about at Cambridge in the next century. Curiously enough, it was in the same year, 1330, that the tale of Cambridge begins.[105] The townsfolk petitioned the king for licence to use the waste ground of the town for their own purposes, evidence enough that in their mind they were not lords of the land. A century later Henry VI is seen buying up waste places in the borough to found King's College. A transmutation had occurred: the king acknowledges the borough as tenant in demesne. What in fact transpired is a mystery. Maitland supposes a licence had been granted in the first place and the right of the borough over the wastes and commons thereby established. But no final opinion was given to determine the true ownership until a law case and enclosure procedure settled the matter once and for all in the early nineteenth century.[106] Cambridge is typical of the confusion of title created by the grant of fee farm to borough communities.

Of far greater importance than a disputed title over the wastes and commons was the strength and character which the grant of the fee farm infused into the personality of the borough. The grant of the farm in fee implied on the part of the Crown, or other grantor as the case may be, an acceptance of an immutable rent in perpetuity and a relationship which virtually made the office of the king's sheriff or other collector of revenue redundant for all time. The burgesses were responsible for collecting the borough income from among themselves and paying the farm out of the proceeds. The permanence of the fee farm engendered the election of borough officers by the enfranchised burgesses and thereby opened the way to self-government with its inevitable concept of a corporate selfhood.[107] Ballard[108] thought that all and

[103] Pollock and Maitland: op. cit., p. 651.
[104] Ballard and Tait: op. cit., p. lxxi.
[105] Maitland: op. cit., p. 83.
[106] Op. cit., p. 2.   [107] Tait: op. cit., p. 234.
[108] Ballard: op. cit., p. lxxxvi.

every grant of the *firma burgi* to burgesses whether in fee or not implied an authority to elect borough reeves or bailiffs by the burgesses. Stephenson[109] doubted whether any grant of the fee farm carried the right of election without an express reference to it. The very fact, however, of concessions of election being linked to grants of fee farm in a number of charters shows clearly the logic binding the two gifts. While authority to elect officers from among themselves did not clothe the burgensic body with corporateness, it undoubtedly stimulated the process leading to that end. Until then the bailiffs of the borough, or other elected officers, were responsible personally for discharging the farm in the name of the burgesses as a whole, for collecting the revenue in their own name from each burgess and burghal institution.[110] The tension of loyalty which such bailiffs experienced and which pulled them two ways between the king, whose officers they were by constitutional theory, and their fellow burgesses whose interests were one with their own, was relieved in time by the organisation of *communes* under a mayor and council acting over a common seal.[111] Along these lines the growth of corporateness can be traced back to the policy of granting the *firma burgi* to the boroughs. An eloquent testimony to the historical process is found among the Year Books of Edward III and Edward IV in two law suits whose findings held that the grant of a vill in fee farm to the men of the vill was an act of incorporateness.[112]

The gild merchant. The contribution which the gift and enjoyment of the gild merchant brought to the development of burghal corporateness has been a matter long under debate. Opinion has oscillated between an early school of thought in which the contribution was everything, the gild merchant was foundation and framework of the borough corporation, and the interpretation of Goss who saw it as a mere incidental in a process of burghal consolidation pivoting about the borough court. Tait[113] gives a more recent view. He sees something in the contentions of both schools; neither the old nor the new are entirely wrong or right. The gild merchant played a marked role in the story of borough corporateness, but not a paramount part. It provided blue prints of a workable constitution. As a general rule the later burghal corporations were modelled upon gilds: "The gild alder-

---

109 Stephenson : op. cit., p. 167.
110 Maitland : op. cit., p. 78.
111 Tait : op. cit., p. 234 et seq.
112 cf. Ballard : *The English Borough in the Twelfth Century*, p. 29.
113 Tait : op. cit., p. 233.

man anticipated the elected mayor or bailiffs, the gild organisation the borough assembly and town council, and the gild
purse the borough treasury."[114] Apart from suggesting the anatomy
of the borough corporation, the gilds provided the animus or
soul of the borough. One mind in one body speaking with one
voice was a potent force wherewith a borough community could
express itself, albeit the claims and inspiration were expounded
in the name of the gild merchant.[115] The gildsman on the other hand
was ready with the name of his borough when among foreign
communities he boasted the liberties of trade his native town
enjoyed.[116] The gild championed the borough and the borough
strengthened the gild. Even where the two institutions were at
variance with one another, the interaction of their two identities
tended to shape the features and integrate the personalities of
each.

The borough court. Historians who stress the importance of
the gild merchant refer to it as the contracting body into whose
hands the king granted the liberty of farming the borough. Ballard[117]
argues very effectively against so unilateral a reading of the
evidence. In his repoussé of the burghal picture it is the borough
court that stands out in clear relief as the centre of early
administration and jurisdiction. Tait follows him in this: "a
regular assembly with a share in the town government only became possible when urban courts were created."[118] The court must
be seen then as the magnet of early borough life about which
gathered the privileges, liberties, obligations and proprietary rights
vested in the burgesses as a whole, awaiting the day when legal
perception would descry the full orb of corporate personality.

The grant of privilege to "all burgesses and every burgess". It
has been noted how the grant of the *firma burgi* to the burgesses
of a borough led to the threshold of self-government because it
provided a benefit and imposed a burden which no single burgess
could fully enjoy or carry. Other gifts likewise required a concept
of a unity beyond the totality of a burghal population; notably
the exercise of the privilege of returning writs, of pleading only
within the borough walls,[119] and the benefit of receiving tolls and
other income which presupposes an indivisible purse.[120] Ancient

[114] Op. cit., p. 234.
[115] Lipson: op. cit., p. 278.
[116] Pollock and Maitland: op. cit., p. 650.
[117] Ballard: *British Borough Charters 1042-1216*, p. cii.
[118] Tait: op. cit., p. 14.
[119] Pollock and Maitland: op. cit., p. 676. [120] Ballard: op. cit.. p. xcvi.

rights of common did not have the same effect. Each burgess severally could enjoy pasturage and pannage by turning his own cattle and swine upon the wastes and into the woodlands. It is when the burgesses start leasing the waste they have *approved* that a different conception of proprietary right develops and the dawn of corporate ownership is close at hand.[121]

The coming of the corporation. These are the urges and movements of the burghal dynamic that finally are comprehended by the *persona ficta* idea, the incorporate person, the borough corporation. The yeast worked slowly. Centuries elapsed before the lawyers framed an adequate formula and found the right word to express their far developed thought. Not until the fifteenth century[122] does the law become precise, and incorporation a universally recognised legal process converting a disarticulate association into an entire personality, a *corporation*. Although corporation in word did not arrive until the fifteenth century, in deed it had been the form of borough existence and activity since the Conquest, if not before. Lawyers of the early days, like Bracton, conveyed the idea of a group-person by the use of *universitas*[123] and the legists of the fourteenth century by *communittas*. It was the corporation of the fifteenth century, however, that was clothed with the final legal pedantries. No new borough could be incorporated without a sovereign act of the king expressed by a creative charter. In the later years, therefore, some boroughs were corporate and others unincorporate.[124] The earliest formal *communitas* was established at Coventry in 1345.[125] The pioneer chartered corporation was the borough of Hull, incorporated in 1479.[126]

The royal and ancient boroughs and others of long standing were said to be incorporate by prescription and were hesitant to accept the indignity of a charter which purported to bestow a status long boasted of. Prejudice was eventually overcome. Dates are immaterial. What is significant is the growth in all leading boroughs of the body corporate, the mayor and corporation, who not only owned property within the borough but by the action of their person moulded the shape of landownership over the entire borough lands.

[121] Maitland : op. cit., p. 84.
[122] Pollock and Maitland : op. cit., p. 669.
[123] Op. cit., p. 676.
[124] Ballard : *The English Borough in the 12th Century*, p. 27.
[125] Tait : op. cit., p. 238.   [126] Maitland : op. cit., p. 18.

CHAPTER VII

SELECT BIBLIOGRAPHY

Ballard, Adolphus: *The English Borough in the 12th Century* (1914).
Ballard, Adolphus: *The Domesday Boroughs* (1904).
Ballard, Adolphus (ed.): *British Borough Charters 1042-1216* (1913).
Ballard, Adolphus, and Tait, J. (ed.): *British Borough Charters 1216-1307* (1923).
Bateson, Mary: *Borough Customs*, Vols. I and II (1904-1906).
Cam, H. M.: *Liberties and Communities in Medieval England. Collected studies in local administration and topography* (1944).
Hemmeon, Morley de W.: *Burgage Tenure in Medieval England* (1914).
Lipson, E.: *The Economic History of England*, Vol. I (8th Ed., 1945).
Maitland, Sir Frederic: *Township and Borough* (1898).
Maitland, Sir Frederic: *Domesday Book and Beyond. Three Essays in the Early History of England* (1907).
Pollock, Sir Frederick, and Maitland, Sir Frederic: *The History of English Law before the Time of Edward I.* Vol. I (2nd Ed., rep. 1952)
Poole, A. L.: *From Domesday Book to Magna Carta 1087-1216* (2nd Ed., 1955).
Stenton, Lady: *English Society in the Early Middle Ages (1066-1307).* Pelican History of England, Vol. 3 (1951).
Stephenson, Carl: *Borough and Town: A Stury of Urban Origins in England* (1933).
Tait, James: *The Medieval English Borough: Studies on its Origins and Constitutional History* (1936).
Weinbaum, M. (ed.): *British Borough Charters 1307-1660* (1943).

INDEX

GEORGE ALLEN & UNWIN LTD
London: 40 Museum Street, W.C.1

Auckland: 24 Wyndham Street
Bombay: 15 Graham Road, Ballard Estate, Bombay 1
Calcutta: 17 Chittaranjan Avenue, Calcutta 13
Cape Town: 109 Long Street
Karachi: 254 Ingle Road, Karachi
New Delhi: 13-14 Ajmeri Gate Extension, New Delhi 1
Sao Paulo: Avenida 9 de Julho 1138-Ap. 51
Sydney, N.S.W.: Bradbury House, 55 York Street
Toronto: 91 Wellington Street West

ESTATE CAPITAL
By D. R. Denman

Agriculture more than any other industry depends upon investment in land and buildings and other forms of fixed equipment. The problem of providing them is fundamentally not an agricultural one but a problem of land proprietorship. *Estate Capital* examines this radical principle and introduces the term "estate capital" to distinguish investment in land and buildings, in which agriculture rests, from investment in agricultural machinery and other forms of capital that are essentially agricultural.

The early chapters are descripitive. The heart of the book is a general review of the formation of estate capital from estate income, the provision of estate capital from other sources and the level of investment on agricultural estates. Concluding chapters describe the influence of estate character upon the formation, provision and investment level of estate capital. Estate duty levy on agricultural estates, tenants' contributions to capital investment, and charity estates receive special attention.

The facts and figures used to illustrate and develop the theme of the book are the fruit of four surveys covering over one and a half million acres of agricultural land in Great Britain. The surveys were conducted by the Department of Estate Management of Cambridge University during the years 1952-1956. Although *Estate Capital* is dependent for its illustrations upon these local surveys, its theme is universal and topical in a day when agriculture in so many countries is straitened for want of capital.

Demy 8vo *About 21s. net*

ECONOMICS OF REAL PROPERTY
By Ralph Turvey

The author is primarily concerned to show the role of analysis, and that there is relatively little descriptive material relating merely to current English land problems. His work will thus be of interest both to general economists, as an application of economic theory, and to specialists in land economics in all countries. The main emphasis is on urban real property.

The book is in two parts. The first discusses the working of the price mechanism in the property market. The second contains an extension and application of the analysis to property taxation and to various aspects of State intervention in the use of property. The chapter on the taxation of site values, for instance, is an original, general equilibrium analysis of the effects of taxation. The chapter on Recoupment concludes the book with an empirical investigation which illustrates the approach outlined in the earlier chapters.

Demy 8vo *16s. net*

GEORGE ALLEN & UNWIN LTD